Nonprofit Accounting

A Practitioner's Guide

Second Edition

Steven M. Bragg

Published by AccountingTools, Inc., Centennial, Colorado.

For more information about AccountingTools® products, visit our Web site at www.accountingtools.com.

ISBN-13: 978-1-938910-81-4

Printed in the United States of America

Table of Contents

Preface

A nonprofit organization is subject to a number of different accounting standards than those applied to for-profit organizations, while also being constrained by limited funding. This combination may lead to incorrect accounting and cash shortages, which can leave a nonprofit in disarray in short order. *Nonprofit Accounting* provides guidance in how to create and operate an accounting system, close the books, and produce financial statements – all while operating in accordance with the unique nonprofit accounting standards. We also describe detailed systems of control, budgeting, and ratio analysis to maintain a proper level of control over funds.

In Chapter 1, we give an overview of the nonprofit entity, and then work through all nonprofit accounting topics in Chapters 2 through 14 – including financial statements, revenue accounting, government grants, investments, inventory, fixed assets, joint costs, and more. We then address several more advanced accounting topics in Chapters 15 through 18, including split-interest agreements, mergers and acquisitions, and tax reporting. The book then switches to management accounting topics, addressing how to close the books, create a budget, install controls, and analyze the financial health of the organization.

You can find the answers to many questions about nonprofit accounting in the following chapters, including:

- What is the structure of nonprofit financial statements?
- How do I account for each type of nonprofit revenue?
- How do I allocate costs to programs funded by government grants?
- What are the options for accounting for a collection?
- How do I account for a defined benefit plan or a defined contribution plan?
- Which joint costs can be allocated?
- How does the accounting vary between a nonprofit merger and a nonprofit acquisition?
- What are the rules for recording a contingent liability?
- What are the different types of split-interest agreements?
- Which tax forms must I file with the IRS?
- Which controls should I build into a nonprofit's accounting systems?

Nonprofit Accounting is designed primarily for professionals, who can use it as a reference tool for developing accounting systems and researching the correct accounting to deal with various transactions and reports. Given its complete coverage of these topics, *Nonprofit Accounting* may earn a permanent place on your book shelf.

Centennial, Colorado
February 2017

ix

About the Author

Steven Bragg, CPA, has been the chief financial officer or controller of four companies, as well as a consulting manager at Ernst & Young. He received a master's degree in finance from Bentley College, an MBA from Babson College, and a Bachelor's degree in Economics from the University of Maine. He has been a two-time president of the Colorado Mountain Club, and is an avid alpine skier, mountain biker, and certified master diver. Mr. Bragg resides in Centennial, Colorado. He has written the following books and courses:

7 Habits of Effective CFOs
7 Habits of Effective Controllers
Accountant Ethics [for multiple states]
Accountants' Guidebook
Accounting Changes and Error Corrections
Accounting Controls Guidebook
Accounting for Casinos and Gaming
Accounting for Derivatives and Hedges
Accounting for Earnings per Share
Accounting for Inventory
Accounting for Investments
Accounting for Intangible Assets
Accounting for Leases
Accounting for Managers
Accounting for Stock-Based Compensation
Accounting Procedures Guidebook
Agricultural Accounting
Behavioral Ethics
Bookkeeping Guidebook
Budgeting
Business Combinations and Consolidations
Business Insurance Fundamentals
Business Ratios
Business Valuation
Capital Budgeting
CFO Guidebook
Change Management
Closing the Books
Coaching and Mentoring
Constraint Management
Construction Accounting
Corporate Cash Management
Corporate Finance
Cost Accounting (college textbook)
Cost Accounting Fundamentals
Cost Management Guidebook
Credit & Collection Guidebook
Developing and Managing Teams
Employee Onboarding

Enterprise Risk Management
Fair Value Accounting
Financial Analysis
Financial Forecasting and Modeling
Fixed Asset Accounting
Foreign Currency Accounting
Fraud Examination
GAAP Guidebook
Hospitality Accounting
How to Run a Meeting
Human Resources Guidebook
IFRS Guidebook
Interpretation of Financial Statements
Inventory Management
Investor Relations Guidebook
Lean Accounting Guidebook
Mergers & Acquisitions
Negotiation
New Controller Guidebook
Nonprofit Accounting
Partnership Accounting
Payables Management
Payroll Management
Project Accounting
Project Management
Public Company Accounting
Purchasing Guidebook
Real Estate Accounting
Records Management
Recruiting and Hiring
Revenue Recognition
Sales and Use Tax Accounting
The MBA Guidebook
The Soft Close
The Statement of Cash Flows
The Year-End Close
Treasurer's Guidebook
Working Capital Management

On-Line Resources by Steven Bragg

Steven maintains the accountingtools.com web site, which contains continuing professional education courses, the Accounting Best Practices podcast, and hundreds of articles on accounting subjects.

Nonprofit Accounting is also available as a continuing professional education (CPE) course. You can purchase the course (and many other courses) and take an on-line exam at:

www.accountingtools.com/cpe

Chapter 1
Overview of the Nonprofit Entity

Introduction

There are more than 1.5 million nonprofit organizations in the United States, according to the National Center for Charitable Statistics. These organizations account for more than 9% of the total wages and salaries paid in the United States. To give the reader a better understanding of this massive part of the economy, we define in this chapter the nonprofit entity, its tax classification, filing requirements, and organizational structure.

Definition of a Nonprofit Entity

Many entities consider themselves to be nonprofits, and advertise themselves as such. But what is a nonprofit? According to the Financial Accounting Standards Board (which issues the accounting standards that govern nonprofits), the key criteria that define a nonprofit are:

- No ownership interests
- An operating purpose other than to earn a profit
- It receives significant contributions from third parties that do not expect a return

Conversely, an entity that cannot be considered a nonprofit is one that is owned by investors, or which provides dividends or other economic benefits to its owners or members. Thus, credit unions and employee benefit plans are not considered nonprofit entities.

To further clarify the status of nonprofits, the following types of organizations are all considered to be nonprofits:

Cemetery organizations	Political parties
Civic and community organizations	Political action committees
Colleges and universities	Private and community foundations
Cultural organizations	Professional associations
Elementary and secondary schools	Public broadcasting stations
Federated fundraising organizations	Religious organizations
Fraternal organizations	Research and scientific organizations
Health care entities	Social and country clubs
Labor unions	Trade associations

Libraries	Voluntary health and welfare entities
Museums	Zoological and botanical societies
Performing arts organizations	

Many nonprofit organizations seek nonprofit status from the Internal Revenue Service (IRS), so that they can avoid paying federal income taxes, and can instead plow these funds back into their core missions. The IRS deals with these organizations in section 501(c) of the Internal Revenue Code. This section of the Code currently provides for 29 types of nonprofit organizations, which are as follows:

Types of Nonprofit Organizations

Section of IRS Code	Organization Type	Activities Conducted
501(c)(1)	Corporations organized under an Act of Congress	Instrumentalities of the United States
501(c)(2)	Title holding corporation for exempt organization	Holds title to property of an exempt organization
501(c)(3)	Religious, educational, charitable, scientific, literary, testing for public safety, to foster national or international sports competition, or prevention of cruelty to children or animals organizations	Activities of a nature implied by the description of the class of organization
501(c)(4)	Civic leagues, social welfare organizations, and local associations of employees	Promotion of community welfare; charitable, educational, or recreational
501(c)(5)	Labor, agricultural, and horticultural organizations	Educational; the purpose being to improve conditions of work, and to improve efficiency
501(c)(6)	Business leagues, chambers of commerce, and real estate boards	Improvement of business conditions of one or more lines of business
501(c)(7)	Social and recreational clubs	Pleasure, recreation, and social activities
501(c)(8)	Fraternal societies and associations	Lodge providing for payment of life, sickness, accident or other benefits to members
501(c)(9)	Voluntary employees beneficiary associations	Providing for payment of life, sickness, accident, or other benefits to members
501(c)(10)	Domestic fraternal societies and associations	Lodge devoting its net earnings to charitable, fraternal, and other specified purposes
501(c)(11)	Teachers' retirement fund associations	Teachers' association for payment of retirement benefits

Section of IRS Code	Organization Type	Activities Conducted
501(c)(12)	Benevolent life insurance associations, mutual ditch or irrigation companies, mutual or cooperative telephone companies, etc.	Activities of a mutually beneficial nature similar to those implied by the description of the organization
501(c)(13)	Cemetery companies	Burials and incidental activities
501(c)(14)	State-chartered credit unions, mutual reserve funds	Loans to members
501(c)(15)	Mutual insurance companies or associations	Providing insurance to members substantially at cost
501(c)(16)	Cooperative organizations to finance crop operations	Financing crop operations in conjunction with activities of a marketing or purchasing association
501(c)(17)	Supplemental unemployment benefit trusts	Provides for payment of supplemental unemployment compensation benefits
501(c)(18)	Employee funded pension trust (created before June 25, 1959)	Payment of benefits under a pension plan funded by employees
501(c)(19)	Post or organization of past or present members of the armed forces	Activities implied by the nature of the organization
501(c)(20)	Formerly used for group legal services plan	No longer used
501(c)(21)	Black lung benefit trusts	Funded by coal mine operators to satisfy their liability for disability or death due to black lung diseases
501(c)(22)	Withdrawal liability payment fund	To provide funds to meet the liability of employers withdrawing from a multi-employer pension fund
501(c)(23)	Veterans' organization (created before 1880)	To provide insurance and other benefits to veterans
501(c)(24)	Formerly used for Section 4049 ERISA trusts	No longer used
501(c)(25)	Title holding corporations or trusts with multiple parent corporations	Holding title and paying over income from property to 35 or fewer parents or beneficiaries
501(c)(26)	State-sponsored organization providing health coverage for high-risk individuals	Provides health care coverage to high-risk individuals
501(c)(27)	State-sponsored workers' compensation reinsurance organization	Reimburse members for losses under workers' compensation acts

Section of IRS Code	Organization Type	Activities Conducted
501(c)(28)	National railroad retirement investment trust	Manages and invests the assets of the Railroad Retirement Account
501(c)(29)	CO-OP health insurance issuers	A qualified health insurance issuer which has received a loan or grant under the CO-OP program

(Extracted from the Organization Reference Chart in IRS Publication 557, *Tax-Exempt Status for Your Organization*)

Most of the subsections of this code deal with very specific types of organizations, and so do not apply to most nonprofits. The area that is applicable to the largest cross-section of nonprofits is 501(c)(3), which applies to religious, educational, charitable, scientific, literary, testing for public safety, fostering of national or international sports competition, or prevention of cruelty to children or animals organizations. Most of the entities granted 501(c)(3) status have operations that are either charitable, educational, or religious in nature. This subset of entities engages in the following types of activities:

Charitable

- Relief of the poor or underprivileged
- Advancement of religion
- Advancement of education or science
- Construction or maintenance of public buildings and other works
- Reduction of the burdens of government
- Reduction of neighborhood tensions
- Elimination of prejudice and discrimination
- Defense of human and civil rights
- Reduction of community deterioration and juvenile delinquency

Educational

- Schools, including primary and secondary schools, colleges, and trade schools
- Public discussion forums, panels, and lectures
- Correspondence instruction via radio or television
- Museums, orchestras, planetariums, and zoos
- Non-profit day-care facilities
- Youth sports organizations

Religious

- Churches, including mosques, synagogues, and temples
- Mission organizations

- Speakers' organizations
- Nondenominational ministries and ecumenical organizations
- Faith-based social agencies

The 501(c)(3) designation is especially important, because donors can make tax-deductible donations to these organizations. Both individuals and corporations are much more likely to donate to a 501(c)(3) entity for this reason. In addition, local governments may grant these organizations exemption from income, sales, or property taxes. Thus, the 501(c)(3) designation is highly prized. Conversely, other types of nonprofit organizations may not qualify for these tax-deductible donations, and so are much less likely to attract contributions from donors. For example, a social or recreational club (designated as a 501(c)(7) organization) does not pay income taxes, but donations to it are not tax-deductible.

The IRS mandates the following requirements for an entity that wishes to apply for the 501(c)(3) designation:

- The entity is organized and operated exclusively for one or more exempt purposes. This means that the entity is organized as a corporation, trust, or unincorporated association. The articles of incorporation (or equivalent) must:
  - Limit the purposes of the entity to exempt activities;
  - Not expressly permit activities unrelated to the exempt mission of the entity; and
  - Permanently dedicate its assets to the designated exempt purposes.

- The entity cannot engage in the following activities:
  - Participation in the political campaigns of candidates for any office
  - Lobbying activities, other than an insubstantial part of total activities
  - Have its earnings benefit an individual
  - Operate for the benefit of any private interests, such as the founder or the founder's family
  - Operate a trade or business not related to its exempt purpose
  - Engage in activities that are illegal or violate public policy

If the 501(c)(3) designation is granted to a nonprofit, the entity then has the following obligations from the perspective of the IRS:

- *Recordkeeping.* Keep sufficiently detailed records that include sources of support, such as contributions, grants, and sponsorships.
- *Filings.* File an annual report with the IRS, which may be either the Form 990, Form 990-EZ, Form 990-N (reserved for entities with gross receipts of $50,000 or less), or Form 990-PF (which is filed by private foundations). The Form 990-T is also filed to report any gross income from an unrelated trade or business of $1,000 or more. A few entities are exempted from filing

these forms. If a nonprofit does not file one of these forms for three consecutive years, it loses its tax-exempt status.

> **Note:** Churches are exempt from filing the Form 990.

- *Public inspection.* A nonprofit must make its 501(c)(3) application and annual returns available for public inspection.
- *Donation documentation.* The entity must provide to donors a written acknowledgement of any donation made of $250 or more. Also, a written disclosure must be made to any donor paying the entity more than $75 that is partly a contribution, and partly for goods and services provided by the entity.

To apply for 501(c)(3) status, an entity must complete and submit to the IRS the Form 1023, *Application for Recognition of Exemption under Section 501(c)(3) of the Internal Revenue Code.* This form must be filed no later than the end of the 27th month after the entity was legally formed. If the status is then granted, the tax exemption is considered to be from the date of creation of the entity. If an entity instead files after the deadline, the tax exemption will take effect only as of the date of the application, though it is possible to request a retroactive exemption.

An IRS examiner will review the Form 1023 and any attached documentation, to see if the submitting entity is worthy of 501(c)(3) status. This can be a prolonged process that calls for the submission of additional documentation to the IRS. If the review is favorable, the IRS will issue a *determination letter* that recognizes the tax-exempt status of the entity. Many larger donors will request a copy of this determination letter before they agree to issue contributions.

> **Tip:** The determination letter is an important document, and so should be stored in a nonprofit's permanent file, where it is less likely to be mislaid or destroyed. Consider retaining copies in several locations. If lost, the letter can be replaced by the IRS with a letter confirming the tax-exempt status of the entity.

When a donor makes a contribution to a nonprofit that can be classified as a charitable deduction, the donor then claims the contribution on his or her individual tax return. It is the responsibility of the donor to determine the amount that can be deducted, and when to do so. The nonprofit has no liability for how a donor uses a tax deduction.

Nonprofit Organizational Structure

Though earning a profit is not the main intent of a nonprofit, it is critical for the organization to be properly run, to ensure that programs are properly administered, contributions are solicited in an effective manner, and expenses are closely monitored. Consequently, a nonprofit may have an organizational structure that is similar in some respects to that of a for-profit entity. There is a board of directors whose members are ultimately responsible for the strategic direction of the organization. The executive director fulfills the role of a chief executive officer, managing the enterprise on behalf of the board of directors. Below the executive director are department managers. Typical manager titles may include several program directors, a controller and an administration director. There is also likely to be a fundraising coordinator, who is also known as a development director. If a large number of volunteers work on behalf of the organization, there may also be a volunteer coordinator. The following organization chart shows the higher levels of a nonprofit.

Nonprofit Organizational Structure

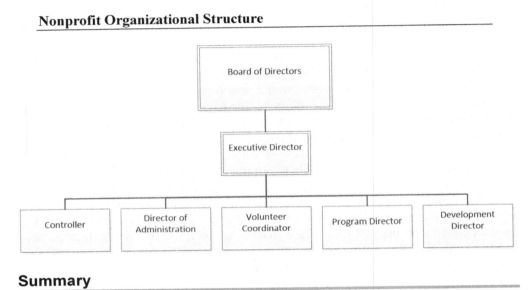

Summary

In this chapter, we have defined the nonprofit entity and pointed out its tax status, filing requirements, and organizational structure. In the following chapters, we turn to the accounting and tax reporting requirements of the nonprofit organization. Some of these topics are highly specific to nonprofits, such as the accounting for government grants, split-interest agreements, and contributions. Other topics, such as lease accounting, budgeting, and closing the books, can be applied to all types of organizations, but are still critical to the proper recordation, reporting, and control of accounting transactions by a nonprofit.

Chapter 2
Basic Nonprofit Accounting Concepts

Introduction

A nonprofit organization shares many of the accounting concepts used by for-profit organizations, though the smaller size of many nonprofits leads them to employ more rudimentary accounting systems than for-profit entities. As we will see in this chapter, the accounting for nonprofits is actually more detailed than for for-profit organizations in some areas. This calls for a *higher* level of accounting effort than might be expected.

In this chapter, we address the basic concepts of double entry bookkeeping, the accrual and cash bases of accounting, the chart of accounts, net assets, and a variety of bookkeeping issues. We close the chapter with a case study that incorporates many of these accounting concepts.

Double Entry Bookkeeping

Double entry accounting is a recordkeeping system under which every transaction is recorded in at least two accounts. There is no limit on the number of accounts used in a transaction, but the minimum is two accounts. There are two columns in each account, with debit entries on the left and credit entries on the right. In double entry accounting, the total of all debit entries must match the total of all credit entries. When this happens, the transaction is said to be *in balance*. If the totals do not agree, the transaction is said to be *out of balance*, and the resulting information cannot be used to create financial statements.

A *debit* is an accounting entry that either increases an asset or expense account, or decreases a liability or net asset account. It is positioned to the left in an accounting entry. A *credit* is an accounting entry that either increases a liability or net asset account, or decreases an asset or expense account. It is positioned to the right in an accounting entry. An account is a separate, detailed record associated with a specific asset, liability, net asset, revenue, expense, gain, or loss. Examples of accounts are:

Account Name	Account Type	Normal Balance
Cash	Asset	Debit
Accounts receivable	Asset	Debit
Fixed assets	Asset	Debit
Accounts payable	Liability	Credit
Accrued liabilities	Liability	Credit
Loans outstanding	Liability	Credit

Account Name	Account Type	Normal Balance
Net assets without donor restrictions	Net asset	Credit
Net assets with donor restrictions	Net asset	Credit
Donor contributions	Revenue	Credit
Compensation expense	Expense	Debit
Gain on sale of asset	Gain	Credit
Loss on sale of asset	Loss	Debit

The Journal Entry

A journal entry is a method used to enter an accounting transaction into the accounting records of an entity. The format of a journal entry is for the first column to contain the account name/number into which the entry is being made, the second column to contain the debit amount being entered, and the third column to contain the credit amount being entered. The account name/number of the account being credited is indented. It is also useful to include a unique journal entry identification number and the date of the entry, as well as a brief narrative description. If there are a large number of journal entries in a typical reporting period, consider adding an approval signature block, as well as a signature and date block for the person who enters the journal entry into the accounting software. The format of a basic journal entry is:

[Journal entry number]	Debit	Credit
Account name / number	$xx,xxx	
Account name / number		$xx,xxx
Narrative description of the reason for the entry		

The basic structural rules of a journal entry are that there must be a minimum of two line items in the journal entry, and that the total amount entered in the debit column equals the total amount entered in the credit column. There are also several best practices related to journal entries, which are:

- *Narrative.* Always provide a complete narrative of why a journal entry has been created. Otherwise, someone reviewing the books at a later date will have no idea why an entry was created.
- *Number of lines.* Do not include too many lines. Whenever possible, try to reduce a complex journal entry into several simpler ones, thereby making it easier to understand the transaction being recorded.
- *Template.* Use a standardized journal entry template for recurring transactions, which reduces the risk of creating an incorrect entry.
- *Reversing entry.* Use an automatically reversing journal entry for accruals whose impact is intended to be for a single accounting period. By doing so, there is no need to manually reverse an entry in the following period.

- *Software module.* Use a transaction module in the accounting software, rather than using manual journal entries. When a transaction is recorded within a transaction module, such as the billing system or accounts payable system, the result is more likely to be correct, since each module is pre-configured to collect and store a particular set of information.

The Accounting Equation

In a for-profit organization, the basic underlying accounting structure is derived from the following formula, which is called the accounting equation:

$$\text{Assets} = \text{Liabilities} + \text{Stockholders' equity}$$

However, there is no equity in a nonprofit, since there are no stockholders to own shares in the business. Instead, the accounting equation is modified as follows:

$$\text{Assets} = \text{Liabilities} + \text{Net assets}$$

The assets in the accounting equation are the resources that a nonprofit has available for its use, such as cash, accounts receivable and fixed assets. The entity pays for these resources by incurring liabilities (which is the Liabilities part of the accounting equation) or by obtaining contributions from donors (which is the Net assets part of the equation). All three components of the accounting equation appear in the statement of financial position, which reveals the financial position of a nonprofit at any given point in time. In the statement of financial position, the total of all assets always equals the sum of the liabilities and net assets sections.

The Liabilities part of the equation is usually comprised of accounts payable that are owed to suppliers, a variety of accrued liabilities, and debt payable to lenders.

The Net Assets part of the equation contains the total amounts of two classifications of donated assets, which are:

- Net assets with donor restrictions
- Net assets without donor restrictions

We address the net assets topic in more detail later, in the Net Assets section.

The reason why the accounting equation is so important is that it is always true – and it forms the basis for all accounting transactions. At a general level, this means that whenever there is a recordable transaction, the choices for recording it all involve keeping the accounting equation in balance.

EXAMPLE

Archimedes Education is a new nonprofit, with no prior activity. Archimedes engages in the following transactions:

1. In January, a donor sends Archimedes a contribution of $10,000 to assist in starting up the organization. The use of these funds is unrestricted.

2. In January, the executive director of Archimedes enters into a one-year lease of office space, and pays the landlord $1,000 for the first month's rent. Of this amount, $400 is actually a security deposit.
3. In January, the same donor contributes $5,000, under the provision that the cash can only be used to pay for a photocopier.
4. In February, Archimedes uses the restricted funds to buy a copier.

To account for the first transaction (the $10,000 donation), Archimedes records the following journal entry:

J/E #1	Debit	Credit
Cash [assets account]	10,000	
Donor contributions – without restrictions [revenue account]		10,000
To record receipt of donor contribution		

To account for the second transaction (the one-year lease), Archimedes records the following journal entry:

J/E #2	Debit	Credit
Deposits [assets account]	400	
Rent expense [expense account]	600	
Cash [assets account]		1,000
To record payment of monthly rent and a related security deposit		

To account for the third transaction (the $5,000 donation), Archimedes records the following journal entry:

J/E #3	Debit	Credit
Cash [assets account]	5,000	
Donor contributions – with restrictions [revenue account]		5,000
To record receipt of restricted donor contribution intended for photocopier purchase		

To account for the fourth transaction (to buy a copier), Archimedes records the following journal entry:

J/E #4	Debit	Credit
Fixed assets – office equipment [assets account]	5,000	
Cash [assets account]		5,000
To record purchase of photocopier, using restricted funds		

These transactions appear in the following table:

Item	(Asset) Cash	(Asset) Deposits	(Asset) Fixed Assets		(Liability) Liabilities	Net Assets
(1)	10,000			=		10,000
(2)	-1,000	400		=		-600
(3)	5,000			=		5,000
(4)	-5,000		5,000	=		
Totals	9,000	400	5,000	=		14,400

In the example, note how every transaction is balanced within the accounting equation – either because there are changes on both sides of the equation, or because a transaction cancels itself out on one side of the equation (as was the case when cash was used to purchase a fixed asset).

What if the totals of all debits and credits in the accounting records do not match? There may be one of three underlying causes to this problem, which are:

- *Rounding error.* If the accounting software is rounding to the nearest dollar or thousand dollars, the rounding function may result in a presentation that appears to be unbalanced, even though the underlying accounts are correct.
- *Unbalanced starting numbers.* If an accountant has just started using the accounting software, beginning balances for the various accounts may have been entered that do not balance under the accounting equation. The software should flag this problem when the beginning balances are being entered.
- *Unbalanced transactions.* A journal entry may have been made in which the debits do not match the credits. This should be impossible as long as accounting software is being used, since the software will not allow entries to be made unless the entries are balanced. However, this situation is entirely possible if accounting records are being maintained manually.

The Chart of Accounts

An account is a record in which is stored financial transactions related to assets, liabilities, revenues, expenses, gains, and losses. A nonprofit will need a number of different accounts in which to store information. The official listing of these accounts is called the chart of accounts. The chart of accounts is sorted in order by account number. Account numbers are usually assigned to accounts based on the following order:

1. Asset accounts first (begin with a "1")
2. Liability accounts second (begin with a "2")
3. Net asset accounts third (begin with a "3")
4. Revenue and gain accounts fourth (begin with a "4")

5. Expense and loss accounts last (begin with a "5")

The intent of this ordering is to list accounts in order of their appearance in the financial statements, starting with the statement of financial position and continuing with the statement of activities. Many nonprofits structure their chart of accounts so that expense information is separately compiled by program; thus, a group of three programs might each have separate expense accounts.

Typical accounts found in the chart of accounts are:

Assets

- Cash
  - o Petty cash
  - o Checking account
  - o Savings account
- Marketable securities
- Accounts receivable | contributions receivable
- Grants receivable
- Prepaid expenses
- Fixed assets
  - o Land
  - o Building
  - o Equipment
  - o Less: Accumulated depreciation
- Other assets

Liabilities

- Accounts payable
- Accrued liabilities
- Wages payable
- Loans payable

Net Assets

- Net assets with donor restrictions
- Net assets without donor restrictions

Revenue

- Donor contributions
- Federal grants
- State grants
- Fundraising events

- Investment income
- Membership fees
- Program revenue

Expenses

- Compensation expense
- Depreciation expense
- Benefits expense
- Payroll tax expense
- Contracted services
- Rent expense
- Repairs and maintenance
- Supplies expense
- Training expense
- Insurance expense
- Travel and entertainment expense
- Utilities expense
- Other expenses

The following points can improve the chart of accounts concept for a nonprofit:

- *Form 990 mapping.* If the nonprofit has to file some variation on the Form 990 with the Internal Revenue Service at year-end, consider setting up the chart of accounts to match the relevant line items in the Form 990. By doing so, account balances will map directly to the form, making it easier to prepare the form.
- *Consistency.* It is of some importance to initially create a chart of accounts that is unlikely to change for several years, so that one can compare the results in the same account over a multi-year period. If an entity instead starts with a small number of accounts and then gradually expands the number of accounts over time, it becomes increasingly difficult to obtain comparable financial information for more than the past year.
- *Size reduction.* Periodically review the account list to see if any accounts contain relatively immaterial amounts. If so, and if this information is not needed for special reports, shut down these accounts and roll the stored information into a larger account. Doing this periodically keeps the number of accounts down to a manageable level.

It can be useful to structure the chart of accounts so that accounts are clearly identified as belonging to unrestricted or restricted funds. For example, a "1" preceding the account number can identify an unrestricted account, while a "2" identifies a restricted account. Further, if there are several restricted accounts, they can be listed with an additional two or three digit code that follows the first digit. For example:

Account Code	Description
2-10-xxx-xx	Restricted – Primary education
2-20-xxx-xx	Restricted – Secondary education
2-30-xxx-xx	Restricted – Facility construction

The Accrual Basis of Accounting

The accrual basis of accounting is the concept of recording revenues when earned and expenses as incurred. This concept differs from the cash basis of accounting, under which revenues are recorded when cash is received, and expenses are recorded when cash is paid. For example, a nonprofit operating under the accrual basis of accounting would record an expense as incurred, while a cash basis entity would instead wait to pay its supplier before recording the expense.

The accrual basis of accounting tends to provide more consistent recognition of revenues and expenses over time, and so is considered by the users of financial statements to be the most valid accounting system for ascertaining the activities, financial position, and cash flows of a nonprofit. In particular, it supports the matching principle, under which revenues and all related expenses are to be recorded within the same reporting period; by doing so, it should be possible to see the full extent of the profits and losses associated with specific business transactions within a single reporting period.

A significant failing of the accrual basis of accounting is that it can indicate an increase in net assets, even though the associated cash inflows have not yet occurred. The result can be a supposedly well-run entity that is starved for cash, and which may therefore go bankrupt despite its reported surge in net assets.

The Cash Basis of Accounting

As just noted, the cash basis of accounting involves recording revenue when cash is received, and expenses when cash is paid. This is the simplest form of accounting, and so is quite appealing for a smaller nonprofit that does not have enough money to pay for a highly skilled accounting staff. In addition, financial statements prepared using the cash basis have the following advantages:

- *Conservative revenue recognition.* Donor contributions are only recognized when the cash is received. This can be useful when donors have committed to make contributions, but have not done so. This form of recognition gives management a better view of the amount of revenue it has to work with.

- *Cash flow view.* A statement of activities prepared under the cash basis is essentially a statement of cash flows (see the Nonprofit Financial Statements chapter), in that it closely parallels actual cash inflows and outflows. As such, it reveals the ability of the organization to generate and use cash.

However, these advantages are offset by several concerns, which are:

- *Not forward looking.* Financial statements prepared under the cash basis do not contain any accounts receivable or accounts payable, so management cannot estimate from the financials any short-term cash inflows or outflows. However, this concern can be mitigated by maintaining a cash forecast that is updated regularly.
- *Revenue and expense mismatches.* There may be a difference of several months between when revenues and expenses are officially recognized. The result can be some months in which a nonprofit appears to be generating huge increases in net assets, and other months in which it appears to be suffering from massive reductions in net assets. This issue is reduced when the financial statements are aggregated over several months, such as when financials are reported on a quarterly basis.

The Modified Cash Basis of Accounting

The modified cash basis of accounting uses elements of both the cash basis and accrual basis of accounting. The modified basis has the following features:

- *Related to cash basis.* Records short-term items when cash levels change. This means that nearly all elements of the statement of activities are recorded using the cash basis. Accounts receivable and inventory are *not* recorded in the statement of financial position.
- *Related to accrual basis.* Records longer-term statement of financial position items. This means that fixed assets and long-term debt are recorded on the statement of financial position, and depreciation and amortization are recorded in the statement of activities.

The modified cash basis provides financial information that is more relevant than can be found with cash basis recordkeeping, and generally does so at less cost than is needed to maintain a set of full-accrual accounting records.

There are no exact specifications for what is allowed under the modified cash basis, since it has developed through common usage. There is no accounting standard that has imposed any rules on its use. If donors still want to see accrual-basis financial statements at the end of the year, financial statements prepared under the modified cash basis will need to be altered, though not to such a comprehensive extent as is needed for financials prepared under the cash basis of accounting.

Converting Cash Basis to the Accrual Basis

Smaller nonprofits may not have the time or accounting expertise to initially record transactions under the accrual basis of accounting. If so, they use the simpler cash basis of accounting. However, donors want to see annual financial statements organized under the accrual basis, so these nonprofits must convert their cash basis financial statements to the accrual basis. The steps involved in this conversion are:

- *Add accrued expenses.* Add all expenses for which the nonprofit has received a benefit but has not yet paid the supplier or employee. This means the accountant should accrue for virtually all types of expenses, such as wages earned but not paid, office supplies received but unpaid, and so forth.
- *Subtract cash payments.* Subtract cash expenditures made for expenses that should have been recorded in the preceding accounting period.
- *Add prepaid expenses.* Some cash payments may relate to assets that have not yet been consumed, such as rent deposits. Review expenditures made during the accounting period to see if there are any prepaid expenses, and move the unused portion of them into an asset account.
- *Add accounts receivable.* Record accounts receivable and revenues for all billings issued to donors and other customers, and for which no cash has yet been received.
- *Subtract cash receipts.* Some revenues originating in a prior period may have been recorded within the current accounting period based on the receipt of cash in that period. If so, reverse the transaction and record it instead as revenue and accounts receivable in the preceding period.

The conversion of cash basis to accrual basis accounting can be a difficult one, for any accounting software that has been configured for the cash basis is not designed to handle accrual basis accounting. This means that all conversion adjustments must be made manually, with journal entries. It may be easier to manage the conversion on a separate spreadsheet, and never include it in the formal accounting records at all.

It is quite possible that some transactions will be missed during the conversion from cash basis to accrual basis accounting. Unfortunately, the only way to be certain of a complete and accurate conversion is to examine all accounting transactions during the year being converted, as well as in the final quarter of the preceding year. This means that the conversion is labor-intensive.

Further, a very complete set of well-documented accounting records is required to convert from the cash basis to the accrual basis. Since a business already on the cash basis is likely to be a small one with less funding for a full-time bookkeeper or controller, it is quite possible that the accounting records are in a sufficient state of disarray that the conversion cannot be made in a reliable manner. If so, the best option is to hire an outside CPA who is skilled in these conversions.

> **Tip:** Arrange with an outside CPA well in advance to convert the records of the organization to the accrual basis; CPAs can be very busy at certain times of the year, so advance planning is needed to obtain their services within the best time slot.

Generally Accepted Accounting Principles (GAAP)

GAAP is short for Generally Accepted Accounting Principles. GAAP is a large group of accounting standards and common industry usage that have been developed over many years, and that are used by organizations to:

- Properly organize their financial information into accounting records;
- Summarize the accounting records into financial statements; and
- Disclose certain supporting information.

One of the reasons for using GAAP is so that anyone reading the financial statements of multiple entities has a reasonable basis of comparison, since all organizations using GAAP have created their financial statements using the same set of rules. GAAP covers a broad array of topics, including:

- Financial statement presentation
- Assets
- Liabilities
- Revenue
- Expenses
- Fair value
- Foreign currency
- Leases
- Nonmonetary transactions
- Subsequent events
- Industry-specific accounting, including a lengthy section for nonprofits

GAAP is derived from the pronouncements of a series of government-sponsored accounting entities, of which the Financial Accounting Standards Board (FASB) is the latest. GAAP is codified into the Accounting Standards Codification (ASC), which is available online and (more legibly) in printed form.

GAAP is used primarily by entities reporting their financial results in the United States. International Financial Reporting Standards, or IFRS, is the accounting framework used in most other countries. GAAP is much more rules-based than IFRS. IFRS focuses more on general principles than GAAP, which makes the IFRS body of work much smaller, cleaner, and easier to understand than GAAP. Since IFRS is still being constructed, GAAP is considered the more comprehensive accounting framework.

Net Assets

We mentioned the net assets concept in the Accounting Equation section. A net asset is the equivalent of retained earnings in the financial statements of a for-profit business. When contributing assets, a donor may impose restrictions on their use. The result is two types of net assets, which are classified as net assets with donor restrictions and net assets without donor restrictions. The accounting for these types of net assets varies, as noted in the following sub-sections.

Net Assets without Donor Restrictions

When a donor imposes no restriction on a contribution made to a nonprofit, the nonprofit records the contribution as an asset and as contribution revenue with no donor restrictions. These funds are used to pay for the general operations of a nonprofit. The fundraising staff strongly encourages donors to make unrestricted donations, since these funds can be put to the broadest possible range of uses. Since this contribution revenue also creates a profit, the profit appears in the statement of financial position as an increase in net assets without donor restrictions.

Net Assets with Donor Restrictions

When a donor imposes a restriction on a contribution made to a nonprofit, the nonprofit records the contribution as contribution revenue with donor restrictions. Only the donor can change this designation; a nonprofit's board of directors is not allowed to do so.

There may be a number of sub-accounts within the net assets with donor restrictions account, for those situations in which donors want to contribute to specific aspects of a project or to release funds for use over a period of time. For example, when a museum is being built, donors may only want to contribute to certain exhibits or rooms within the museum. Or, donors may want their contributions to be spent evenly over the next five years. It is also possible that donors will require that an asset be held by a nonprofit in perpetuity, usually allowing the nonprofit to only spend any interest income derived from the funds.

Net Assets Summary

The following example shows various situations in which contributions fall into the two classifications.

EXAMPLE

Mr. Davis Templeton is a major contributor to Newton Education. He is aware that Newton needs $25,000 for laptop computers for use in one of its classes. He therefore contributes $25,000 to Newton, under the provision that the funds will be used to buy laptops. This contribution increases both the cash account of Newton and the net assets with donor restrictions account by $25,000. Newton uses the money to acquire laptops. The result is a shift of $25,000 from the cash account to the fixed assets account, as well as a shift of $25,000 from the net assets with donor restrictions account to the net assets without donor restrictions account.

Mrs. Martha Anglesey is a lifetime devotee of ballet, and so contributes $500,000 to the Kansas Ballet, under the provision that only the interest on the contribution can be spent. This contribution increases the Ballet's net assets with donor restrictions account by $500,000.

Mrs. Anglesey further restricts the interest earned on her endowment to fund scholarships for aspiring ballet dancers. In the first year of the endowment, $15,000 in interest is earned from the endowment. The Ballet records the $15,000 as a net asset with donor restrictions, until such time as the cash is awarded as scholarships.

The totals of each of these classifications are reported within the net assets section of the statement of financial position, along with a grand total for all net assets.

A final thought regarding net assets is that they do not refer to *assets*. An asset is an item of economic value that is expected to yield a benefit in future periods. A net asset is more like a separate project, for which a separate set of financial statements can be generated.

The Release from Restriction Concept

When funds are used in accordance with the wishes of a donor who had initially restricted the funds, they are considered to have been *released* from their initial restriction. This is a common event, and is reported within the revenue section of the statement of activities. In essence, funds released from restriction are stated as a fund reduction in the column for net assets with donor restrictions, and as a fund addition in the net assets without donor restrictions column. The net effect is zero. This concept appears in the case study at the end of this chapter. We show a portion of the statement of activities in that case study next, to show how $5,000 is released from the net assets with donor restrictions column and shifted to the net assets without donor restrictions column, with no effect on the nonprofit's revenues.

Archimedes Education
Statement of Activities
For the month ended February 28, 20X1

	Net Assets without Donor Restrictions	Net Assets with Donor Restrictions	Totals
Revenues:			
Contributions	$-	$-	$-
Net assets released from restrictions	5,000	-5,000	-
Total revenues	$5,000	-$5,000	$-

Inter-Fund Receivables and Payables

When funds are spent that are tied to a restricted account, it would be excessively complex to immediately tie the payments back to the funding accounts. Instead, funds are initially spent from the general checking account of a nonprofit. An inter-fund receivable and payable is then set up, indicating that the related restricted fund owes cash to the unrestricted checking account. Typically, the accounting staff settles up these inter-fund receivables at the end of each month by transferring cash from the restricted accounts to the unrestricted checking account. By the time the period-end financial statements have been issued, there should be no inter-fund receivables and payables remaining in the accounting records.

Board-Designated Funds

The board of directors can choose to set aside funds for a specific purpose, such as the construction of a facility. An outcome of this decision can be a journal entry to move these funds from net assets without donor restrictions to a separate account. The intent behind this restriction is to make it clear that certain funds are being set aside for a specific purpose. However, the board can just as easily terminate this special designation, even if the underlying reason for the change was never completed.

The board-designated funds concept is essentially an accounting fiction. These funds are still part of net assets without donor restrictions, and are not really restricted. Only donors can place restrictions on contributed funds.

Program Identification

The reason why a nonprofit exists is to provide some kind of service, which is called a *program*. Examples of programs are providing meals to the elderly, offering free training classes, and distributing printed materials about safety hazards. Whatever the program may be, the accounting system should be designed to accumulate information about program revenues and expenses, so that management can determine how resources are being allocated to fulfill a nonprofit's mission. It is particularly important to separate revenues and expenses for programs from the other activities of a nonprofit, especially the fundraising area and the management and administration area. When a sophisticated donor wants to see how well a nonprofit is managing its resources, it will likely want to see a breakdown of results that separates each individual program, and which separately shows fundraising expenses and management and administration expenses. Doing so reveals the relative proportions of resources being spent on the core mission of the entity.

Clearly then, the identification of programs is a key consideration when setting up an accounting system. When doing so, try to introduce some recordation stability for the programs. This means that identified programs are not changed much from year to year. By doing so, someone examining the financial results of a nonprofit can trace back its commitment to specific programs over a number of years.

It is easier to identify programs if the mission statement of a nonprofit is highly focused. With a focused statement, it is simpler to determine if a cluster of expenses should be classified as being part of a program, or whether it is more of an administrative or fundraising item.

EXAMPLE

The mission statement of Focus on the Poor states that the organization exists to improve the condition of low-income people. The controller is trying to identify how many programs the organization is managing. In the past year, Focus spent $100,000 on the maintenance of low-income housing, $25,000 on a food collection drive, and $40,000 on a car used in a raffle sale that was intended to bring in funds for the organization. The controller decides to classify the $40,000 expenditure as a fundraising cost, since it is really designed to raise cash. Also, the controller complains to the board of directors that the vague mission statement makes it difficult for her to identify programs, which (based on the identified expenditures) are Housing Support and Food Support. The board decides to recast the mission statement to "improve the housing of low-income people." By doing so, Focus can eliminate the Food Support program, leaving just one program for which financial information must be aggregated.

The Management and Administration Classification

Those activities not directly related to fundraising or programs are considered to fall within the management and administration classification. This classification provides operational support to the entire organization, and ensures that other activities run as smoothly as possible. The main activity areas provided by it include:

- Accounting and finance services
- Facility maintenance
- Human resources services
- Information technology maintenance
- Risk management and legal services
- Strategic planning and budgeting

The proportion of expenditures assigned to this classification is of deep concern to donors, who do not want to see their contributions "squandered" on areas outside of the core programs offered by a nonprofit. For this reason, the executive directors of nonprofits pay considerable attention to paring back management and administration expenses. They also have a deep understanding of the extent to which management and administration expenses can be allocated to programs. When activities involve the direct conduct or supervision of a program, the cost of those activities should be allocated to the relevant programs from the management and administration classification.

The Fundraising Classification

Fundraising is the sales and marketing component of a nonprofit, tasked with raising funds via a variety of methods to support the expenditure level of the organization. The activities of this group can include:

- Grant proposals
- Direct solicitation of individuals and businesses for contributions
- E-mail solicitations through a mailing list of donors
- Passive solicitation via a nonprofit's website
- Seminars regarding estate planning
- Fundraising events, such as charity balls and art auctions
- Contacting employers regarding matching contributions

Fundraising is primarily intended to support programs, but must also be directed at funding the management and administration classification; indeed, some nonprofits require that a certain proportion of all contributions be targeted at management and administration expenditures, just to ensure that the organization can be properly run.

A key component of fundraising is its marketing activities. Nonprofit marketing involves creating an image of the entity that makes it an attractive target for donors. Marketing can involve advertising, printed materials, hands-on contact with donors, interviews on the radio or television, local presentations, the creation of an attractive website, and so forth.

A key accounting consideration in the fundraising area is to track fundraising expenses at the level of the individual fundraising activity. By doing so, one can determine whether the amount of funds generated exceeds the associated fundraising cost. Without this level of detail, it is quite likely that the development director will continue to spend time and money on fundraising activities that do not generate an adequate return. This fine-grained level of expense tracking can be conducted by storing expense information in accounts for individual fundraising activities. However, given the ongoing changes in the types of fundraising activities used, it can make more sense to use a more informal tracking system, such as an electronic spreadsheet.

The fundraising classification may also appear in the statement of activities as the "development" classification.

Bookkeeping Concerns

The bookkeeping for a nonprofit can be complicated, since donors may specify that their contributions only be used in certain ways. To make matters more complex, a donor may specify that certain proportions of their contributions be allocated to different types of expenditures. For example, a $10,000 donation may have attached to it a mandate that $1,000 can be spent on management and administration activities, while the remainder must be evenly split between two different programs. In this section, we note several options for reducing the bookkeeping burden on the accounting staff when dealing with these difficult tracking chores. Possible options are:

- *Review reporting requirements in advance.* The reporting requirements imposed by some donors can be quite difficult to comply with, especially when a nonprofit's accounting systems are primitive. Accordingly, it can make sense to review a donor's reporting requirements prior to accepting any contributions from it (or even applying for the funds in the first place). If the reporting is too difficult, consider not accepting the related contribution.
- *Restricted sub-accounts.* Create a small number of sub-accounts within the general classification of net assets with donor restrictions and encourage donors to contribute into these prearranged sub-accounts. Doing so keeps a nonprofit from having to create a plethora of restricted accounts, each one dealing with the different restrictions imposed by each donor.

EXAMPLE

The Munro Arts Festival finds that its donors continually contribute funds under the provision that they be used only for the presentation of specific art exhibits. This has resulted in the use of more than 40 sub-accounts within the general classification of net assets with donor restrictions. To improve the situation, the development director authorizes the creation of just three sub-accounts, which are for portraits, landscapes, and still lifes. Donors are encouraged to contribute to these sub-accounts, from which funds will be disbursed based on the art classifications indicated by their names.

- *Separate bank accounts.* Open a separate bank account for each program and move funds into the account based on what donors are allowing. The accounting staff can then focus on the remaining cash balance in each account to determine what can be spent on a program. If this approach is used, be sure to tie the balance in the bank account back to the accounting records on a regular basis, to keep any irregularities from creeping into the system.
- *Flag negative balances.* The balance in any restricted net asset account should never drop below zero, since this implies that the organization has spent more money than it has available. The accounting software should warn the accounting staff when a transaction will drop one of these account

balances below zero. If not, an ongoing staff activity should be to scan the account balances for negative amounts.

- *Document restrictions.* A nonprofit can get into trouble with its donors if it does not spend money in accordance with their wishes. To improve the odds of spending donated funds correctly, create a detailed listing of the restrictions placed on fund usage by donors, including the dates (if any) on which these restrictions are terminated. This document should be updated regularly, whenever funds with new restrictions are received, and when old restrictions are removed or the associated funds are spent.

Case Study

The use of journal entries and how they impact the financial statements of a nonprofit can be confusing, so we present in this section a case study that uses the preceding example concerning the activities of Archimedes Education to show what happens to the statement of activities and statement of financial position when each entry is made. More information about financial statements is included in the Nonprofit Financial Statements chapter.

In the first transaction, a donor contributed $10,000 to assist in the startup of the organization. The related journal entry was:

J/E #1	Debit	Credit
Cash [assets account]	10,000	
Donor contributions - unrestricted [revenue account]		10,000
To record receipt of donor contribution		

Since this is the first transaction that Archimedes has ever had, the entry is the only one impacting the financial statements, which are as follows:

Archimedes Education
Statement of Financial Position
As of January 31, 20X1

ASSETS		LIABILITIES AND NET ASSETS	
Cash and cash equivalents	$10,000	Accrued expenses	$-
Accounts receivable	-	Net assets:	
Fixed assets	-	Net assets without donor restrictions	10,000
Other assets	-	Net assets with donor restrictions	-
Total assets	$10,000	Total liabilities and net assets	$10,000

Archimedes Education
Statement of Activities
For the month ended January 31, 20X1

	Net Assets without Donor Restrictions	Net Assets with Donor Restrictions	Totals
Revenues:			
Contributions	$10,000	$-	$10,000
Net assets released from restrictions	=		
Total revenues	$10,000	$-	$10,000
Expenses:			
Program expenses	$-		$-
Management and administration expenses	-		-
Fundraising expenses	=		=
Total expenses	$-		$-
Change in net assets	$10,000	$-	$10,000
+ Beginning net assets	=	=	=
= Ending net assets	$10,000	$0	$10,000

In the second transaction, Archimedes pays $1,000 to a landlord for office space. Of this amount, $400 is a deposit and $600 is the rent for the first month. The related journal entry was:

J/E #2	Debit	Credit
Deposits [assets account]	400	
Rent expense [expense account]	600	
Cash [asset account]		1,000
To record payment of monthly rent and a related security deposit		

This transaction reduces the cash balance, recognizes a $600 expense, and creates a deposit asset, as shown in the following financial statements. Also, note that these transactions are net of the previous $10,000 contribution that already appeared in the statements.

Archimedes Education
Statement of Financial Position
As of January 31, 20X1

ASSETS		LIABILITIES AND NET ASSETS	
Cash and cash equivalents	$9,000	Accrued expenses	$-
Accounts receivable	-	Net assets:	
Fixed assets	-	Net assets without donor restrictions	9,400
Other assets	400	Net assets with donor restrictions	-
Total assets	$9,400	Total liabilities and net assets	$9,400

Archimedes Education
Statement of Activities
For the month ended January 31, 20X1

	Net Assets without Donor Restrictions	Net Assets with Donor Restrictions	Totals
Revenues:			
Contributions	$10,000	$-	$10,000
Net assets released from restrictions	=		
Total revenues	$10,000	$-	$10,000
Expenses:			
Program expenses	$-		$-
Management and administration expenses	600		600
Fundraising expenses	=		=
Total expenses	$-		$-
Change in net assets	$9,400	$-	$9,400
+ Beginning net assets	=	=	=
= Ending net assets	$9,400	$0	$9,400

In the third transaction, the donor contributes another $5,000, but this time mandates that the funds only be used to purchase a photocopier. This means that the funds are categorized as being restricted, as noted in the following journal entry.

J/E #3	Debit	Credit
Cash [assets account]	5,000	
Donor contributions – restricted [revenue account]		5,000
To record receipt of restricted donor contribution intended for photocopier purchase		

The impact on the January financial statements is that the funds are separately categorized from net assets without donor restrictions, as shown next.

Archimedes Education
Statement of Financial Position
As of January 31, 20X1

ASSETS		LIABILITIES AND NET ASSETS	
Cash and cash equivalents	$14,000	Accrued expenses	$-
Accounts receivable	-	Net assets:	
Fixed assets	-	Net assets without donor restrictions	9,400
Other assets	400	Net assets with donor restrictions	5,000
Total assets	$14,400	Total liabilities and net assets	$14,400

Archimedes Education
Statement of Activities
For the month ended January 31, 20X1

	Net Assets without Donor Restrictions	Net Assets with Donor Restrictions	Totals
Revenues:			
Contributions	$10,000	$5,000	$15,000
Net assets released from restrictions	-		
Total revenues	$10,000	$5,000	$15,000
Expenses:			
Program expenses	$-		$-
Management and administration expenses	600		600
Fundraising expenses	-		-
Total expenses	$-		$-
Change in net assets	$9,400	$5,000	$14,400
+ Beginning net assets	-	-	-
= Ending net assets	$9,400	$5,000	$14,400

In the fourth transaction, Archimedes uses the contributed $5,000 to purchase a photocopier, and records the event with the following journal entry:

J/E #4	Debit	Credit
Fixed assets – office equipment [assets account]	5,000	
Cash [assets account]		5,000
To record purchase of photocopier, using restricted funds		

This transaction shifts cash into a fixed asset, and also shifts the funds in net assets with donor restrictions to net assets without donor restrictions, as shown in the following financial statements. Note that the month in which the transaction occurs is February, which impacts the presentation in the statement of activities.

Archimedes Education
Statement of Financial Position
As of February 28, 20X1

ASSETS		LIABILITIES AND NET ASSETS	
Cash and cash equivalents	$9,000	Accrued expenses	$-
Accounts receivable	-	Net assets:	
Fixed assets	5,000	Net assets without donor restrictions	14,400
Other assets	400	Net assets with donor restrictions	-
Total assets	$14,400	Total liabilities and net assets	$14,400

Archimedes Education
Statement of Activities
For the month ended February 28, 20X1

	Net Assets without Donor Restrictions	Net Assets with Donor Restrictions	Totals
Revenues:			
Contributions	$-	$-	$-
Net assets released from restrictions	5,000	-5,000	-
Total revenues	$5,000	-$5,000	$-
Expenses:			
Program expenses	$-		$-
Management and administration expenses	-		-
Fundraising expenses	-		-
Total expenses	$-		$-
Change in net assets	$5,000	-$5,000	$-
+ Beginning net assets	9,400	5,000	14,400
= Ending net assets	$14,400	$-	$14,400

In all cases, note that the ending net asset total in the statement of financial position matches the ending net asset total in the statement of activities.

Summary

The accounting staff of a nonprofit must spend time creating the most appropriate recordkeeping structure when the system is first organized. This means deciding whether to use an accrual or cash basis system, developing an effective chart of accounts, and deciding how to account for each transaction type.

Nonprofit accounting is quite similar to project accounting, in that revenues and expenses are generally traceable to specific activities, such as programs and fundraising activities. This is a more fine-grained level of detail than many for-profit organizations engage in. This means that more accounting effort is needed for a given level of activity in a nonprofit entity than in a for-profit business.

This chapter has only addressed the most basic accounting concepts that pertain to a nonprofit. In the following chapters, we delve into a number of topics for which the accounting requirements for nonprofits are quite specific, including financial statements, revenue, investments, fixed assets, and pensions.

Chapter 3
Nonprofit Financial Statements

Introduction

Though a nonprofit does not have shareholders, there are a number of individuals and other entities that want to view its financial condition and ability to provide services, such as volunteers, donors, and lenders. This information is provided through the financial statements, which use a standardized format to describe the financial results, financial position, and cash flows of an organization. The purpose of these statements is to provide information about the following issues:

- The amount and types of assets, liabilities, and net assets held by a nonprofit, particularly in regard to the liquidity and financial flexibility of the entity
- The effects of certain events on the amount and nature of a nonprofit's net assets
- The amounts and types of inflows and outflows of economic resources
- How cash is obtained and spent
- The efforts made by a nonprofit to provide services

A nonprofit issues financial statements that are somewhat different in name and structure from those used by for-profit entities. The following table compares the financial statements used by these two types of organizations:

Nonprofit Statement	Comparable For-Profit Statement
Statement of Activities	Income Statement
Statement of Financial Position	Balance Sheet
Reporting of expenses by nature and function	(no comparable document)
Statement of Cash Flows	Statement of Cash Flows
(no comparable document)	Statement of Stockholders' Equity

In this chapter, we explore the format and content of each of the financial statements used by nonprofits.

The Statement of Financial Position

A nonprofit needs to report the state of its assets and liabilities as of the end of each reporting period, as well as provide an indication of its ability to meet its financial obligations. In a for-profit business, the financial statement used to report this information is the balance sheet. A nonprofit entity reports similar information in the *statement of financial position*. The main difference between a balance sheet and a nonprofit's statement of financial position is that the balance sheet contains a shareholders' equity section, which is replaced by a net assets section in the statement of financial position.

A simplified statement of financial position format follows.

Archimedes Education
Statement of Financial Position
As of April 30, 20X1

ASSETS		LIABILITIES AND NET ASSETS	
Cash and cash equivalents	$25,000	Accounts payable	$49,000
Accounts receivable	63,000	Net assets:	
Fixed assets	180,000	Net assets without donor restrictions	114,000
Other assets	15,000	Net assets with donor restrictions	120,000
Total assets	$283,000	Total liabilities and net assets	$283,000

The main intent of reporting this information is to show to donors that the entity is relatively liquid, and so will not go out of business after a large donation is made. If a nonprofit is borrowing money from a lender, the lender may examine this statement to see if the nonprofit is liquid enough to pay back borrowed funds.

Note: If the reported cash balance is negative, this implies that the entity probably issued checks to suppliers prior to having the offsetting cash in its bank account. The situation is remedied by using a journal entry to shift sufficient funds from the cash account back to accounts payable to bring the reported cash balance up to zero.

The types of information most likely to be found on this statement include the following items, which are presented in the order in which they are found on the statement. This organizational structure is designed to present the most liquid assets first, followed by less liquid assets, and then liabilities in order of their maturity, with the most immediate obligations listed first. Net assets are noted last. The line items are:

- *Cash and cash equivalents* [asset]. This is cash or assets readily convertible into cash. Examples of cash are coins, currency, cash in checking accounts, cash in savings accounts, bank drafts, money orders, and petty cash. Examples of cash equivalents are commercial paper, marketable securities, money market funds, short-term government bonds, and treasury bills. The two primary criteria for classification as a cash equivalent are that an asset be readily convertible into a known amount of cash, and that it be so near its maturity that there is an insignificant risk of changes in value due to changes in interest rates. A key point is that, if a donor restricts the use of cash to a longer-term purpose, this cash must be presented as a longer-term asset, not as part of the cash line item. Otherwise, a reader of the financial statements would assume that this cash is available to pay for immediate liabilities.

- *Accounts / pledges receivable* [asset]. A nonprofit may have a business in which it bills customers, in which case all unpaid billings are considered accounts receivable. In the more common case where donors pledge money to a nonprofit, these unpaid amounts are classified as pledges receivable.
- *Prepaid expenses* [asset]. This is expenditures made in advance of consumption. For example, a nonprofit may pay a landlord at the end of the month for the following month's rent. Since the rent has not yet been consumed, it is initially classified as a prepaid expense. This is also a common classification for prepaid insurance.
- *Investments* [asset]. This is the fair value of all investments made by a nonprofit, such as in corporate stocks and bonds.
- *Fixed assets* [asset]. This is the amounts paid for assets having a longer-term useful life, net of any accumulated depreciation taken against them.
- *Accounts payable* [liability]. This is the aggregate amount of any liabilities payable to suppliers, which have been incurred but not yet paid.
- *Accrued expenses* [liability]. This is the amounts of any liabilities payable to third parties, for which invoices have not yet been received but for which a liability has been incurred and no payment has yet been made.
- *Grants payable* [liability]. This is a promise of payment made to issue a grant to a third party.
- *Deferred revenue* [liability]. This is deposits made by third parties that the nonprofit has not yet earned, or where there is a condition attached to a donation.
- *Debt [liability]*. This is the amount of any unpaid principal and interest associated with a loan.
- *Net assets without donor restrictions* [net asset]. This is the unrestricted amount of residual assets.
- *Net assets with donor restrictions* [net asset]. This is the remaining balance of those donations received that have conditions attached to them. Separate line items may be reported to distinguish between different types of donor-imposed restrictions, such as:
  - Assets that must be invested to provide a permanent source of income
  - Assets intended to support specific operating activities
  - Assets to be used in a specific future period
  - Assets that are to be preserved and not sold

A more comprehensive statement of financial position that includes all of the preceding items is as follows:

Archimedes Education
Statement of Financial Position
As of April 30, 20X1

ASSETS		LIABILITIES AND NET ASSETS	
Cash and cash equivalents	$25,000	Accounts payable	$12,000
Accounts and pledges receivable	63,000	Accrued expenses	5,000
Prepaid expenses	5,000	Grants payable	14,000
Investments	10,000	Deferred revenue	8,000
Fixed assets	180,000	Debt	10,000
		Net assets:	
		Without donor restrictions	114,000
		With donor restrictions	120,000
Total assets	$283,000	Total liabilities and net assets	$283,000

A statement of financial position might contain extra line items that identify current assets and current liabilities. A current asset is either cash or an asset that can be converted into cash within one year. A current liability is a liability that is payable within one year. If this identification is used, all items considered current assets or current liabilities are indented beneath the applicable line item. For example:

Current Assets:	Current Liabilities:
Cash and cash equivalents	Accounts payable
Accounts and pledges receivable	Accrued expenses
Prepaid expenses	Grants payable
Investments	Deferred revenue

It can make sense to arrange the format of the statement of financial position to match the reporting requirements of the Internal Revenue Service (IRS) in its annual Form 990. The following exhibit is an extract from the form that shows the reporting structure that the IRS expects to see.

Form 990 Reporting Requirement for the Statement of Financial Position

Part X	Balance Sheet			
Check if Schedule O contains a response or note to any line in this Part X . . . . ☐				

				(A) Beginning of year		(B) End of year
Assets	1	Cash—non-interest-bearing			1	
	2	Savings and temporary cash investments			2	
	3	Pledges and grants receivable, net			3	
	4	Accounts receivable, net			4	
	5	Loans and other receivables from current and former officers, directors, trustees, key employees, and highest compensated employees. Complete Part II of Schedule L			5	
	6	Loans and other receivables from other disqualified persons (as defined under section 4958(f)(1)), persons described in section 4958(c)(3)(B), and contributing employers and sponsoring organizations of section 501(c)(9) voluntary employees' beneficiary organizations (see instructions). Complete Part II of Schedule L			6	
	7	Notes and loans receivable, net			7	
	8	Inventories for sale or use			8	
	9	Prepaid expenses and deferred charges			9	
	10a	Land, buildings, and equipment: cost or other basis. Complete Part VI of Schedule D	10a			
	b	Less: accumulated depreciation	10b		10c	
	11	Investments—publicly traded securities			11	
	12	Investments—other securities. See Part IV, line 11 . .			12	
	13	Investments—program-related. See Part IV, line 11 .			13	
	14	Intangible assets			14	
	15	Other assets. See Part IV, line 11			15	
	16	**Total assets.** Add lines 1 through 15 (must equal line 34) . . .			16	
Liabilities	17	Accounts payable and accrued expenses			17	
	18	Grants payable			18	
	19	Deferred revenue			19	
	20	Tax-exempt bond liabilities			20	
	21	Escrow or custodial account liability. Complete Part IV of Schedule D .			21	
	22	Loans and other payables to current and former officers, directors, trustees, key employees, highest compensated employees, and disqualified persons. Complete Part II of Schedule L			22	
	23	Secured mortgages and notes payable to unrelated third parties . .			23	
	24	Unsecured notes and loans payable to unrelated third parties . . .			24	
	25	Other liabilities (including federal income tax, payables to related third parties, and other liabilities not included on lines 17-24). Complete Part X of Schedule D			25	
	26	**Total liabilities.** Add lines 17 through 25			26	
Net Assets or Fund Balances		Organizations that follow SFAS 117 (ASC 958), check here ▶ ☐ and complete lines 27 through 29, and lines 33 and 34.				
	27	Unrestricted net assets			27	
	28	Temporarily restricted net assets			28	
	29	Permanently restricted net assets			29	
		Organizations that do not follow SFAS 117 (ASC 958), check here ▶ ☐ and complete lines 30 through 34.				
	30	Capital stock or trust principal, or current funds			30	
	31	Paid-in or capital surplus, or land, building, or equipment fund . . .			31	
	32	Retained earnings, endowment, accumulated income, or other funds .			32	
	33	Total net assets or fund balances			33	
	34	Total liabilities and net assets/fund balances			34	

Form **990** (2016)

A donor-restricted endowment fund may be an underwater endowment fund. This classification arises when a fund's fair value is less than the original gift amount or the amount that the donor or the law requires must be maintained. In this situation, the accumulated losses associated with the fund are to be included together with that fund in the line item for net assets with donor restrictions.

The Statement of Activities

The primary intent of a nonprofit is (as the name implies) something other than earning a profit. Consequently, a nonprofit does not issue an income statement, as does a for-profit business. Instead, a nonprofit issues an alternative called a *statement of activities*. This statement quantifies the revenue and expenses of a nonprofit for a reporting period. These revenues and expenses are broken down into the "without donor restrictions" and "with donor restrictions" classifications that were referred to earlier for the statement of financial position, and which are divided into separate columns across the statement. The rows in the statement reveal revenues and expenses. Though it is possible to compress these rows down to just a few line items, it is customary to be more expansive in detailing revenues and expenses. For example, line items that may be separately presented for nonprofit revenues can include:

- Contributions
- Fundraising events
- Gain on sale of investments
- Grants
- Investment income
- Member dues
- Program fees

Explanations for these line items are noted in the following Revenue Accounting chapter. In addition, nonprofit revenues can include net assets released from restriction. This is funds received in an earlier period that had restrictions placed on them, and for which the restrictions have now been lifted. When these funds are shifted from the "with donor restrictions" column to the "without donor restrictions" column, the net effect on revenues during the reporting period is always zero, since this is just a change in classification.

Line items for expenses may also be separately presented, and in considerable detail. At a minimum, the statement of activities usually includes the following line items:

- *Program expenses*. Those expenses incurred in order to deliver specific programs in accordance with the mission of the nonprofit. The presentation may include additional line items to break out the expenses associated with each individual program.
- *Support services expenses*. Those expenses used to manage the organization and raise funds.

The net effect of all revenues and expenses is a change in net assets, rather than the profit or loss figure found in the income statement of a for-profit entity. A sample statement of activities format follows.

Archimedes Education
Statement of Activities
For the month ended June 30, 20X1

	Without Donor Restrictions	With Donor Restrictions	Totals
Revenues, gains, and other support:			
Contributions	$48,000	$10,000	$58,000
Net unrealized and realized gains on long-term investments	2,000		2,000
Net assets released from restrictions	12,000	-$12,000	
Total revenues, gains, and other support	$62,000	-$2,000	$60,000
Expenses and losses:			
Program expenses	$29,000		$29,000
Management and administration expenses	11,000		11,000
Fundraising expenses	6,000		6,000
Total expenses	$46,000		$46,000
Change in net assets	$16,000	-$2,000	$14,000
+ Beginning net assets	32,000	12,000	44,000
= Ending net assets	$48,000	$10,000	$58,000

In the sample, Archimedes has obtained $48,000 of unrestricted revenues that it is allowed to use in any way, such as to pay for current operations. In addition, a donor restriction on revenues received in an earlier period has been lifted, allowing Archimedes to spend $12,000 that had been contributed in a prior period; this involves a reclassification from the donor restrictions category to the without donor restrictions category. In addition, $10,000 of contributions have been received, and for which there is a donor restriction. There are also unrealized gains of $2,000 on investments.

Despite the implication that a nonprofit is not supposed to earn a profit, it may need to generate substantial profits in order to guard against shortfalls in donor funding or unexpected increases in expenses. Consequently, the results appearing in the statement of activities are closely perused by the managers of a nonprofit, to see if the business is generating sufficient profit to guard against future financial difficulties.

The ending net assets figure in the statement of activities should tie back to the information in the statement of financial position. This is the beginning amount of net assets, net of any changes in net assets during the reporting period.

The IRS requires that a subset of the information in the statement of activities related to revenues be presented in a specific format in its annual Form 990. The following exhibit is an extract from the form that shows the reporting structure that the IRS expects to see. It can make sense to design a chart of accounts for a nonprofit so that the required information can be easily extracted in the IRS-mandated format.

Form 990 Reporting Requirement for the Statement of Revenue

Part VIII	Statement of Revenue			(A) Total revenue	(B) Related or exempt function revenue	(C) Unrelated business revenue	(D) Revenue excluded from tax under sections 512-514
	Check if Schedule O contains a response or note to any line in this Part VIII ☐						
Contributions, Gifts, Grants and Other Similar Amounts	1a Federated campaigns	1a					
	b Membership dues	1b					
	c Fundraising events	1c					
	d Related organizations	1d					
	e Government grants (contributions)	1e					
	f All other contributions, gifts, grants, and similar amounts not included above	1f					
	g Noncash contributions included in lines 1a-1f: $						
	h Total. Add lines 1a-1f						
Program Service Revenue			Business Code				
	2a						
	b						
	c						
	d						
	e						
	f All other program service revenue						
	g Total. Add lines 2a-2f						
Other Revenue	3 Investment income (including dividends, interest, and other similar amounts)						
	4 Income from investment of tax-exempt bond proceeds						
	5 Royalties						
		(i) Real	(ii) Personal				
	6a Gross rents						
	b Less: rental expenses						
	c Rental income or (loss)						
	d Net rental income or (loss)						
	7a Gross amount from sales of assets other than inventory	(i) Securities	(ii) Other				
	b Less: cost or other basis and sales expenses						
	c Gain or (loss)						
	d Net gain or (loss)						
	8a Gross income from fundraising events (not including $ ____ of contributions reported on line 1c). See Part IV, line 18	a					
	b Less: direct expenses	b					
	c Net income or (loss) from fundraising events						
	9a Gross income from gaming activities. See Part IV, line 19	a					
	b Less: direct expenses	b					
	c Net income or (loss) from gaming activities						
	10a Gross sales of inventory, less returns and allowances	a					
	b Less: cost of goods sold	b					
	c Net income or (loss) from sales of inventory						
	Miscellaneous Revenue		Business Code				
	11a						
	b						
	c						
	d All other revenue						
	e Total. Add lines 11a-11d						
	12 Total revenue. See instructions.						

Form **990** (2016)

The Statement of Cash Flows

The *statement of cash flows* contains information about the flows of cash into and out of a nonprofit; in particular, it shows the extent of those nonprofit activities that generate and use cash. This information is useful for donors, who may want to know how their contributed funds are used. The primary activities are:

- *Operating activities.* These are an entity's primary revenue-producing activities. Examples of operating activities are the provision of program services and the receipt of donations from contributors, as well as disbursements to contractors and employees.
- *Investing activities.* These involve the purchase and sale of investment instruments, as well as the acquisition of fixed assets.
- *Financing activities.* These activities include the incurrence and repayment of debt. Financing activities can also include the earning of interest and dividends associated with net assets with donor restrictions.

A nonprofit can use the *direct method* or the *indirect method* to present the statement of cash flows. These methods are described next.

The Direct Method

The direct method of presenting the statement of cash flows presents the specific cash flows associated with items that affect cash flow. Items that typically do so include:

- Cash collected from customers
- Interest and dividends received
- Cash paid to employees
- Cash paid to suppliers
- Interest paid
- Income taxes paid

The format of the direct method appears in the following example. If the direct method is used, a nonprofit can provide a reconciliation to the indirect method (as explained next), but it is not required.

EXAMPLE

Newton Education constructs the following statement of cash flows using the direct method:

Newton Education
Statement of Cash Flows
For the year ended 12/31/20X1

Cash flows from operating activities		
Cash receipts from donors	$45,800,000	
Cash paid to suppliers	-29,800,000	
Cash paid to employees	-11,200,000	
Interest paid	-310,000	
Grants paid	-1,700,000	
Net cash provided by operating activities		$2,790,000
Cash flows from investing activities		
Purchase of fixed assets	-580,000	
Proceeds from sale of investments	110,000	
Net cash used by investing activities		-470,000
Cash flows from financing activities		
Proceeds from new mortgage	1,500,000	
Payment of mortgage	-460,000	
Net cash provided by financing activities		1,040,000
Net increase in cash and cash equivalents		3,360,000
Cash and cash equivalents at beginning of period		1,640,000
Cash and cash equivalents at end of period		$5,000,000

Reconciliation of change in net assets to net cash provided by operating activities:

Change in net assets		$2,665,000
Adjustments to reconcile change in net assets to net cash provided by operating activities:		
Depreciation and amortization	$125,000	
Provision for losses on pledges receivable	15,000	
Gain on sale of equipment	-155,000	
Increase in grants payable	32,000	
Increase in accounts payable	90,000	
Increase in other liabilities	18,000	
Total adjustments		125,000
Net cash provided by operating activities		$2,790,000

The standard-setting bodies encourage the use of the direct method, but it is rarely used, for the excellent reason that the information in it is difficult to assemble; nonprofits usually do not collect and store information in the manner required for this format. Instead, they use the indirect method, which is described next.

The Indirect Method

Under the indirect method of presenting the statement of cash flows, the presentation begins with the change in net assets, with subsequent additions to or deductions from that amount for non-cash revenue and expense items, resulting in cash generated from operations. The cash flows are further adjusted for cash flows from investing and financing activities. The format of the indirect method appears in the following example.

EXAMPLE

Newton Education constructs the following statement of cash flows using the indirect method:

Newton Education
Statement of Cash Flows
For the year ended 12/31/20X1

Cash flows from operating activities		
Change in net assets		$3,000,000
Adjustments to reconcile change in net assets to net cash provided by operating activities:		
Depreciation and amortization	$125,000	
Provision for losses on pledges receivable	20,000	
Gain on sale of facility	-65,000	
		80,000
Increase in pledges receivable	-250,000	
Decrease in inventories	325,000	
Decrease in trade payables	-50,000	
		25,000
Cash generated from operations		3,105,000
Cash flows from investing activities		
Purchase of fixed assets	-500,000	
Proceeds from sale of equipment	35,000	
Net cash used in investing activities		-465,000

Cash flows from financing activities

Proceeds from new mortgage	325,000	
Payment of mortgage	-45,000	
Net cash used in financing activities		280,000
Net increase in cash and cash equivalents		2,920,000
Cash and cash equivalents at beginning of period		2,080,000
Cash and cash equivalents at end of period		$5,000,000

The indirect method is very popular, because the information required for it is relatively easily assembled from the accounts that a nonprofit normally maintains.

How to Prepare the Statement of Cash Flows

The most commonly used format for the statement of cash flows is the indirect method. The general layout of an indirect method statement of cash flows is shown below, along with an explanation of the source of the information in the statement.

Nonprofit Name
Statement of Cash Flows
For the year ended 12/31/20X1

Line Item	Derivation
Cash flows from operating activities	
Change in net assets	From the change in net assets line on the statement of activities
Adjustment for:	
Depreciation and amortization	From the corresponding line items in the statement of activities
Provision for losses on pledges receivable	From the change in the allowance for doubtful accounts in the period
Gain/loss on sale of facility	From the gain/loss accounts in the statement of activities
Increase/decrease in pledges receivable	Change in pledges receivable during the period, from the statement of financial position
Increase/decrease in inventories	Change in inventories during the period, from the statement of financial position
Increase/decrease in trade payables	Change in trade payables during the period, from the statement of financial position
Cash generated from operations	Summary of the preceding items in this section

Line Item	Derivation
Cash flows from investing activities	
Purchase of fixed assets	Itemized in the fixed asset accounts during the period
Proceeds from sale of fixed assets	Itemized in the fixed asset accounts during the period
Net cash used in investing activities	Summary of the preceding items in this section
Cash flows from financing activities	
Proceeds from new mortgage	Itemized in the long-term debt account during the period
Payment of mortgage	Itemized in the long-term debt account during the period
Net cash used in financing activities	Summary of the preceding items in this section
Net change in cash and cash equivalents	Summary of all preceding subtotals

The general layout of a direct method statement of cash flows is shown next, along with an explanation of the source of the information in the statement.

Nonprofit Name
Statement of Cash Flows
For the year ended 12/31/20X1

Line Item	Derivation
Cash flows from operating activities	
Cash receipts from customers	Summary of the cash receipts journal for the period
Cash paid to suppliers	Summary of the cash disbursements journal for the period (less the financing payments noted below)
Cash paid to employees	Summary of the payroll journal for the period
Cash generated from operations	Summary of the preceding items in this section
Interest paid	Itemized in the cash disbursements journal
Grants paid	Itemized in the cash disbursements journal
Net cash from operating activities	Summary of the preceding items in this section

Line Item	Derivation
Cash flows from investing activities	
Purchase of fixed assets	Itemized in the fixed asset accounts during the period
Proceeds from sale of fixed assets	Itemized in the fixed asset accounts during the period
Net cash used in investing activities	Summary of the preceding items in this section
Cash flows from financing activities	
Proceeds from new mortgage	Itemized in the long-term debt account during the period
Payment of mortgage	Itemized in the long-term debt account during the period
Net cash used in financing activities	Summary of the preceding items in this section
Net change in cash and cash equivalents	Summary of all preceding subtotals

As can be seen from the explanations for either the indirect or direct methods, the statement of cash flows is much more difficult to create than the statement of activities and statement of financial position. In fact, a complete statement may require a substantial supporting spreadsheet that shows the details for each line item in the statement.

If the nonprofit's accounting software contains a template for the statement of cash flows, use it! The information may not be aggregated quite correctly, and it may not contain all of the line items required for the statement, but it *will* produce most of the information needed, and is much easier to modify than the alternative of creating the statement entirely by hand.

Reporting of Expenses by Nature and Function

It can be useful for a nonprofit to report its expenses by nature and function. This presentation is used to show how expenses are incurred for each functional area of the business. Information reported by nature means that a line item is presented that contains expense results, such as for salaries, rent, electricity, supplies, interest expense, and so forth. This information must be reported in one place, which can be on the face of the statement of activities, as disclosure notes, or in a separate financial statement.

Functional areas typically include the following:

- Management and administration
- Fundraising
- Programs

A possible presentation of this information is as a matrix, where each functional area is listed across the top row of the report, and the expense types are listed down the left side. This approach presents the relationship between the functional and natural classifications for all expenses. An example follows:

Newton Education
Expenses by Nature and Function
for the year ended 12/31/xx

	Management and Administration	Fundraising	Secondary Education Program	Primary Education Program	Totals
Compensation	$225,000	$190,000	815,000	$1,230,000	$2,460,000
Rent and utilities	78,000	25,000	100,000	190,000	393,000
Supplies	26,000	12,000	65,000	83,000	186,000
Depreciation	15,000	10,000	29,000	34,000	88,000
Total	$344,000	$237,000	$1,009,000	$1,537,000	$3,127,000

If a nonprofit has a number of programs, it is permissible to aggregate and report their functional expenses. When aggregating programs for reporting purposes, do so by the function of each set of programs. Also, consistently aggregate this information from period to period, so that a reader can track changes in expense levels over time.

Expenses reported by nature and function should tie back to the information in the statement of activities.

It can make sense to arrange the reporting of expenses by nature and function to match the reporting requirements of the IRS in its annual Form 990. The following exhibit is an extract from the form that shows the reporting structure that the IRS expects to see.

Form 990 Reporting Requirement for the Statement of Functional Expenses

Part IX **Statement of Functional Expenses**

Section 501(c)(3) and 501(c)(4) organizations must complete all columns. All other organizations must complete column (A).

Check if Schedule O contains a response or note to any line in this Part IX . . . . ☐

Do not include amounts reported on lines 6b, 7b, 8b, 9b, and 10b of Part VIII.	(A) Total expenses	(B) Program service expenses	(C) Management and general expenses	(D) Fundraising expenses
1 Grants and other assistance to domestic organizations and domestic governments. See Part IV, line 21 . .				
2 Grants and other assistance to domestic individuals. See Part IV, line 22				
3 Grants and other assistance to foreign organizations, foreign governments, and foreign individuals. See Part IV, lines 15 and 16 . . .				
4 Benefits paid to or for members				
5 Compensation of current officers, directors, trustees, and key employees				
6 Compensation not included above, to disqualified persons (as defined under section 4958(f)(1)) and persons described in section 4958(c)(3)(B) . .				
7 Other salaries and wages				
8 Pension plan accruals and contributions (include section 401(k) and 403(b) employer contributions)				
9 Other employee benefits				
10 Payroll taxes				
11 Fees for services (non-employees):				
a Management				
b Legal				
c Accounting				
d Lobbying				
e Professional fundraising services. See Part IV, line 17				
f Investment management fees . . .				
g Other. (If line 11g amount exceeds 10% of line 25, column (A) amount, list line 11g expenses on Schedule O.) . .				
12 Advertising and promotion				
13 Office expenses				
14 Information technology				
15 Royalties				
16 Occupancy				
17 Travel				
18 Payments of travel or entertainment expenses for any federal, state, or local public officials				
19 Conferences, conventions, and meetings .				
20 Interest				
21 Payments to affiliates				
22 Depreciation, depletion, and amortization .				
23 Insurance				
24 Other expenses. Itemize expenses not covered above (List miscellaneous expenses in line 24e. If line 24e amount exceeds 10% of line 25, column (A) amount, list line 24e expenses on Schedule O.)				
a				
b				
c				
d				
e All other expenses				
25 Total functional expenses. Add lines 1 through 24e				
26 **Joint costs.** Complete this line only if the organization reported in column (B) joint costs from a combined educational campaign and fundraising solicitation. Check here ▶ ☐ if following SOP 98-2 (ASC 958-720)				

Form **990** (2016)

Financial Statement Disclosures

When issuing financial statements to outside parties, it is usually necessary to attach a set of disclosures to the financial statements that describe additional issues. The most common disclosure addresses the accounting policies used by the organization, such as whether it uses the cash or accrual basis of accounting. There may also be a set of subsidiary-level tables that provide further information about certain line items in the financial statements, such as a breakdown of the classifications of fixed assets listed in the statement of financial position. These additional disclosures are noted at the end of other chapters that pertain to more specific accounting topics.

In addition, there are several general disclosures that must be made when nonprofit financials are released. These general disclosures are:

- *Nature of activities.* State what the nonprofit does; if there are several different programs, describe them in general terms. This description can instead be included in the statement of activities by listing them within the column headers.
- *Endowment funds.* If there are endowment funds, disclose how they are classified within net assets, how net assets have changed in the reporting period, the spending policies associated with net assets, and any related policies pertaining to how these funds are invested.
- *Legal interpretation.* If there are laws governing the classification of net assets and restricted endowment funds, clarify the board's interpretation of these laws. For example:

The entity is subject to the State Prudent Management of Institutional Funds Act (SPMIFA), and so classifies the amounts in its donor-restricted endowment funds as net assets with donor restrictions because those net assets are time-restricted until the Board appropriates the amounts for expenditure. The Board has interpreted SPMIFA as not requiring the maintenance of purchasing power of the original amount contributed, unless a donor stipulates to the contrary. As a result of this interpretation, the Board considers a fund to be underwater if the fair value of the fund is less than the sum of the original value of donated gifts and any accumulations to the fund that are required to be maintained in perpetuity, as noted in the directions accompanying the applicable gift instrument.

- *Spending policy.* Clarify the entity's spending policy for how endowment assets are used, including its interpretation of the ability to spend from underwater endowment funds. For example:

The entity spending policy is to appropriate all of the excess return from its endowments over the amount needed to maintain the value of those endowments, less 20% of this excess return, which is added back to the endowments. The intent of this policy is to continue to increase the endowment valuation over time, thereby improving the financial security of the entity.

- *Investment policy.* Note the details of the entity's investment policy, including return objectives and risk parameters, how these objectives relate to the spending policy, and the strategies used to achieve the return objectives. For example:

The entity seeks to achieve a consistent rate of return over time, so that it can provide some predictability to the cash inflow available to its programs. Accordingly, all funds are used to purchase highly-rated bonds, with maturities designed to match the needs of the programs to which the funds are linked. To diversify risk, bonds are purchased from a variety of industry and government sectors.

- *Endowment composition.* State the composition of the endowments by class of net assets. Separately show donor-restricted funds from board-restricted funds. For example:

Net assets with donor restrictions, the income from which is expendable to support:	
Program A activities	$400,000
Program B activities	120,000
Program C activities	1,250,000
Total	$1,770,000

- *Reconciliation.* Provide a reconciliation that shows all changes in the period from the beginning endowment to the ending endowment, by net asset class. The reconciliation should be broken down into investment income, net appreciation or depreciation of assets, contributions, appropriations, reclassifications, and any other changes. For example:

	Net Assets without Donor Restrictions	Net Assets with Donor Restrictions	Total
Endowment net assets, beginning of year	$2,000,000	$5,200,000	$7,200,000
Net investment return	90,000	240,000	330,000
Contributions	200,000	600,000	800,000
Appropriations for expenditure that contain no purpose restrictions	210,000	240,000	450,000
Endowment net assets, end of year	$2,080,000	$5,800,000	$7,880,000

- *Deficiencies.* Note the fair value of underwater endowment funds, the original amount required to be maintained, and the aggregate deficiency in these funds. For example:

Certain of the entity's endowment funds stipulate that any changes in the consumer price index that deflate the value of an endowment be added back into the endow-

47

ment, thereby preserving the inflation-adjusted value of the endowment. In the presented year of results, the fair value of the entity's underwater endowment funds was $1,150,000, as compared to $1,270,000 that was required to be maintained. The difference was an aggregate deficiency of $120,000 in these funds.

- *Fundraising ratio.* If a fundraising expense to contributions received ratio is presented, also reveal how the ratio is calculated.
- *Purchasing power.* If a nonprofit is subject to a donor restriction or law that requires the maintenance of purchasing power for donor-restricted endowment funds, the nonprofit should periodically adjust the disclosed amount that must be maintained in order to uphold the purchasing power of the endowment fund.
- *Liquidity.* Describe the liquidity or maturity of assets and liabilities, including any restrictions and/or self-imposed limits on the use of certain items. Note how the nonprofit makes its liquid resources available to meet cash needs for general expenditures within the next year. If applicable, include the following additional information:
  - o Unusual circumstances restricting the use of cash
  - o Significant liquidity problems
  - o Any circumstances under which the nonprofit has not maintained sufficient cash to comply with donor-imposed restrictions
  - o Information about material limitations resulting from contractual agreements with business partners, including loan covenants

For example:

The entity has $250,000 of financial assets available within one year of the balance sheet date to meet its cash needs for general expenditures, consisting of cash of $50,000, contributions receivable of $80,000 and short-term investments of $120,000. None of these assets are subject to contractual or donor restrictions that would make them unavailable for general expenditure within one year of the balance sheet date.

The entity has a goal to maintain financial assets, which consist of cash and short-term investments, on hand to meet 75 days of normal operating expenses, which are usually $100,000. As part of its liquidity management processes, the entity invests cash in excess of daily requirements in Board-approved short-term investments, including money market funds and certificates of deposit. In addition, the entity has a committed line of credit for $25,000, which it can draw upon to meet any unanticipated liquidity needs.

- *Board designations.* If the financial statements include internal board designations or appropriations, include in the accompanying notes an appropriate level of disaggregation of these actions.
- *Cost allocations.* Describe the methods used to allocate costs among the various program and support functions.

- *Asset restrictions.* If there are restrictions on the assets presented within the statement of financial position, clarify the nature of these restrictions in the notes accompanying the financial statements. Also, note any contractual limitations on the use of assets, such as:
  - o Assets set aside to satisfy reserve requirements under charitable gift annuity agreements
  - o Assets set aside under collateral arrangements
  - o Assets set aside under self-insurance funding arrangements
  - o Restricted cash set aside under debt agreements

Summary

This chapter described the nature and content of the financial statements that a nonprofit is expected to produce. It is critical to fully understand each line item in these statements at a level of detail where they can be explained to contributors. Otherwise, ignorance of the financial statements can lead to the loss of contributions from key donors. It is helpful to examine the Analysis of a Nonprofit's Financial Health chapter to gain a greater understanding of how additional information can be teased out of the financial statements.

A crucial issue when constructing financial statements is to adopt a consistent method for recording revenues and charging expenses to the same functions and programs from period to period. This is much more of an issue than with for-profit organizations, since a nonprofit needs to assign revenues and expenses at a more detailed level. If these assignments are made incorrectly or are deliberately skewed, the result can be financial statements that give an incorrect impression of how funds are being used, which can impact the amount of contributions received from donors.

Chapter 4
Revenue Accounting

Introduction

A nonprofit's management is likely to be especially concerned with the amount of revenues that the organization can recognize, since an upward trend of revenues is an indicator of an organization's health that may attract additional donors. Also, an organization with higher revenue levels may qualify for a larger proportion of available government grants. Consequently, there is likely to be great interest in the accounting rules related to revenue. In this chapter, we address the various types of revenue, pass-through contributions, exchange value, revenue journal entries, and similar topics.

Types of Revenue

Revenue is the "top line" income that a nonprofit receives from third parties. A nonprofit can receive a variety of revenue types, which include:

- *Donor contributions.* This is a payment made by a third party, where the third party does not expect to receive any compensation in exchange for the payment. A donor contribution may be unrestricted or restricted. The payment may be in cash, or in the form of some other asset, or by paying off a liability owed by a nonprofit. Contributions received that have donor-imposed restrictions are reported as donor-restricted support that increases net assets with donor restrictions. When contributions have no donor-imposed restrictions, they are reported as support that increases net assets without donor restrictions. Donor-restricted contributions for which the conditions are met in the same reporting period can be reported as support within net assets without donor restrictions.

- *Fundraising proceeds.* A nonprofit routinely engages in events that are designed to raise money for its general operations or for specific programs. Sample fundraising events are art shows, dinners, and periodic mailings. These activities may involve the transfer of some item of value back to a donor, such as art work, a dinner, or a trip. The value of these items of value is termed *exchange value*, which is dealt with in a later section.

- *Fee for services.* A nonprofit may have operations similar to those of a for-profit enterprise, where it provides goods or services in exchange for a fee. If so, the fee is treated as revenue, while the cost of the goods or services provided are recognized within the cost of goods (or services) sold line item. These fees are recognized during the period when goods are sold or services are provided. Examples of fee for service arrangements are:

- o An institute of higher learning charges tuition in exchange for providing a degree program. The tuition fee is recognized over the period during which the education is provided.
- o A state CPA society charges its members a fee for continuing professional education classes that they attend. The fee is recognized in the period when the classes are attended.
- o A ballet company charges attendees a fee for their performances. The fee is recognized in the period when the performance is completed.

- *Promises to give.* Donors may commit in writing to making payments to a nonprofit, perhaps over several years. See the following Promises to Give section for more information.
- *Stock donations.* Donors may contribute some portion of their stock holdings to nonprofits in order to take a tax deduction on the fair value of the stock. When this happens, the nonprofit records the value of the stock received at its fair value on the date of receipt. See the Investment Accounting chapter for more information.
- *Collections.* A group of artworks intended for public use is considered a collection. There are multiple options for how to recognize a collection (if at all), which are dealt with in the Fixed Asset Accounting chapter.
- *In-kind service donations.* Volunteers routinely donate large amounts of their time to the operations of a nonprofit. A nonprofit can record the value of their time using a reasonable valuation, but only if both of the following conditions are met:
  - o The services create or enhance non-financial assets; and
  - o The services require specialized skills, are provided by persons with those skills, and would otherwise need to be purchased.

If these conditions are met, the nonprofit recognizes the value of the services as both revenue and an expense, so that the net effect on the statement of activities is zero. The accounting is somewhat different if a fixed asset is involved; see the Fixed Asset Accounting chapter for more information.

Tip: Since there is no net change in the statement of financial activities as a result of recording in-kind service donations (with the exception of fixed assets), it is usually easiest to not record these types of donations at all.

- *In-kind materials donations.* A donor may contribute assets other than cash. For example, foodstuffs or used cars may be donated. These donations are to be recorded at their fair values. The fair value of any inventory items contributed can be derived from published catalogs, vendors, appraisers, and so forth. The amount of effort that goes into the determination of fair value will likely depend on the extent of the donation; for example, a nonprofit is more likely to engage the services of an appraiser if a facility is donated than if a bag of used clothes is received.

Tip: When it is difficult to assign a value to a donation, it is best not to assign a value at all. For example, it can be difficult to assign a value to a gift of used clothing, and the value is also likely to be so small that ascertaining a valuation is not worthwhile.

- *Items to be used in fundraising.* Donors may contribute such items as gift certificates, trips, and concert tickets to a nonprofit, to be used as prizes in fundraising campaigns. These items are to be recorded as revenue at their fair values when received. Once these items are given away as part of a fundraising event, the nonprofit can also recognize as revenue the difference between the fundraising total and the previously recorded revenue associated with the items used in the fundraising event.
- *Memberships.* Nonprofits may have a large membership base that pays an annual membership fee. If so, the entity recognizes this revenue ratably over the period covered by a membership.

A gain can be comprised of any of the preceding items, but only when the item does not constitute one of the ongoing major operations of the organization. For example, the gain on sale of an asset is likely to be recorded as a gain, rather than revenue, unless the entity is in the business of selling assets. Thus, revenue in one nonprofit might be considered a gain in another nonprofit.

Promises to Give

A donor may promise a nonprofit to contribute money to it in the future. This promise is called a *pledge*. There are many types of pledges, such as ones that are to be fulfilled all at one time, in increments, and with or without restrictions. The accounting for a pledge depends upon the conditions attached to it. The variations are:

- *Unconditional pledge.* When a donor commits to a pledge without reservation, the nonprofit receiving the funds records the pledge as revenue and an account receivable.
- *Conditional pledge.* When a donor commits to a pledge, but only when a condition is met, the nonprofit does not record anything. Instead, it waits for the condition to be fulfilled and then records the pledge as revenue and an account receivable. If the probability that a condition will *not* be fulfilled is remote, the pledge can be treated as an unconditional pledge.

EXAMPLE

Mole Industries has a standing policy of matching all donations made by its employees to Archimedes Education. The offer of Mole Industries is a conditional pledge, since it is contingent upon donations being made by its employees. In May, Mole's employees contribute $500 to Archimedes, so Mole pays Archimedes an additional $500. This matching amount can be recognized by Archimedes upon receipt.

EXAMPLE

The president of Mole Industries promises to give Archimedes an additional $10,000 donation if Archimedes provides him with its year-end financial statements. Since the probability that Archimedes will withhold this information is remote, Archimedes could treat the promise as an unconditional one, and recognize the revenue and an offsetting receivable at once.

When in doubt, a nonprofit should not record a pledge in the accounting records. Instead, wait for the situation to resolve itself, so that it can tell with certainty the circumstances under which a donor will make a contribution. In many cases, a simple notification of a forthcoming payment is not sufficient proof that a pledge exists. Instead, there should be a well-documented pledge that itemizes the amount to be paid and any conditions that must be fulfilled prior to payment.

If a pledge commitment is unconditional and legally enforceable, the nonprofit is required to recognize the present value of the entire series of payments. Present value is the current worth of the cash to be received in the future with one or more payments, which has been discounted at a market rate of interest. The present value requirement is subject to the following variations:

- If the funds are to be received within one year, it is permissible to recognize the entire amount of the pledge, rather than just its present value.
- The estimated amount of cash flows can be used in the present value calculation, rather than the pledged amount. This allows management to be more conservative and recognize a lesser amount of revenue if it is uncertain about the total amount to be received or the timing of the receipt.

Tip: When a donor pledges that a contribution will be made in a certain amount and then fulfills the pledge with a stock donation, it is possible that the fair value of the stock will be less than the amount of the pledge. If so, contact the donor to determine how the remainder of the pledge will be fulfilled. Otherwise, the donor may assume that the obligation has been fulfilled, and will contribute no additional assets.

Tip: It is best to develop standardized pledge agreements for donors to sign, so that pledges can be recognized as revenue.

Pass-Through Contributions

A special condition is situations in which a nonprofit raises money on behalf of other nonprofits, to which it passes through all funds received. For example, a nonprofit may have a separate foundation whose sole purpose is to raise funds for the nonprofit. If these transactions were to be passed through to the ultimate recipient at once with no accounting for the revenue by the pass-through entity, this means the entity would show management and administration and fundraising expenses in its statement of activities, but no revenues. Financial statements containing such an imbalance would hardly encourage donors to contribute money.

Under GAAP, when a donor contributes to a pass-through organization and mandates that the funds be forwarded to a third party, the funds are to be recorded by the pass-through entity as a cash asset and a liability to forward the funds to the third party. This means that the donation only appears in the statement of financial position of the pass-through entity; it never appears as revenue in the statement of activities. However, there are two situations in which the pass-through organization can instead record the donation as revenue and the subsequent forwarding of funds to the third party as an expense. These situations are:

- *Variance power is granted.* The donor explicitly grants variance power to the pass-through organization. This is the unilateral power to redirect funds. The variance power must allow the pass-through organization to unilaterally override the instructions of the donor.
- *Financially interrelated.* The pass-through entity and the ultimate beneficiary are financially interrelated. In addition, the beneficiary organization is not a trustee of the pass-through organization. This financial interrelationship is considered to be present when one entity has the ability to influence the financial and operating decisions of the other, *and* one entity has an ongoing economic interest in the net assets of the other. Examples of situations in which an entity can influence the decisions of another entity include:
  - o Having significant representation on the board of directors of the other entity
  - o The charter or bylaws of the pass-through entity restrict its activities to benefit the other entity
  - o An agreement allows one entity to actively participate in the policy-making decisions of the other entity

A further question when dealing with pass-through contributions is *when* the ultimate beneficiary of the funds can recognize the revenue. Is it when the funds are actually received by the beneficiary, or at an earlier date? In brief, a beneficiary can recognize its interest in the assets held by a pass-through organization, but only if the pass-through entity does not have variance power over how the funds are used. If there is no variance power and the organizations are interrelated, the beneficiary essentially uses the equity method to record its interest in the net assets of the pass-through organization. The equity method is described in the Investment Accounting chapter.

EXAMPLE

The Arcadia Mountaineering Club (AMC) is a nonprofit organization that has been in existence for over a century, and provides free escorted hikes through the Maine wilderness. Several members of the club decide to form a pass-through organization called the Arcadia Foundation to raise funds for the AMC. The two entities are closely intertwined, since the charter of the Foundation specifically restricts its activities to fundraising on behalf of the AMC. In addition, two members of the AMC board of directors currently sit on the board of the Foundation. Since the entities are clearly interrelated, the Foundation can recognize all contributions received as revenue. When these funds are sent to the AMC, the Foundation records them as an expense. The AMC can record its interest in any changes in the net assets of the Foundation.

EXAMPLE

The South Face Corporation sends mountaineering supplies to the Kansas Mountaineering Foundation, to be used by members of the Kansas Mountaineering Club (KMC). The bylaws of the Foundation state that it is organized to obtain monetary and other types of assets to support the training mission of the KMC. The Foundation can decide when to transfer assets to the KMC. The KMC does not exercise any direct control over the Foundation, but the entities are financially interrelated, since the Foundation exists to benefit the KMC.

The Foundation initially recognizes the fair value of the mountaineering supplies as an increase in its assets and contribution revenue. This is classified as a restricted net asset, since the donor has specified the use to which the supplies must be put. When the Foundation eventually transfers the supplies to the KMC, the Foundation recognizes an expense and reduces its recorded assets.

As part of the preparation of its periodic financial statements, the KMC recognizes its interest in any changes in its interest in the Foundation. Thus, the Foundation's receipt of supplies from the South Face Corporation increases the KMC's recognized amount of its interest in the net assets of the Foundation. When the KMC receives the supplies from the Foundation, it recognizes the fair value of the assets received, and reduces its interest in the net assets of the Foundation.

EXAMPLE

A business transfers $100,000 to The Rescue Foundation, with the attached proviso that The Foundation uses the gift to support the activities of search and rescue operations in the Rocky Mountain region. The bylaws of The Foundation state that it is organized to provide financial support for the benefit of Colorado Springs Rescue, Denver Helicopter Search, and Boulder Terrain Search. All four entities are affiliates that are controlled by American Search and Rescue.

The Foundation recognizes the $100,000 as an unrestricted net asset, since the donating business did not identify a specific beneficiary for its gift. When The Foundation eventually transfers the money to another nonprofit, The Foundation recognizes an expense and reduces its recorded assets.

As part of the preparation of their financial statements, Colorado Springs Rescue, Denver Helicopter Search, and Boulder Terrain Search recognize any changes in their interests in the net assets of The Foundation. When doing so, each affiliate is only allowed to include those net assets of The Foundation that are specifically restricted to the use of that affiliate. Since The Foundation is allowed to choose how it disburses the $100,000 donation, none of the affiliates can recognize any portion of this donation. American Search and Rescue can recognize as its interest in the net assets of The Foundation the assets resulting from the $100,000 donation, as well as all other changes in the net assets of The Foundation.

If the three affiliates of The Foundation had instead entered into an agreement that stated how unrestricted gifts to The Foundation should be distributed amongst the group, each of the affiliates could then recognize its share of The Foundation's net assets without donor restrictions. The same result could be achieved if American Search and Rescue, which controls the affiliates, were to mandate a specific formula under which such donations would be distributed amongst the affiliates.

Exchange Value

Donors may agree to make a contribution to a nonprofit in exchange for an item or service. For example, a person paying $100 might receive a book in exchange. The item or service given to a donor has an assigned exchange value. When a donor accepts this exchange, the value of the received item or service reduces the tax-deductible amount of the donor's contribution. For example, if a donor bids $50,000 at a charity auction for a used vehicle that has a fair value of $30,000, the donor can only take a tax deduction of $20,000; this represents the net amount of contribution paid.

When a donor makes a contribution and does not accept any item or service in return, the donor can then use the entire amount of the contribution as a tax deduction.

Transfers of Assets

A donor may transfer assets to a nonprofit, along with a conditional promise to actually contribute them to the nonprofit at a later date. In this situation, the nonprofit can only record the transaction as a refundable advance, which is not revenue. Instead, the advance is considered a liability. If the donor later makes the transfer unconditional or waives any conditions, the nonprofit can then eliminate the advance and instead record the assets as revenue.

Discounts from Revenue

A nonprofit may sometimes provide discounts to the users of its goods or services. For example, a college might offer a deserving student a tuition reduction, or a museum may offer low-income children a steep discount from its usual entry fee. When these discounts are granted, they must be subtracted from gross revenue, so that the revenues reported in the statement of activities appear net of discounts. The presentation can be as a single net revenue line item, or the organization may elect to show gross revenues, discounts, and net revenues in separate line items.

Sales Taxes

When a nonprofit conducts a fundraising auction, certain states may require that the auctioned items be taxed. If so, the nonprofit deducts the amount of the tax from the revenue it would otherwise have garnered from the auction, and forwards it to the applicable government entity. This involves extra accounting effort by the nonprofit to obtain a sales tax license, track the amount of the tax, and remit it to the government.

Related Podcast Episode: Episode 229 of the Accounting Best Practices Podcast discusses sales and use taxes. The episode is available at: **accounting-tools.com/podcasts** or **iTunes**

The Allowance for Uncollectible Pledges

There tends to be a relatively large proportion of pledges made that are never paid by donors. This is because there is no incentive for donors to fulfill their pledges, and because nonprofits are reluctant to pursue donors about late payments. Since such a large part of pledges receivable are never paid, it is necessary to use an allowance for uncollectible pledges. This account offsets the pledges receivable account, and contains management's best estimate of the proportion of outstanding receivables that will never be paid by donors. The result is a net receivables balance that should fairly reflect the amount of receivables that will actually be collected.

The allowance is typically based on a historical analysis of receivables that could not be collected in the past. For example, if a nonprofit has traditionally been unable to collect eight percent of all outstanding receivables, then create an allowance for uncollectible pledges that contains a balance that is eight percent of the total ending receivable balance. A more detailed approach to deriving the allowance is to divide the outstanding receivables report into 30-day buckets, so that receivables are listed by 0-30 days, 31-60 days, 61-90 days, and 90+ days. Then develop an allowance based on the proportion of receivables in each bucket that has historically proven to be uncollectible. The latter approach is likely to reveal a relatively low uncollectible percentage for current receivables, while there may be an extremely high uncollectible percentage for receivables in the 90+ day bucket.

Restricted Fund Releases

When revenues are initially recorded as donor-restricted and the restrictions are later released, the result is a shifting of the funds from the net assets with donor restrictions column in the statement of activities to the unrestricted column. The net result for the total amount of revenue presented in the statement does not change – this is just a reclassification. The following extract from a statement of activities shows how this release of funds appears.

Archimedes Education
Statement of Activities
For the month ended February 28, 20X1

	Net Assets without Donor Restrictions	Net Assets with Donor Restrictions	Totals
Revenues:			
Contributions	$-	$-	$-
Net assets released from restrictions	5,000	-5,000	-
Total revenues	$5,000	-$5,000	$-

Tip: When funds are released from donor restrictions due to the passage of time, this can be discerned by examining the expenses in the unrestricted column of the statement of activities – there will be no increase in expenses to correspond to the release of funds.

Revenue Journal Entries

When revenue is received that is unrestricted and the revenue is a cash payment, the related journal entry is:

	Debit	Credit
Cash [asset account]	xxx	
Revenue – without donor restrictions [revenue account]		xxx
To record $____ of unrestricted revenue		

When revenue is received that is donor-restricted and the revenue is a cash payment, the related journal entry is:

	Debit	Credit
Cash [asset account]	xxx	
Revenue – with donor restrictions [revenue account]		xxx
To record $____ of restricted revenue		

When revenues stored in a donor-restricted fund are eventually released for use, the funds are shifted from the net assets with donor restrictions account to the net assets without donor restrictions account. The related journal entry is:

	Debit	Credit
Net assets without donor restrictions [net asset account]	xxx	
Net assets with donor restrictions [net asset account]		xxx
To release $____ for unrestricted usage		

When volunteers provide contributed services, this can be recognized as revenue and an offsetting expense. The related journal entry is:

	Debit	Credit
Revenue – without donor restrictions [revenue account]	xxx	
Expenses – contributed services [expense account]		xxx
To record the value of contributed services		

When there is a reasonable likelihood that some pledges receivable will not be collected, create a reserve account that contains an estimate of the amount that will not be paid. The related journal entry is:

	Debit	Credit
Bad debt expense [expense account]	xxx	
Allowance for uncollectible pledges [contra asset account]		xxx
To create a reserve for uncollectible pledges receivable		

When a state government charges a sales tax on auctioned items, the nonprofit records a liability to remit the tax to the government. The related journal entry, which is part of the entry to record auction proceeds, is:

	Debit	Credit
Cash [asset account]	xxx	
Sales taxes payable [liability account]		xxx
Revenue – without donor restrictions [revenue account]		xxx
To create a reserve for uncollectible pledges receivable		

Special Reporting Considerations

When a nonprofit earns revenue from a special event, there are two ways to report the revenue in the statement of activities. The options are based on the amount of the proceeds. If the proceeds are relatively minimal, the revenue and any direct expenses associated with the special event can be netted together and reported in a single line item. For example:

	Net Assets without Donor Restrictions	Net Assets with Donor Restrictions	Totals
Revenues:			
Contributions	$-	$-	$-
Special event, net of direct donor benefits of $5,000	12,000	-	12,000

For a major event that recurs on a regular basis, the related revenues are to be presented in the revenue block of the statement of activities within two line items. The first line states the gross amount of special event revenue. Immediately after it is the gross amount of the direct expenses associated with the event, followed by a net revenue line item. For example:

	Net Assets without Donor Restrictions	Net Assets with Donor Restrictions	Totals
Revenues:			
Contributions	$-	$-	$-
Special event, revenue	50,000		50,000
Less: Cost of direct benefits to donors	-8,000		-8,000
Net revenue of special event	$42,000	-	$42,000

The direct donor costs noted in the two examples can also be reported within the expenses block lower in the statement of activities. However, doing so makes it more difficult for a reader of the financial statements to discern how much a nonprofit is spending on its fundraising events.

Revenue Recordkeeping

When a donor makes a contribution of less than $250, the receiving nonprofit has no obligation to issue a receipt to the donor. However, for larger amounts, the IRS mandates that a receipt be issued that contains the following information:

- The donor name
- The amount paid or a description of the asset contributed
- A statement indicating whether any goods or services were provided in compensation; if so, an estimate of the value of the goods or services provided

When a nonprofit provides goods or services in exchange for a contribution (known as a *quid pro quo* contribution), a receipt must be issued when the amount contributed exceeds $75. The receipt must contain the following information:

- Inform the donor that the amount of the contribution that is deductible for federal income tax purposes is limited to the excess of any money (or the value of other assets) contributed by the donor over the value of goods or services provided by the nonprofit; and

- Provide the donor with a good faith estimate of the value of the goods or services that the donor received.

Tip: Keep copies of donor receipts, since donors are likely to lose their copies and request replacements.

When revenue is received and a donor includes a stipulation on its use, the funds are recorded as net assets with donor restrictions. If not used promptly, net assets with donor restrictions may linger in the accounting records for years. These funds can only be used if management knows what the restrictions are that are associated with them. This calls for excellent recordkeeping for all restricted revenue. There should be a report that is regularly perused by management, showing exactly which funds are still restricted and unused. The total funds in this report should match the total balance in the net assets with donor restrictions account; otherwise, management does not really know how to use the funds it has been given. Two additional reasons to fully document net assets with donor restrictions are:

- *For future contact with donors.* There are cases where donors may eventually be willing to re-designate prior contributions for other purposes. If so, the nonprofit should know how to contact them, and in regard to how much money.
- *For use of invested funds.* Some restricted funds also have restrictions placed on the use of the investment income derived from these funds. If so, documentation of the restrictions is needed.

Donors who commit to large contributions may want to keep their existence and the size of their donations out of the public eye. If so, it can make sense to store donor information in a secure location, where it cannot be accessed without management approval.

It is a rare nonprofit that elects to track the hours worked by their volunteers and translate this into a revenue and expense journal entry for services provided (see the Types of Revenue section). It is simply too time-consuming to engage in this activity, though it may still be necessary to track volunteer hours as part of the reporting system required by some donors.

A nonprofit is under no obligation to assign a value to any donated property; this is the responsibility of the donor. However, a nonprofit may be called upon to fill out a portion of the tax forms that a donor submits to the IRS. For larger donations, a donor fills out the Form 8283, which identifies donated property of various valuations. The nonprofit must complete Part IV of this form, in which it acknowledges that it has indeed received the property identified by the donor in the previous sections of the form. We include a copy of this form, so that the accountant will be familiar with its content if called upon by a donor to complete Part IV.

Form 8283 – Noncash Charitable Contributions (page 1)

Form **8283** (Rev. December 2014) Department of the Treasury Internal Revenue Service	**Noncash Charitable Contributions** ▶ Attach to your tax return if you claimed a total deduction of over $500 for all contributed property. ▶ Information about Form 8283 and its separate instructions is at www.irs.gov/form8283.	OMB No. 1545-0908 Attachment Sequence No. **155**
Name(s) shown on your income tax return		Identifying number

Note. Figure the amount of your contribution deduction before completing this form. See your tax return instructions.

Section A. Donated Property of $5,000 or Less and Publicly Traded Securities—List in this section only items (or groups of similar items) for which you claimed a deduction of $5,000 or less. Also list publicly traded securities even if the deduction is more than $5,000 (see instructions).

Part I — Information on Donated Property—If you need more space, attach a statement.

1	(a) Name and address of the donee organization	(b) If donated property is a vehicle (see instructions), check the box. Also enter the vehicle identification number (unless Form 1098-C is attached).	(c) Description of donated property (For a vehicle, enter the year, make, model, and mileage. For securities, enter the company name and the number of shares.)
A		☐	
B		☐	
C		☐	
D		☐	
E		☐	

Note. If the amount you claimed as a deduction for an item is $500 or less, you do not have to complete columns (e), (f), and (g).

	(d) Date of the contribution	(e) Date acquired by donor (mo., yr.)	(f) How acquired by donor	(g) Donor's cost or adjusted basis	(h) Fair market value (see instructions)	(i) Method used to determine the fair market value
A						
B						
C						
D						
E						

Part II — Partial Interests and Restricted Use Property—Complete lines 2a through 2e if you gave less than an entire interest in a property listed in Part I. Complete lines 3a through 3c if conditions were placed on a contribution listed in Part I; also attach the required statement (see instructions).

2a Enter the letter from Part I that identifies the property for which you gave less than an entire interest ▶ _____
If Part II applies to more than one property, attach a separate statement.

b Total amount claimed as a deduction for the property listed in Part I: (1) For this tax year ▶ _____
(2) For any prior tax years ▶ _____

c Name and address of each organization to which any such contribution was made in a prior year (complete only if different from the donee organization above):
Name of charitable organization (donee)

Address (number, street, and room or suite no.)

City or town, state, and ZIP code

d For tangible property, enter the place where the property is located or kept ▶ _____
e Name of any person, other than the donee organization, having actual possession of the property ▶ _____

		Yes	No
3a	Is there a restriction, either temporary or permanent, on the donee's right to use or dispose of the donated property?		
b	Did you give to anyone (other than the donee organization or another organization participating with the donee organization in cooperative fundraising) the right to the income from the donated property or to the possession of the property, including the right to vote donated securities, to acquire the property by purchase or otherwise, or to designate the person having such income, possession, or right to acquire?		
c	Is there a restriction limiting the donated property for a particular use?		

For Paperwork Reduction Act Notice, see separate instructions.   Cat. No. 62299J   Form **8283** (Rev. 12-2014)

Revenue Accounting

Form 8283 – Noncash Charitable Contributions (page 2)

When a donor gifts property to a nonprofit that is valued at more than $5,000, the nonprofit must later file a Form 8282 with the IRS if it sells, exchanges, consumes, or otherwise disposes of the property at any time within the next three years. A copy of the form must also be sent to the donor. There is a $50 penalty if this form is not filed. A copy of the form is noted next.

Form 8282 – Donee Information Return (page 1)

Form **8282** (Rev. April 2009) Department of the Treasury Internal Revenue Service	**Donee Information Return** (Sale, Exchange, or Other Disposition of Donated Property) ▶ See instructions.	OMB No. 1545-0908 Give a Copy to Donor

Parts To Complete

- If the organization is an **original donee**, complete *Identifying Information*, Part I (lines 1a–1d and, if applicable, lines 2a–2d), and Part III.
- If the organization is a **successor donee**, complete *Identifying Information*, Part I, Part II, and Part III.

Identifying Information

Print or Type	Name of charitable organization (donee)	Employer identification number
	Address (number, street, and room or suite no.) (or P.O. box no. if mail is not delivered to the street address)	
	City or town, state, and ZIP code	

Part I — Information on ORIGINAL DONOR and SUCCESSOR DONEE Receiving the Property

1a Name of original donor of the property	1b Identifying number(s)
1c Address (number, street, and room or suite no.) (P.O. box no. if mail is not delivered to the street address)	
1d City or town, state, and ZIP code	

Note. Complete lines 2a–2d only if the organization gave this property to another charitable organization (successor donee).

2a Name of charitable organization	2b Employer identification number
2c Address (number, street, and room or suite no.) (or P.O. box no. if mail is not delivered to the street address)	
2d City or town, state, and ZIP code	

Part II — Information on PREVIOUS DONEES. Complete this part only if the organization was not the first donee to receive the property. See the instructions before completing lines 3a through 4d.

3a Name of original donee	3b Employer identification number
3c Address (number, street, and room or suite no.) (or P.O. box no. if mail is not delivered to the street address)	
3d City or town, state, and ZIP code	
4a Name of preceding donee	4b Employer identification number
4c Address (number, street, and room or suite no.) (or P.O. box no. if mail is not delivered to the street address)	
4d City or town, state, and ZIP code	

For Paperwork Reduction Act Notice, see page 4.   Cat. No. 62307Y   Form **8282** (Rev. 4-2009)

Form 8282 – Donee Information Return (page 2)

Form 8282 (Rev. 4-2009)   Page **2**

Part III   Information on DONATED PROPERTY

	2. Did the disposition involve the organization's entire interest in the property?		3. Was the use related to the organization's exempt purpose or function?		4. Information on use of property.
1. Description of the donated property sold, exchanged, or otherwise disposed of and how the organization used the property. (If you need more space, attach a separate statement.)	Yes	No	Yes	No	• If you answered "Yes" to question 3 and the property was tangible personal property, describe how the organization's use of the property furthered its exempt purpose or function. Also complete Part IV below. • If you answered "No" to question 3 and the property was tangible personal property, describe the organization's intended use (if any) at the time of the contribution. Also complete Part IV below, if the intended use at the time of the contribution was related to the organization's exempt purpose or function and it became impossible or infeasible to implement.
A					
B					
C					
D					

		Donated Property			
		A	B	C	D
5	Date the organization received the donated property (MM/DD/YY)	/ /	/ /	/ /	/ /
6	Date the original donee received the property (MM/DD/YY)	/ /	/ /	/ /	/ /
7	Date the property was sold, exchanged, or otherwise disposed of (MM/DD/YY)	/ /	/ /	/ /	/ /
8	Amount received upon disposition	$	$	$	$

Part IV   Certification

You must sign the certification below if any property described in Part III above is tangible personal property and:
- You answered "Yes" to question 3 above, or
- You answered "No" to question 3 above and the intended use of the property became impossible or infeasible to implement.

Under penalties of perjury and the penalty under section 6720B, I certify that either: (1) the use of the property that meets the above requirements, and is described above in Part III, was substantial and related to the donee organization's exempt purpose or function; or (2) the donee organization intended to use the property for its exempt purpose or function, but the intended use has become impossible or infeasible to implement.

▶ _____   _____   ▶ _____
Signature of officer   Title   Date

Sign Here

Under penalties of perjury, I declare that I have examined this return, including accompanying schedules and statements, and to the best of my knowledge and belief, it is true, correct, and complete.

▶ _____   _____   ▶ _____
Signature of officer   Title   Date

Type or print name

Form **8282** (Rev. 4-2009)

Revenue Disclosures

The following disclosures regarding revenues should be included in the notes to the financial statements of a nonprofit:

- *Nature of contributed services.* If a nonprofit recognizes revenue from contributed services, it must describe the programs or activities for which those services were used, as well as the related amount of revenues recognized. The nature and extent of these services are to be described; for example, by the number of donated hours.
- *Unrecognized contributed services.* If a nonprofit has received contributed services but has chosen not to recognize it as revenue, the entity is encouraged (but not required) to disclose the fair value of these services. The nature and extent of these services are to be described; for example, by the number of donated hours.
- *Time restrictions.* If the organization has a policy for implying a time restriction on the use of donated long-term assets, state the policy.
- *Pass-through receipts.* A pass-through entity must disclose its policy concerning the recognition of nonfinancial assets accepted on behalf of a specified beneficiary.

Summary

A key concern when accounting for revenues is to adopt an accounting position that is approved by the entity's auditors, and then follow that position consistently over time. Doing so results in financial statements that are considered reliable by outsiders, and which can be used to derive long-term trends in revenue levels. This level of consistency can be difficult if there are many types of revenue being recognized, so be sure to adopt a standard set of policies and procedures, as well as adequate staff training, to ensure that revenue transactions are dealt with in the same manner, time after time.

A nonprofit may be in the unique position of being given a substantial part of its total revenues in the form of assets other than cash, such as real estate, securities, or equipment. In these situations, the entity is required to record revenue at the fair value of the assets. For a detailed discussion of what fair value means and how it can be derived, see the Fair Value chapter.

Chapter 5
Government Grants

Introduction

The primary source of revenue for some nonprofits is the government, which routinely funds them with grants. If so, the accounting discussion in this chapter is likely to be of overriding importance, compared to all other nonprofit accounting topics.

Overview of Government Grants

A major source of funds for a nonprofit may be the government, which provides it with grants of various types. If so, it may be necessary to organize the recordation of accounting transactions by grant contract, so that incoming and outgoing funds can be traced to specific grants. For the larger grants, it may be necessary to create budgets for how funds are to be spent, and then trace actual expenditures back to the budget. Some governments want to see exactly how their funds were used, so the nonprofit may also need to develop a unique report format for each grant, which is to be used when discussing fund usage with the applicable government representative.

In some instances, a nonprofit may function as a general contractor. In this role, the nonprofit takes in government grants and disburses it to other entities that perform the actual work. If so, the nonprofit takes a portion of the grant in order to pay for its administrative costs in managing the disbursement of funds and how those funds are used. This situation typically arises when research is being conducted.

When a nonprofit subsists on government grants, the tracking and reporting of grant-related funds is likely to be the central responsibility of the accounting department – to the point where the accounting staff can be considered key to obtaining and retaining government grants. If so, it may be necessary to assign some of the accounting staff to specific government contracts, so that they can closely monitor activity. These personnel are specialists, and are not involved in the more general functional activities of the department.

Grant Accounting

A government grant is essentially a contribution, in that the funds are not to be repaid. However, the grant concept differs from a contribution in that the grant is tied to the provision of goods or services by the nonprofit, usually in relation to a specific program.

Grants may be paid in advance; if so, the related funds are booked into net asset with donor restriction accounts. When funds are spent against these grants, an equivalent amount of funds are released from the applicable net asset accounts. Thus, the amount released matches the amount spent. Alternatively, a nonprofit may spend the funds first and then apply for a drawdown of a matching amount from the applicable grant.

Whenever possible, costs should be designated as direct costs; this means that they are directly related to a specific activity, and so would not be incurred if the related activity did not exist. For example, the salaries of technical staff, project supplies, project publications, computer costs, travel costs, and specialized services can usually be treated as direct costs when they can be linked to a specific program. However, the salaries of administrative staff are usually *not* treated as a direct cost, except when a project or activity explicitly requires and budgets for administrative services and individuals can be specifically identified with the project or activity.

> **Tip:** Office supplies, postage, periodicals and memberships cannot usually be treated as direct costs.

A nonprofit is typically allowed to charge an additional amount of expense against a grant, called the *indirect rate*. The indirect rate is an overhead charge. The compilation of the indirect rate is based on one of two formulas allowed by the federal government. The first is called the *simplified allocation method*, and is described as follows in Circular 122 of the Office of Management and Budget:

> The allocation of indirect costs may be accomplished by (i) separating the organization's total costs for the base period as either direct or indirect, and (ii) dividing the total allowable indirect costs (net of applicable credits) by an equitable distribution base. The result of this process is an indirect cost rate which is used to distribute indirect costs to individual awards. The rate should be expressed as the percentage which the total amount of allowable indirect costs bears to the base selected.

The preceding description of the simplified allocation method refers to indirect costs, which are costs not directly associated with a specific activity or program. The "equitable distribution base" noted in the description is usually considered to be the total amount of direct costs charged to a program. Direct costs are most commonly the salaries of those people working on a program.

EXAMPLE

Cancer Resolution has total indirect costs of $3,500,000 and total direct costs of $15,900,000. Direct costs are considered an equitable distribution base. Accordingly, the indirect cost rate is derived by dividing total indirect costs into total direct costs, for an allocation rate of 22%.

Cancer Resolution has obtained $1,000,000 of funding from the federal government to engage in research regarding cancer of the pancreas. Seven researchers will work full-time on this project, at a cost of $750,000. The $750,000 is the total direct cost associated with the project, and is considered the base upon which indirect costs will be allocated to the project. The entity's indirect cost rate is 22%, so the direct cost figure is multiplied by 22% to arrive at an indirect cost allocation of $165,000.

A considerably more complex approach is the *multiple allocation base method*, which is described in the same publication as follows:

Aggregate indirect costs are accumulated into separate cost groupings. Each grouping is then allocated individually to benefitting functions by means of a base which best measures the relative benefits. Each grouping constitutes a pool of expenses that are of like character in terms of functions they benefit and in terms of the allocation base which best measures the relative benefits provided to each function. The indirect cost pools are defined as follows:

- *Depreciation and use allowances.* The portion of the costs of the organization's buildings, capital improvements to land and buildings, and equipment.
- *Interest.* Interest on debt associated with certain buildings, equipment and capital improvements.
- *Operation and maintenance expenses.* Those costs that have been incurred for the administration, operation, maintenance, preservation, and protection of the organization's physical plant. They include expenses normally incurred for such items as: janitorial and utility services; repairs and ordinary or normal alterations of buildings, furniture and equipment; care of grounds; maintenance and operation of buildings and other plant facilities; security; earthquake and disaster preparedness; environmental safety; hazardous waste disposal; property, liability and other insurance relating to property; space and capital leasing; facility planning and management; and, central receiving. The operation and maintenance expenses category shall also include its allocable share of fringe benefit costs, depreciation and use allowances, and interest costs.
- *General and administrative expenses.* Those costs that have been incurred for the overall general executive and administrative offices of the organization and other expenses of a general nature which do not relate solely to any major function of the organization. This category shall also include its allocable share of fringe benefit costs, operation and maintenance expense, depreciation and use allowances, and interest costs. Examples of this category include central offices, such as the director's office, the office of finance, business services, budget and planning, personnel, safety and risk management, general counsel, management information systems, and library costs.

Given the increased level of accounting difficulty associated with the multiple allocation base method, one should be knowledgeable about when its use can be avoided. The key factors to consider are:

- *One major function.* When a nonprofit has just one major function that may encompass several projects, use the simplified allocation method.
- *Minimal funding.* When the level of federal awards to a nonprofit is relatively small, use the simplified allocation method.
- *Differing levels of benefit.* When a nonprofit's indirect costs benefit its major functions in the same degree, use the simplified allocation method.

If any of these issues are *not* the case, use the multiple allocation base method instead.

There are situations where a nonprofit may want to use an indirect cost rate that is not derived precisely from either of the two preceding methods. If so, it can submit an allocation plan to the federal agency from which it obtains the largest proportion of its government grants. If approved, the result is an official indirect cost rate that can be applied to most grants originating from federal agencies, and sometimes also from state and local agencies.

Income from Government Grants

There are situations in which government funds result in the generation of additional revenue. For example, there may not be an immediate need for all of the funds in a grant, so they are parked in an interest-bearing investment account. Alternatively, the funds may result in a profit-making endeavor that generates its own cash flow. In either case, how is this additional income to be handled in the accounting records? There are several possibilities:

- Add the additional income to the amount of the government grant, thereby resulting in more cash being made available for the applicable program.
- Use the cash to fund the other parts of the applicable program that are not being paid for by a government grant, thereby reducing the fundraising burden of the nonprofit.
- Subtract the extra income from the expenses associated with the applicable program, thereby reducing the amount of expenses, and allowing for additional expenditures.

The contract associated with a grant will typically state which of these alternatives can be used.

Credits on Expenditures

A nonprofit may occasionally receive a credit from a supplier in relation to expenditures made in relation to a government grant. Perhaps the nonprofit is being paid at year-end for the volume of total purchases made during the year, or perhaps the nonprofit took advantage of an early payment discount offer from a supplier. In these situations, the credits should be netted against the expenditures associated with the affected grant. Doing so reduces the amount of expenditures matched against a grant.

Grant Reporting

The government will likely require that a separate report be issued to it regarding the uses to which its grants have been put. If there are different granting agencies within the government, this is likely to mean that each report is formatted differently and requires that different information be reported. A particular concern is that the government may have a different fiscal year than the nonprofit, in which case the government may expect to see reports that span its own fiscal year, rather than that of the nonprofit.

The government may withdraw additional funding if a nonprofit does not issue reports to it in a timely manner. Accordingly, it is essential that the controller monitor the dates when all reports are due, as well as the progress of each report toward completion. This can be accomplished by maintaining a schedule of reports, on which is noted the following information:

- Report name
- Date when report must be issued
- Person responsible for compiling the report
- The name and address of the person to whom the report is to be delivered

Proper use of this tracking system reduces the risk that a report will not be delivered in a timely manner.

Some grants require that the funds supplied are only available if a nonprofit can match the funds with gifts from other donors. The intent is to maximize the amount of funding generated. To comply with this matching requirement, a nonprofit needs a reporting system in place that traces each incoming contribution to a matching grant, so that the matching detail can be reported back to the government when applying for a grant drawdown. In some instances, donors may gift with in-kind contributions, such as free labor or materials. If so, the reporting system must encompass how these in-kind contributions are valued and assigned to matching grants.

When applying for grants from the federal government, a nonprofit must comply with the requirements of Circular A-110 of the Office of Management and Budget. A key requirement is that the financial management systems of the nonprofit provide for the following:

- *Budget comparison*. Compare outlays to budgeted amounts for each award.
- *Controls*. There must be effective control over and accountability for all funds, property and other assets. All assets are to be adequately safeguarded and used only for authorized purposes.

- *Disclosure.* There must be accurate, current and complete disclosure of the financial results of each federally-sponsored program.
- *Procedures.* Written procedures are required to minimize the time elapsed between the transfer of funds to the nonprofit and the issuance or redemption of payments for program purposes by the nonprofit. Also, there must be written procedures for determining the reasonableness, allocations, and allowability of costs in accordance with federal rules.
- *Sources and uses.* Records must be available that identify the source and application of funds for federally-sponsored activities, including information about awards, authorizations, obligations, unobligated balances, assets, outlays, income and interest.
- *Supporting documentation.* Accounting records must be kept that are supported by source documentation.

In short, the government wants to deal with nonprofits that have reliable accounting systems that consistently store and report information, as well as controls and budgets that ensure that funds are used as intended.

Summary

There can be a large amount of complexity in the government grant arena, which makes it especially difficult for a newer nonprofit to obtain funding. The guidance given in this chapter only provides an overview of the topic. For more information, consult Circulars 110 (*Uniform Administrative Requirements for Grants and Agreements with Institutions of Higher Education, Hospitals, and Other Non-Profit Organizations*) and 122 (*Cost Principles for Non-profit Organizations*) of the Office of Management and Budget, which provide significant detail that may be illuminating for a nonprofit trying to break into the government grant arena.

Chapter 6
Investment Accounting

Introduction

Nonprofits have a strong interest in accumulating funding that can be used as a long-term source of investment income. This means they are likely to have significant investments in a variety of debt and equity instruments. In this chapter, we address how to account for and disclose information pertaining to these investments.

Contributed Investments

Donors may sometimes contribute equity or debt securities to a nonprofit. When this happens, the nonprofit should recognize the contribution as an asset, and record the receipt as either revenue or a gain. The investment is to be recognized at its fair value if the securities are quoted on a securities exchange. See the Fair Value chapter for alternative methods that can be used to derive the fair value of contributed investments.

Purchased Investments

When a nonprofit purchases investment instruments, it initially records them at their acquisition cost. This cost is considered to include any brokerage or other transaction fees associated with the purchase.

Subsequent Measurement of Investments

Once investments in equity and debt securities have been acquired (by whatever means), they are to be measured in subsequent periods at their fair values. This is only the case for equity securities when they have readily determinable fair values, which is the case when their price is quoted on a securities exchange. Or, if the investment is in a mutual fund, when the price of the fund is published and used as the basis for current transactions in the marketplace.

If an investment is in restricted stock, its fair value is to be derived based on the quoted price of an unrestricted security from the same issuer that is identical to the restricted stock in all other respects. In this case, the valuation is adjusted for the effect of the restriction, which will reduce its fair value.

Other types of investments do not have a readily discernible fair value. For example, it can be quite difficult to ascertain the value of a partnership interest or an investment in real estate. These investments are to be reported as follows, depending on the nature of the nonprofit entity:

- *Institutions of higher learning.* Report these investments at either their fair value or at their carrying value. If reported at their carrying value, adjust subsequently for any non-temporary value impairment.
- *Voluntary health and welfare entities.* Report these investments at either their fair value or carrying value. If a loss on disposition is expected, recognize an impairment loss when the decline in fair value occurs.
- *Health care entities.* Report these investments at their amortized cost and periodically review them for impairment.
- *All other nonprofits.* Report these investments at either their fair value or the lower of their cost or fair value.

There may also be equity securities that do not have readily determinable fair values. These securities are to be reported at cost, and also examined periodically to see if there has been an impairment loss. A security is considered to be impaired if its fair value is less than its cost. If this impairment is considered to be other-than-temporary, recognize an impairment loss in the amount of the difference between the fair value and cost. The result is the new cost basis of the investment, which cannot be subsequently adjusted upward for any recoveries of fair value.

The preceding guidance is much simpler than the investment accounting mandated for for-profit businesses, which are required to classify investments into trading securities, held-to-maturity securities, or available-for-sale securities; each of these classifications carries with it different accounting requirements.

Gains and Losses on Investment

Gains and losses on investment may be *realized*, which occurs when an investment is sold. The gains and losses may also be *unrealized*, which is when the investment is still held, but there is a change in the value of the investment. In both cases, gains and losses are to be reported in the statement of activities as part of investment income. The requirement to report unrealized gains and losses can cause heartburn among nonprofit managers, since there is not yet any actual decline in cash flows from an investment, even though the recognition will trigger a decline in net assets.

Any gains and losses on investments are to be reported in the statement of activities as changes in net assets without donor restrictions. If the use of these investments is restricted in some way by donor stipulations or legal restrictions, the gains and losses may instead be recognized as changes in net assets with donor restrictions.

Investment income should be reported net of investment expenses, including both external and direct internal expenses. Direct internal investment expenses relate to the direct conduct or direct supervision of the activities involved in generating a return on investment. Examples of these expenses are:

- The compensation, benefits, travel, and other costs associated with the personnel responsible for developing and executing investment strategy.
- Those allocated costs associated with the internal investment management of external investment management firms.

It is allowable to present the amounts of net investment returns in separate line items on the statement of activities, if the related portfolios are managed differently or derived from different sources.

The Equity Method of Accounting

In rare cases, a nonprofit may receive so much stock from a donor that the nonprofit can gain a certain amount of control over the for-profit entity whose stock it now owns. In this case, the nonprofit may use the equity method to account for its ownership interest. This treatment is not available for reporting an interest in another nonprofit entity.

The equity method is designed to measure changes in the economic results of the investee, by requiring the investor to recognize its share of the profits or losses recorded by the investee. The equity method is a more complex technique of accounting for ownership, and so is typically used only when there is a significant ownership interest that enables an investor to have influence over the decision-making of the investee.

The key determining factor in the use of the equity method is having significant influence over the operating and financial decisions of the investee. The primary determinant of this level of control is owning at least 20% of the voting shares of the investee, though this measurement can be repudiated by evidence that the investee opposes the influence of the investor. Other types of evidence of significant influence are controlling a seat on the board of directors, active participation in the decisions of the investee, or swapping management personnel with the investee.

The investor can avoid using the equity method if it cannot obtain the financial information it needs from the investee in order to correctly account for its ownership interest under the equity method.

The essential accounting under the equity method is to initially recognize an investment in an investee at cost, and then adjust the carrying amount of the investment by recognizing its share of the earnings or losses of the investee in net assets over time. The following additional guidance applies to these basic points:

- *Dividends.* The investor should subtract any dividends received from the investee from the carrying amount of the investor's investment in the investee.
- *Financial statement issuance.* The investor can only account for its share of the earnings or losses of the investee if the investee issues financial statements. This may result in occasional lags in reporting.

- *Funding of prior losses.* If the investor pays the investee with the intent of offsetting prior investee losses, and the carrying amount of the investor's interest in the investee has already been reduced to zero, the investor's share of any additional losses can be applied against the additional funds paid to the investee.

- *Investee losses.* It is possible that the investor's share of the losses of an investee will exceed the carrying amount of its investment in the investee. If so, the investor should report losses up to its carrying amount, as well as any additional financial support given to the investee, and then discontinue use of the equity method. However, additional losses can be recorded if it appears assured that the investee will shortly return to profitability. If there is a return to profitability, the investor can return to the equity method only after its share of the profits has been offset by those losses not recognized when use of the equity method was halted.

- *Other write-downs.* If an investor's investment in an investee has been written down to zero, but it has other investments in the investee, the investor should continue to report its share of any additional investee losses, and offset them against the other investments, in sequence of the seniority of those investments (with offsets against the most junior items first). If the investee generates income at a later date, the investor should apply its share of these profits to the other investments in order, with application going against the most senior items first.

- *Share calculation.* The proportion of the investee's earnings or losses to be recognized by the investor is based on the investor's holdings of common stock and in-substance common stock.

- *Share issuances.* If the investee issues shares, the investor should account for the transaction as if a proportionate share of its own investment in the investee had been sold. If there is a gain or loss resulting from the stock sale, recognize it in earnings.

- *Ownership increase.* If an investor increases its ownership in an investee, this may qualify it to use the equity method, in which case the investor should retroactively adjust its financial statements for all periods presented to show the investment as though the equity method had been used through the entire reporting period.

- *Ownership decrease.* If an investor decreases its ownership in an investee, this may drop its level of control below the 20% threshold, in which case the investor may no longer be qualified to use the equity method. If so, the investor should retain the carrying amount of the investment as of the date when the equity method no longer applies, so there is no retroactive adjustment.

EXAMPLE

Archimedes Education purchases 30% of the common stock of Titanium Barriers, Inc. Archimedes controls two seats on the board of directors of Titanium as a result of this investment, so it uses the equity method to account for the investment. In the next year, Titanium earns $400,000. Archimedes records its 30% share of the profit with the following entry:

	Debit	Credit
Investment in Titanium Barriers	120,000	
Equity in Titanium Barriers income		120,000

A few months later, Titanium issues a $50,000 cash dividend to Archimedes, which the organization records with the following entry:

	Debit	Credit
Cash	50,000	
Investment in Titanium Barriers		50,000

EXAMPLE

Archimedes Education has a 35% ownership interest in the common stock of Arlington Research. The carrying amount of this investment has been reduced to zero because of previous losses. To keep Arlington solvent, Archimedes has purchased $250,000 of Arlington's preferred stock, and extended a long-term unsecured loan of $500,000.

During the next year, Arlington incurs a $1,200,000 loss, of which Archimedes' share is 35%, or $420,000. Since the next most senior level of Arlington's capital after common stock is its preferred stock, Archimedes first offsets its share of the loss against its preferred stock investment. Doing so reduces the carrying amount of the preferred stock to zero, leaving $170,000 to be applied against the carrying amount of the loan. This results in the following entry by Archimedes:

	Debit	Credit
Equity method loss	420,000	
Preferred stock investment		250,000
Loan		170,000

In the following year, Arlington records $800,000 of profits, of which Archimedes' share is $280,000. Archimedes applies the $280,000 first against the loan write-down, and then against the preferred stock write-down with the following entry:

	Debit	Credit
Preferred stock investment	110,000	
Loan	170,000	
Equity method income		280,000

The result is that the carrying amount of the loan is fully restored, while the carrying amount of the preferred stock investment is still reduced by $140,000 from its original level.

Investment Disclosures

The following information must be disclosed in the notes accompanying the financial statements that pertain to investments:

- *Composition.* The types of investment return must be reported. This means the total return must be broken down into at least the following:
    - Investment income
    - Net gains or losses on investments reported at fair value
    - Net realized gains or losses on investments reported at other than fair value

For example:

	Net Assets without Donor Restrictions	Net Assets with Donor Restrictions	Total
Dividends and interest (net of $300 in expenses)	$18,000	$4,000	$22,000
Net gains on investments reported at fair value	40,000	83,000	123,000
Net realized gains on investments reported at other than fair value		30,000	30,000
Total investment return	$58,000	$117,000	$175,000
Investment return designated for current operations	40,000	72,000	112,000
Investment return in excess of amounts designated for current operations	$18,000	$45,000	$63,000

- *Reconciliation.* If the investment return is separated into operating and non-operating amounts, reconcile these amounts to the total investment return. Also note the policy used to determine how much of the total investment return is reported as operating or non-operating, as well as any changes to that policy.

- *Aggregate carrying amounts.* Separately present the aggregate carrying amount of each major type of investment. For example, there may be separate line items for real estate, corporate debt securities, and U.S. treasury securities.
- *Market risk.* If there is a significant concentration of market risk (such as when securities all come from the same industry or all real estate investments are clustered within a single geographic location), disclose the nature of the risk and the related carrying amount of the investment.
- *Credit risk.* Note significant concentrations of credit risk related to all financial instruments. The disclosure should include the maximum amount of potential loss if counterparties fail, as well as the policies used to require collateral on financial instruments subject to credit risk.
- *Other investments.* Note the basis used to determine the carrying amount of other investments. Also describe the methods and assumptions used to estimate investment fair values when those investments were reported at their fair value.

Though not mandatory, it is also possible to report on realized and unrealized gains and losses on investments. This reporting can be useful if there is an applicable law mandating that only realized gains can be spent.

If a nonprofit is an institution of higher education, it must also disclose the total performance of its other investments portfolio, which is comprised of both investment income and realized and unrealized gains and losses.

A nonprofit using the equity method to account for an investment should disclose the following information:

- *Identification.* The name of each investee and the nonprofit's ownership percentage in it.
- *Market value.* The value of each investment at its quoted market price (if such a price is available).
- *Policies.* The nonprofit's policies regarding its investments in common stock, including cases where the nonprofit owns a 20% or more interest in a business but does not use the equity method. Also describe any situations where the nonprofit uses the equity method despite owning less than 20% of an investee. Further, note any difference between the carrying amount of an investment and the amount of underlying equity in net assets.
- *Change in ownership.* If there is a potentially material impact on the nonprofit's share of reported investee earnings from the conversion of convertible securities, the conversion of warrants, or similar transactions, disclose this information.

Summary

Even a smaller nonprofit may find that it has a broad range of investments in its portfolio, since many types of investments can be contributed by donors. If the more unusual investments cannot be liquidated (as per donor instructions), this means that the accounting staff will need to acquire a deep knowledge of the rules relating to investment accounting. This chapter has only given an overview of the general concepts associated with investment accounting. If a nonprofit is the recipient of an unusual investment whose fair value is especially difficult to ascertain, it can make sense to bring the organization's auditors into the initial accounting for the investment, to ensure that the situation is handled correctly from the start.

Chapter 7
Inventory Accounting

Introduction

The typical nonprofit does not deal with large amounts of inventory. Typically, it acquires merchandise from third parties and resells it. Only in rare cases does a nonprofit create goods within a production facility. Given this low-usage assumption, we are restricting the discussion of inventory accounting in this chapter to the two types of inventory tracking systems, the basic concepts of cost layering, and when to write down the recorded cost of inventory.

> **Related Podcast Episodes:** Episodes 56, 66, 177, and 200 of the Accounting Best Practices Podcast discuss inventory record accuracy, obsolete inventory, freight costs, and the revised lower of cost or market rule, respectively. These episodes are available at: **accountingtools.com/podcasts** or **iTunes**

The Periodic Inventory System

The minimum inventory accounting system is the periodic system. It is impossible to devise an ending inventory valuation without having a functioning periodic inventory system in place. The system is dependent upon just two activities, which are:

- Compiling the cost of all inventory-related purchases during the reporting period; and
- Conducting a physical count of the ending inventory.

The compilation of inventory-related purchases is quite easy in any accounting system, and is only dependent upon recording targeted purchases in an inventory purchases account as the offsetting debit to each accounts payable transaction.

Since physical inventory counts are time-consuming, few organizations do them more than once a quarter or year. In the meantime, the inventory asset account continues to show the cost of the inventory that was recorded as of the last physical inventory count; the balance is not adjusted until there is another physical count or an ending valuation is estimated. The longer it takes to conduct a replacement physical inventory count, the longer the time period in which errors and inventory losses of various kinds can pile up undetected. As a result, there is an increasing risk of overstating ending inventory and understating the cost of goods sold over time. Given this problem, we recommend fairly frequent physical counts. To operate a periodic inventory system, follow these steps:

1. Compile all inventory-related purchases during the reporting period in a separate account.
2. At the end of the period, conduct a physical count to derive the ending inventory valuation.
3. Calculate the cost of goods sold for the period, using the following formula:

Beginning inventory + Purchases = Cost of goods available for sale

Cost of goods available for sale – Ending inventory = Cost of goods sold

4. Complete the following entry to zero out the balance in the purchases account, adjust the inventory account to match the ending physical count, and record the cost of goods sold:

	Debit	Credit
Cost of goods sold	xxx	
Inventory purchases		xxx
Inventory		xxx

EXAMPLE

Senior Care Home Supplies (SCHS) has beginning inventory of $100,000, has paid $170,000 for purchases, and its physical inventory count reveals an ending inventory cost of $80,000. The calculation of its cost of goods sold is:

$100,000 Beginning inventory + $170,000 Purchases - $80,000 Ending inventory

= $190,000 Cost of goods sold

SCHS' controller records the following journal entry to document this calculation:

	Debit	Credit
Cost of goods sold	190,000	
Purchases		170,000
Inventory		20,000

The periodic inventory system is most useful for smaller organizations that maintain minimal amounts of inventory. For them, a physical inventory count is easy to complete, and they can estimate cost of goods sold figures for interim periods. However, there are several problems with the system:

- *Inaccuracy in the absence of a count.* The system does not yield any information about the cost of goods sold or ending inventory balances during interim periods when there has been no physical inventory count.

- *Subsequent catch-up adjustments.* The accounting staff must estimate the cost of goods sold during interim periods, which will likely result in a significant adjustment to the actual cost of goods whenever the entity eventually completes a physical inventory count.
- *Obsolete inventory and scrap adjustments.* There is no way to adjust for obsolete inventory or scrap losses during interim periods, so there tends to be a significant (and expensive) adjustment for these issues when a physical inventory count is eventually completed.

A more up-to-date and accurate alternative to the periodic inventory system is the perpetual inventory system, which is described in the next section.

The Perpetual Inventory System

Under the perpetual inventory system, an entity continually updates its inventory records to account for additions to and subtractions from inventory for such activities as received inventory items and goods sold from stock. Thus, a perpetual inventory system has the advantages of both providing up-to-date inventory balance information and requiring a reduced level of physical inventory counts. However, the calculated inventory levels derived by a perpetual inventory system may gradually diverge from actual inventory levels, due to unrecorded transactions or theft, so the warehouse staff should periodically compare book balances to actual on-hand quantities. The following example shows how a perpetual system functions.

EXAMPLE

This example contains several journal entries used to account for transactions in a perpetual inventory system. Senior Care Home Supplies (SCHS) records a purchase of $1,500 of widgets that are stored in inventory:

	Debit	Credit
Inventory	1,500	
Accounts payable		1,500

SCHS records $250 of inbound freight cost associated with the delivery of widgets:

	Debit	Credit
Inventory	250	
Accounts payable		250

SCHS records the sale of widgets from inventory for $2,000, for which the associated inventory cost is $800:

	Debit	Credit
Accounts receivable	2,000	
Revenue		2,000
Cost of goods sold	800	
Inventory		800

SCHS records a downward inventory adjustment of $300, caused by inventory theft, and detected during a periodic count:

	Debit	Credit
Inventory shrinkage expense	300	
Inventory		300

The net effect of these entries, assuming a zero beginning balance, is an ending inventory balance of $650.

The downside of using a perpetual inventory system is a massive increase in the number of inventory-related transactions that must be recorded. This burden may require the addition of warehouse clerks to record transactions, or the use of bar code scanning, portable data entry terminals, or other labor-saving devices.

The initial comparison of a perpetual system's recorded inventory valuation to the physical count will likely reveal a significant disparity. This variance will be caused by a number of transactions not being recorded or recorded incorrectly. If the causes of these variances are tracked down and corrected (usually with procedural changes and training updates), the perpetual system will eventually become quite reliable. However, if a nonprofit has a small and low-cost inventory that rarely experiences much turnover, it is possible that the increased reliability of a perpetual system will not be worth its added cost. If so, the periodic inventory system may be the more applicable system.

Inventory Cost Layering Overview

The typical inventory asset is comprised of many identical parts that may have been acquired during different time periods. In each of these time periods, it is likely that the costs incurred varied somewhat from those incurred in other time periods. The result is a mish-mash of inventory items that all look the same, but which have different costs associated with them. How is the accountant to decide which costs to assign to goods when they are sold? A possible solution is the cost layering concept. Under cost layering, we assume that different tranches of costs have been incurred to construct or acquire certain clusters of inventory. The following example illustrates the concept.

EXAMPLE

Senior Care Home Supplies acquires wheel chairs from a contract manufacturer, for sale through SCHS' on-line store. An especially popular wheel chair is a battery-powered model. Over the past three months, Milford made the following purchases of this model from its contract manufacturer:

Date	Quantity	Price/each
1/05/X3	320	$89.00
1/29/X3	85	90.25
2/15/X3	170	91.00
3/09/X3	135	91.00

Since the first two purchases were made at different prices, the units in each of these purchases can be considered a separate cost layer. Since the last two purchases were made at the same price, they can be aggregated into the same cost layer, or they may be treated as separate cost layers.

Depending on the cost layering system that SCHS chooses to use, the organization can assume that the cost of a wheel chair that is charged to the cost of goods sold may come from the first of these cost layers (the first in, first out system) or from the last of the cost layers (the last in, first out system).

Two methods for calculating the cost of inventory that employ the cost layering concept are shown in this chapter. Of the methods presented, the first in, first out method has gained worldwide recognition. The last in, first out method cannot realistically be justified based on the actual flow of inventory, and is only used in the United States under the sanction of the Internal Revenue Service; it is specifically banned under international financial reporting standards. We also make passing note of the specific identification method, which is an acceptable alternative to the cost layering methods, but which is usually only applicable to a small number of entities.

The First in, First Out Method

The first in, first out (FIFO) method of inventory valuation operates under the assumption that the first goods purchased are also the first goods sold. In most organizations, this accounting assumption closely matches the actual flow of goods, and so is considered the most theoretically correct inventory valuation method.

Under the FIFO method, the earliest goods purchased are the first ones removed from the inventory account. This results in the remaining items in inventory being accounted for at the most recently incurred costs, so that the inventory asset recorded on the statement of financial position contains costs quite close to the most recent costs that could be obtained in the marketplace. Conversely, this method also results in older historical costs being matched against current revenues and recorded in the cost of goods sold, so the gross margin does not necessarily reflect a proper matching of revenues and costs.

EXAMPLE

Senior Care Home Supplies (SCHS) decides to use the FIFO method for the month of January. During that month, it records the following transactions:

	Quantity Change	Actual Unit Cost	Actual Total Cost
Beginning inventory (layer 1)	+100	$210	$21,000
Sale	-75		
Purchase (layer 2)	+150	280	42,000
Sale	-100		
Purchase (layer 3)	+50	300	15,000
Ending inventory	= 125		$78,000

The cost of goods sold in units is calculated as:

100 Beginning inventory + 200 Purchased – 125 Ending inventory = 175 Units

SCHS' controller uses the information in the preceding table to calculate the cost of goods sold for January, as well as the cost of the inventory balance as of the end of January. The calculations appear in the following table:

	Units	Unit Cost	Total Cost
Cost of goods sold			
FIFO layer 1	100	$210	$21,000
FIFO layer 2	75	280	21,000
Total cost of goods sold	175		$42,000
Ending inventory			
FIFO layer 2	75	280	$21,000
FIFO layer 3	50	300	15,000
Total ending inventory	125		$36,000

Thus, the first FIFO layer, which was the beginning inventory layer, is completely used up during the month, as well as half of Layer 2, leaving half of Layer 2 and all of Layer 3 to be the sole components of the ending inventory.

Note that the $42,000 cost of goods sold and $36,000 ending inventory equals the $78,000 combined total of beginning inventory and purchases during the month.

From a database management perspective, the FIFO method results in the smallest number of cost layers to track, since the oldest layers are constantly being eliminated.

The Last in, First Out Method

The last in, first out (LIFO) method operates under the assumption that the last item of inventory purchased is the first one sold. Picture a store shelf where a clerk adds items from the front, and customers also take their selections from the front; the remaining items of inventory that are located further from the front of the shelf are rarely picked, and so remain on the shelf – that is a LIFO scenario.

The trouble with the LIFO scenario is that it is rarely encountered in practice. If an entity were to use the process flow embodied by LIFO, a significant part of its inventory would be very old, and likely obsolete. Nonetheless, an organization does not actually have to experience the LIFO process flow in order to use the method to calculate its inventory valuation.

EXAMPLE

Senior Care Home Supplies (SCHS) decides to use the LIFO method for the month of March. The following table shows the various purchasing transactions for the organization's First Alert electronic ambulance notification product. The quantity purchased on March 1 actually reflects the inventory beginning balance.

Date Purchased	Quantity Purchased	Cost per Unit	Units Sold	Cost of Layer #1	Cost of Layer #2	Total Cost
March 1	150	$210	95	(55 × $210)		$11,550
March 7	100	235	110	(45 × $210)		9,450
March 11	200	250	180	(45 × $210)	(20 × $250)	14,450
March 17	125	240	125	(45 × $210)	(20 × $250)	14,450
March 25	80	260	120	(25 × $210)		5,250

The following bullet points describe the transactions noted in the preceding table:

- *March 1.* SCHS has a beginning inventory balance of 150 units, and sells 95 of these units between March 1 and March 7. This leaves one inventory layer of 55 units at a cost of $210 each.

- *March 7.* SCHS buys 100 additional units on March 7, and sells 110 units between March 7 and March 11. Under LIFO, we assume that the latest purchase was sold first, so there is still just one inventory layer, which has now been reduced to 45 units.
- *March 11.* SCHS buys 200 additional units on March 11, and sells 180 units between March 11 and March 17, which creates a new inventory layer that is comprised of 20 units at a cost of $250. This new layer appears in the table in the "Cost of Layer #2" column.
- *March 17.* SCHS buys 125 additional units on March 17, and sells 125 units between March 17 and March 25, so there is no change in the inventory layers.
- *March 25.* SCHS buys 80 additional units on March 25, and sells 120 units between March 25 and the end of the month. Sales exceed purchases during this period, so the second inventory layer is eliminated, as well as part of the first layer. The result is an ending inventory balance of $5,250, which is derived from 25 units of ending inventory, multiplied by the $210 cost in the first layer that existed at the beginning of the month.

Before implementing the LIFO system, consider the following points:

- *Covenant compliance.* When LIFO has been used for a long period of time and materials prices have increased during that period, the reported inventory asset may be so low that an organization has trouble meeting the terms of its loan covenants that require a certain amount of current assets.
- *Layering.* Since the LIFO system is intended to use the most recent layers of inventory, the accountant may never access earlier layers, which can result in an administrative problem if there are many layers to document.
- *Profit fluctuations.* If early layers contain inventory costs that depart substantially from current market prices, a nonprofit could experience sharp changes in its net assets if those layers are ever accessed.

In summary, LIFO does not usually reflect the actual flow of inventory, and may even yield unusual financial results that differ markedly from reality.

The Specific Identification Method

The cost layering concept operates under the assumption that costs cannot be traced to specific inventory items. This assumption is largely true, since there may be hundreds of identical items in stock. However, in cases where a nonprofit only retains uniquely identifiable inventory items, it is perfectly acceptable to assign a cost to each individual unit of inventory. When an item is sold, the cost specifically linked to that item is charged to the cost of goods sold. The result is a highly accurate inventory accounting system that precisely matches inventory costs with revenues. For this system to work, it should have the following attributes:

- *Unique inventory items.* Each item in stock must be uniquely identified. This typically limits use of the specific identification method to custom-made or uniquely-configured items.
- *Cost linkage.* When goods are acquired or built, the costing system must accumulate costs at the individual unit level.
- *Expensive items.* Because of the extra cost of accumulating and tracking costs at the individual unit level, this system is only cost-effective when the items being tracked are quite expensive.

The Lower of Cost or Market Rule

The lower of cost or market rule (LCM) is required by GAAP, and essentially states that the cost of inventory be recorded at whichever cost is lower – the original cost or its current market price (hence the name of the rule). More specifically, the rule mandates that the recognized cost of an inventory item should be reduced to a level that does not exceed its replacement cost as derived in an open market. This replacement cost is subject to the following two conditions:

- The recognized cost cannot be greater than the likely selling price minus costs of disposal (known as net realizable value).
- The recognized cost cannot be lower than the net realizable value minus a normal profit percentage.

This situation typically arises when inventory has deteriorated, or has become obsolete, or market prices have declined. The following example illustrates the concept.

EXAMPLE

Senior Care Home Supplies (SCHS) resells five major brands of portable emergency alert devices, which are noted in the following table. At the end of its reporting year, SCHS calculates the upper and lower price boundaries of the LCM rule for each of the products, as noted in the table:

Product	Selling Price	-	Completion/ Selling Cost	=	Upper Price Boundary	-	Normal Profit	=	Lower Price Boundary
Full Spectrum	$250		$25		$225		$75		$150
Gander Elite	190		19		171		57		114
Hi-Volume	150		15		135		45		90
Night Alert	1,000		100		900		300		600
Titanium	700		70		630		210		420

The normal profit associated with these products is a 30% margin on the original selling price.

The information in the preceding table for the upper and lower price boundaries is then included in the following table, which completes the LCM calculation:

Product	Upper Price Boundary	Lower Price Boundary	Existing Recognized Cost	Replacement Cost*	Market Value**	Lower of Cost or Market
Full Spectrum	$225	$150	$140	$260	$225	$140
Gander Elite	171	114	180	175	171	171
Hi-Volume	135	90	125	110	110	110
Night Alert	900	600	850	550	600	600
Titanium	630	420	450	390	420	420

* The cost at which the item could be acquired on the open market
** The replacement cost, as limited by the upper and lower pricing boundaries

The LCM decisions noted in the last table are explained as follows:

- *Full Spectrum.* It would cost SCHS $260 to replace these items, which is above the upper price boundary of $225. This means the market value for the purposes of this calculation is $225. Since the market price is higher than the existing recognized cost, the LCM decision is to leave the recognized cost at $140 each.
- *Gander Elite.* The replacement cost of these items has declined to a level below the existing recognized cost, so the LCM decision is to revise the recognized cost to $171. This amount is a small reduction from the unadjusted replacement cost of $175 to the upper price boundary of $171.
- *Hi-Volume.* The replacement cost is less than the recognized cost, and is between the price boundaries. Consequently, there is no need to revise the replacement cost. The LCM decision is to revise the recognized cost to $110.
- *Night Alert.* The replacement cost of these items is below the existing recognized cost, but is below the lower price boundary. Thus, the LCM decision is to set the market price at the lower price boundary, which will be the revised cost of the items.
- *Titanium.* The replacement cost is much less than the existing recognized cost, but also well below the lower price boundary. The LCM decision is therefore to set the market price at the lower price boundary, which is also the new product cost.

If the amount of a write-down caused by the LCM analysis is minor, charge the expense to the cost of goods sold, since there is no reason to separately track the information. If the loss is material, track it in a separate account (especially if such losses are recurring), such as "Loss on LCM adjustment." A sample journal entry for a large adjustment is:

	Debit	Credit
Loss on LCM adjustment	147,000	
Merchandise inventory		147,000

Additional factors to consider when applying the LCM rule are:

- *Analysis by category.* The LCM rule is normally applied to a specific inventory item, but it can be applied to entire inventory categories. In the latter case, an LCM adjustment can be avoided if there is a balance within an inventory category of items having market below cost and in excess of cost.
- *Hedges.* If inventory is being hedged by a fair value hedge, add the effects of the hedge to the cost of the inventory, which frequently eliminates the need for an LCM adjustment.
- *Last in, first out layer recovery.* A write-down to the lower of cost or market can be avoided in an interim period if there is substantial evidence that inventory amounts will be restored by year end, thereby avoiding recognition of an earlier inventory layer.
- *Raw materials.* Do not write down the cost of raw materials if the finished goods in which they are used are expected to sell either at or above their costs.
- *Recovery.* A write-down to the lower of cost or market can be avoided if there is substantial evidence that market prices will increase before the inventory is sold.
- *Sales incentives.* If there are unexpired sales incentives that will result in a loss on the sale of a specific item, this is a strong indicator that there may be an LCM problem with that item.

Tip: When there is an LCM adjustment, it must be taken at once – the expense cannot be recognized over multiple reporting periods.

Inventory Disclosures

The following information should be disclosed about an organization's inventory practices in its financial statements:

- *Basis.* Note the basis on which inventories are stated. If there is a significant change in the basis of accounting, the nature of the change and the effect on net assets (if material) shall be stated.
- *Lower of cost or market losses.* If there are substantial and unusual losses caused by the lower of cost or market rule, disclose this amount separately in the statement of activities. This is not a requirement.
- *Goods above cost.* Disclose the particulars concerning any inventory items that have been stated above cost.
- *Goods at sales prices.* Disclose the particulars concerning any inventory items that have been stated at their sales prices.
- *Firm purchase commitments.* Separately note in the statement of activities the amounts of any net losses that have been accrued on firm purchase commitments.

- *Estimate*. Disclose any significant estimates related to inventory.

Summary

The information provided in this chapter should be sufficient for a nonprofit to deal with the basic accounting for its merchandise inventory. We made note of the periodic and perpetual systems for tracking aggregate inventory levels, as well as several ways to assign costs to units of inventory. The discussion of the lower of cost or market rule is one that a nonprofit will need to address at least once a year, before it completes its annual financial statements.

This chapter did not address a large number of more advanced inventory accounting topics, such as cycle counting, backflushing, physical inventory counts, inventory estimation, standard costing, job costing, and overhead allocation. For a more complete discussion of inventory that includes these other topics, see the author's *Accounting for Inventory* book.

Chapter 8
Fixed Asset Accounting

Introduction

A fixed asset is an item with a useful life greater than one reporting period, and which exceeds an organization's minimum capitalization limit. The capitalization limit is the amount paid for an asset, above which the item is recorded as a fixed asset. If an entity pays less than the capitalization limit for an asset, it charges the expenditure to expense in the period incurred. The following are examples of general categories of fixed assets:

- Buildings
- Computer equipment
- Computer software
- Furniture and fixtures
- Intangible assets
- Land
- Leasehold improvements
- Machinery
- Vehicles

> **Related Podcast Episodes:** Episodes 122, 139, and 196 of the Accounting Best Practices Podcast discuss fixed asset disposals, a lean system for fixed assets, and fixed asset counting, respectively. The episodes are available at: **accounting-tools.com/podcasts** or **iTunes**

Initial Recognition of Fixed Assets

When a not-for-profit entity receives a fixed asset contribution, it records the asset with an offsetting entry to a revenue or gain account. Record a contribution as revenue if it is part of the entity's ongoing major activities, or record it as a gain if the contribution is part of peripheral or incidental activity.

If a contributor places a restriction on the use of a fixed asset, this does not impact the underlying value of the donation, so the entity records the same amount for such a contributed asset as it would for one without a restriction, with no change in the timing of recognition.

If a nonprofit receives a contributed asset for which there is a major uncertainty about its value, do not recognize it in the accounting records. Examples of such assets are those of historical value, photographs, or items that may be of use solely for scientific research.

Conversely, an organization should record an asset that has a future economic benefit or service potential (usually by exchanging it for cash or using it to generate goods or services).

EXAMPLE

Newton Enterprises provides free science classes to high school students. It receives the following contributions:

- A philosopher's stone. The stone is of historical significance, but probably does not transmute lead into gold. Since there is considerable uncertainty about its value, Newton does not record the asset.
- A used lawn mower. The lawn mower is of no direct use to Newton's primary operations, and will be sold. Newton accordingly records the lawn mower as a gain.
- An electron microscope. The microscope is of direct use in Newton's primary operations, so Newton records it as revenue.

As an example of the journal entries to be used for a donated asset, if the microscope in the preceding example were to be valued at $50,000, the journal entry might be:

	Debit	Credit
Scientific devices	50,000	
Revenue		50,000

If the lawn mower in the preceding example were to be valued at $1,000, the journal entry might be:

	Debit	Credit
Maintenance equipment	1,000	
Gain on contributed assets		1,000

The initial recognition of a fixed asset shall include the costs incurred to place the asset in use. For example, the cost to install and test contributed equipment is considered part of the asset cost. Similarly, the cost to catalog library books is considered part of the cost of the books.

The Capitalization Limit

One of the most important decisions to be made in the initial recognition of a fixed asset is what minimum cost level to use, below which an expenditure is recorded as an expense in the period incurred, rather than recording it as a fixed asset and depreciating it over time. This capitalization limit, which is frequently abbreviated as the *cap limit*, is usually driven by the following factors:

- *Asset tracking.* If an expenditure is recorded as a fixed asset, the fixed asset tracking system may impose a significant amount of control over the newly-recorded fixed asset. This can be good, if it is useful to know where an asset is at any time. Conversely, there is not usually a tracking system in place for an expenditure that is charged to expense, since the assumption is that such items are consumed at once, and so require no subsequent tracking.
- *Fixed asset volume.* The number of expenditures that will be recorded as fixed assets will increase dramatically as the cap limit is lowered. For example, there may only be one fixed asset if the cap limit is $100,000, 50 assets if the cap limit is $10,000, and 500 assets if the cap limit is $1,000. Analyze historical expenditures to estimate a cap limit that will prevent the accounting staff from being deluged with additional fixed asset records.
- *Record keeping cost.* What is the lowest asset cost at which it becomes burdensome to track an individual fixed asset? There is a labor cost associated with each fixed asset, which includes depreciation, derecognition, impairment, and auditing transactions.

From an efficiency perspective, a high cap limit is always best, since it greatly reduces the work of the accountant. From an asset tracking perspective, the reverse is desirable, with a very low cap limit. These conflicting objectives call for some discussion within the management team about the most appropriate cap limit – it should not simply be imposed on the entity by the accounting department.

EXAMPLE

Newton Enterprises is reviewing its capitalization limit, which is currently set at $250. A review of this limit reveals that the organization has capitalized several hundred tables, none of which it actively tracks. There are also a number of servers that were acquired for its data storage facility, each of which cost about $5,000 each. These servers are occasionally subject to failure, and so are monitored closely. Finally, there are several large training facilities, with each building costing several million dollars.

Upon review of this information, management concludes that it should re-set the capitalization limit to $1,000, so that it excludes all tables, but continues to include the servers that it has more interest in tracking. This change in policy will also eliminate roughly 20 percent of all assets tracked, which will reduce the cost of record keeping. Though there will be an additional expense associated with immediately charging tables to expense, the increase is considered immaterial to Newton's overall change in net assets.

Restrictions on Contributed Assets

If a donor makes a contribution that is an *unconditional promise to give*, recognize the contribution when received. This calls for sufficient verifiable documentation that the promise was both made and received. The promise should be legally enforceable. If a contributor is able to rescind the promise to give, do not recognize the asset being contributed.

If a contributor makes a contribution that is a conditional promise to give, only recognize the asset when the underlying conditions have been substantially met (e.g., at the point when the promise becomes unconditional).

EXAMPLE

Newton Enterprises receives an offer from a contributor to pay $2 million for a new classroom building, but only if Newton can raise matching funds from other contributors within one year. Given the conditional nature of this offer, Newton cannot record the asset until the matching funds have been raised within the specified time period.

A donor may contribute a fixed asset with restrictions placed on the use of that asset. If so, record the asset within the net assets with donor restrictions classification. This amount may be reclassified to net assets without donor restrictions at a later date, if the restrictions expire.

The following contributed assets should be reclassified from net assets with donor restrictions to net assets without donor restrictions when the assets are placed in service:

- Cash contributed for the acquisition or construction of fixed assets.
- Fixed assets contributed with purpose restrictions, for which there is no stipulation stating how long the asset must be used.

Valuation of Contributed Assets

Recognize a donated asset at its fair value as of the receipt date. The following techniques are available for deriving fair value:

- *Market approach*. Use information from actual market transactions to arrive at an estimated fair value. Ideally, this information is based on quoted prices in an active market for identical items, but may also use information from transactions for similar items, or just the best available information.
- *Income approach*. Use discounted cash flows to derive the present value of an asset.
- *Cost approach*. Use an asset's current replacement cost. This is essentially the cost of acquiring or building a substitute asset that has comparable utility.

If the election is made to use the income approach, and the asset being contributed will not be received for at least a year, use the projected fair value of the asset as of the date when it is expected to be received, discounted back to its present value. When it is impossible to determine fair value as of a future date, use the fair value of the asset at the initial recognition date, though without any discounting to present value.

EXAMPLE

Newton Enterprises is given an office building for use as a training center by a city government that has no use for the building. The city is suffering through a severe downturn, and the government was unable to find a buyer for the building. In general, there is very little market information available for the valuation of similar buildings, given the paucity of sale transactions. Newton also has trouble using the income approach to derive a value for the building, since it gives science classes for free. Thus, it elects to use the cost approach to value the building, under which it determines that the cost to create a substitute building of comparable utility would be $700,000.

Valuation of Contributed Services

What if volunteers donate their time to construct a fixed asset? Record the value of these services in either of the following situations:

- The services create or enhance non-financial assets; or
- The services require specialized skills, are provided by persons with those skills, and would otherwise need to be purchased.

Value these services at either their fair value or at the fair value of the fixed asset created or the change in value of the fixed asset being improved.

EXAMPLE

Newton Enterprises constructs a science school, using the services of a large group of volunteers, which include architects, carpenters, electricians, and plumbers. Newton spends $800,000 on materials for the building project. Once the asset is placed in service, a third-party appraiser estimates that the fair value of the building is now $1.2 million. Newton can therefore record the building asset at a cost of $1.2 million, of which $400,000 is the value of contributed services.

Valuation of Art, Historical Treasures, and Similar Items

If a donor contributes works of art, historical treasures, or similar items, a nonprofit can recognize them as assets, with offsetting revenue or gains. This only applies if the items contributed are not part of a collection. A *collection* is defined as art works that are for public use, are safeguarded and cared for, and are protected by a policy to replace items that are sold from the collection. If contributions are part of a collection, use any of the following alternatives for reporting them:

- Record them as fixed assets; or
- Record as fixed assets only those items received after a specific date; or

- Do not record them.

It is not allowable to record only *selected* collections or items as fixed assets; instead, any recordation policy must be consistently applied to *all* collections or items.

Capitalize the cost of major preservation or restoration projects, and assign them useful lives that extend until the next expected preservation or restoration project for the same asset.

EXAMPLE

Newton Enterprises maintains a small science museum, to which a donor contributes an original quadruplex telegraph built by Thomas Edison. An independent appraisal establishes that the device has a fair value of $150,000. Newton adds the telegraph to its Edison collection and records it as a fixed asset. This results in revenue of $150,000, as well as a new fixed asset.

If a collection is to be capitalized, a possible issue is what value to assign to the collection items. The amount to recognize should be the fair value of the items, but this can be difficult to ascertain. As noted in the preceding example and in the prior Valuation of Contributed Assets section, one approach is to have an appraiser develop a valuation, which is usually derived from the quoted market prices of similar items. The amount of the valuation will be of great interest to the donor, who may use this information to claim a tax deduction for the value of the contributed items.

If a nonprofit contributes a previously recognized collection item to another entity, the nonprofit recognizes the contribution as an expense, using the fair value of the item as the recognized expense. However, if the collection item was never recognized as an asset, it is not recognized as an expense when contributed elsewhere.

Depreciation of Fixed Assets

Depreciation is the concept of gradually charging the cost of an asset to expense as the asset is consumed over time, rather than charging the entire amount to expense as soon as the asset is acquired. Doing so more accurately represents asset consumption.

A nonprofit entity should depreciate any contributed assets that it has recorded as fixed assets, if they have a useful life. If an asset's useful life is extremely long (as would be the case for a work of art), a nonprofit does not have to recognize depreciation for it. Only avoid depreciation in this manner if both of the following conditions exist:

- The asset should be preserved perpetually, due to its cultural, aesthetic, or historical value; and

- The entity has the ability to preserve the asset (such as by preserving it in a protected environment), and is currently doing so.

It is necessary to depreciate art collections, on the grounds that they experience wear and tear during their intended uses that requires periodic major restoration efforts.

If the cost of a major restoration project has been capitalized, depreciate this cost over the expected period before the next restoration project is expected. Do this even if the asset being restored or preserved is not depreciated.

There are a number of complex depreciation methods available, but it is rarely necessary for a nonprofit to use them. Instead, use the simplest depreciation method, which is called the straight-line method. Under this approach, recognize depreciation expense evenly over the estimated useful life of an asset. The straight-line calculation steps are:

1. Subtract the estimated salvage value of the asset from the amount at which it is recorded on the books.
2. Determine the estimated useful life of the asset.
3. Divide the estimated useful life (in years) into 1 to arrive at the straight-line depreciation rate.
4. Multiply the depreciation rate by the asset cost (less salvage value).

EXAMPLE

Newton Education purchases a cold fusion training lab for $60,000. The lab has an estimated salvage value of $10,000 and a useful life of five years. Newton calculates the annual straight-line depreciation for the machine as:

1. Purchase cost of $60,000 – Estimated salvage value of $10,000 = Depreciable asset cost of $50,000
2. 1 ÷ 5-Year useful life = 20% Depreciation rate per year
3. 20% Depreciation rate × $50,000 Depreciable asset cost = $10,000 Annual depreciation

---

If it is necessary to recognize depreciation expense on an accelerated basis, the double-declining balance (DDB) method is most commonly used. This approach is most logical when the use of an asset is expected to be most heavy in the early years of its useful life, and to then taper off over time.

To calculate the double-declining balance depreciation rate, divide the number of years of useful life of an asset into 100 percent, and multiply the result by two. The formula is:

$$(100\%/\text{Years of useful life}) \times 2$$

The DDB calculation proceeds until the asset's salvage value is reached, after which depreciation ends.

EXAMPLE

Newton Education purchases a machine for $50,000. It has an estimated salvage value of $5,000 and a useful life of five years. The calculation of the double declining balance depreciation rate is:

$$(100\%/\text{Years of useful life}) \times 2 = 40\%$$

By applying the 40% rate, Newton arrives at the following table of depreciation charges per year:

Year	Book Value at Beginning of Year	Depreciation Percentage	DDB Depreciation	Book Value Net of Depreciation
1	$50,000	40%	$20,000	$30,000
2	30,000	40%	12,000	18,000
3	18,000	40%	7,200	10,800
4	10,800	40%	4,320	6,480
5	6,480	40%	1,480	5,000
Total			$45,000	

Note that the depreciation in the fifth and final year is only for $1,480, rather than the $3,240 that would be indicated by the 40% depreciation rate. The reason for the smaller depreciation charge is that Newton stops any further depreciation once the remaining book value declines to the amount of the estimated salvage value.

Depreciation Accounting Entries

The basic depreciation entry is to debit the depreciation expense account (which appears in the statement of activities) and credit the accumulated depreciation account (which appears in the statement of financial position as an offset to the fixed assets line item). Over time, the accumulated depreciation balance will continue to increase as more depreciation is added to it, until such time as it equals the original cost of the asset. At that time, stop recording any depreciation expense, since the cost of the asset has now been reduced to zero.

The journal entry for depreciation can be a simple two-line entry designed to accommodate all types of fixed assets, or it may be subdivided into separate entries for each type of fixed asset.

EXAMPLE

Newton Education calculates that it should have $25,000 of depreciation expense in the current month. The entry is:

	Debit	Credit
Depreciation expense	25,000	
Accumulated depreciation		25,000

In the following month, Newton's controller decides to show a higher level of precision at the expense account level, and instead elects to apportion the $25,000 of depreciation among different expense accounts, so that each class of asset has a separate depreciation charge. The entry is:

	Debit	Credit
Depreciation expense – Automobiles	4,000	
Depreciation expense – Computer equipment	8,000	
Depreciation expense – Furniture and fixtures	6,000	
Depreciation expense – Office equipment	5,000	
Depreciation expense – Software	2,000	
Accumulated depreciation		25,000

Accumulated Depreciation

When an asset is sold or otherwise disposed of, remove all related accumulated depreciation from the accounting records at the same time. Otherwise, an unusually large amount of accumulated depreciation will build up on the statement of financial position.

EXAMPLE

Newton Education has $1,000,000 of fixed assets, for which it has charged $380,000 of accumulated depreciation. This results in the following presentation on Newton's statement of financial position:

Fixed assets	$1,000,000
Less: Accumulated depreciation	(380,000)
Net fixed assets	$620,000

Newton then sells a training machine for $80,000 that had an original cost of $140,000, and for which it had already recorded accumulated depreciation of $50,000. It records the sale with this journal entry:

	Debit	Credit
Cash	80,000	
Accumulated depreciation	50,000	
Loss on asset sale	10,000	
Fixed assets		140,000

As a result of this entry, Newton's statement of financial position presentation of fixed assets has changed, so that fixed assets before accumulated depreciation have declined to $860,000, and accumulated depreciation has declined to $330,000. The new presentation is:

Fixed assets	$860,000
Less: Accumulated depreciation	(330,000)
Net fixed assets	$530,000

The amount of net fixed assets declined by $90,000 as a result of the asset sale, which is the sum of the $80,000 cash proceeds and the $10,000 loss resulting from the asset sale.

Asset Impairment

Fixed assets should be periodically tested to see if they are still as valuable as the costs at which they are now recorded in the accounting records. If not, reduce the recorded cost of these assets by recognizing a loss. The basic rule is to recognize an impairment loss on a fixed asset if its carrying amount is not recoverable and exceeds its fair value. The carrying amount is the cost of an asset, minus any accumulated depreciation and impairments. Once impairment has been recognized, it cannot be reversed in a later period.

The carrying amount of an asset is not recoverable if it exceeds the sum of the undiscounted cash flows expected to result from the use of the asset over its remaining useful life and the final disposition of the asset. These cash flow estimates should incorporate assumptions that are reasonable in relation to the assumptions the entity uses for its budgets, forecasts, and so forth. If there are a range of possible cash flow outcomes, consider using a probability-weighted cash flow analysis.

The amount of an impairment loss is the difference between an asset's carrying amount and its fair value. Once an impairment loss is recognized, this reduces the carrying amount of the asset, so it may be necessary to alter the amount of periodic depreciation being charged against the asset to adjust for this lower carrying amount (otherwise, an excessively large depreciation expense will be incurred over the remaining useful life of the asset).

Our treatment of asset impairment is intentionally limited, since the impairment test is designed for organizations whose assets have discernible cash flows associated with them. Nonprofits do not necessarily operate in this manner, and so are effectively exempt from the asset impairment concept. However, if a non-profit has a business-type activity, such as a bookstore, café, or fee-generating training program where assets *do* generate cash flows, the related assets will be subject to asset impairment testing.

Recordation of Fixed Assets

The record keeping for a fixed asset may be relatively minimal, perhaps with just an authorizing purchase order copy attached to a supplier invoice. However, for more expensive fixed assets, management might want to track a considerably larger pool of information. Consider whether the following information might be needed:

- *Description.* This is a description of the asset that is sufficient to identify it.
- *Tag number.* This is the identification number of the asset tag that the entity affixes to its assets.
- *Serial number.* If no tag numbers are used, instead list the serial number of the asset, as assigned by the manufacturer.
- *Location.* Note the location where the asset resides.
- *Responsible party.* This is the name or position of the person who is responsible for the equipment.
- *In service date.* This is the date on which the asset is ready for its intended use, and is the traditional trigger date for the start of depreciation.
- *Cost.* The cost may simply be the original purchase price, or it may be a more extensive record of additions to the asset over time as high-cost items are replaced.
- *Useful life.* This can be the manufacturer's recommended equipment life, or it can be supplemented it over time if management concludes that the useful life should be changed, with notations regarding the impact on the depreciation rate.
- *Asset class.* Note the class of assets in which the asset is categorized. Since a standard depreciation method is typically assigned to an asset class, it is not necessary to also state the depreciation method. If a standard useful life is used for an asset class, it is not necessary to separately record an asset's useful life.
- *Warranty period.* This is the period during which the manufacturer will pay for repairs to the equipment. If there is a cost-effective warranty extension option, note it here.
- *Supplier contact information.* This may include several addresses for the supplier, such as for its field servicing, customer service, warranty, and sales departments.
- *Impairment circumstances.* If there has been a write down in the value of the equipment due to impairment, note the circumstances of the impairment,

and when it occurred. This may require extensive documentation if there have been several impairments or impairment reversals.

By retaining this additional asset information, one can more easily track down assets, determine who is responsible for them, and determine if the manufacturer is responsible for any repairs. It is useful to consolidate this record with any manufacturer's warranty documents, as well as a copy of key maintenance records.

In addition, consider maintaining the following information that relates specifically to nonprofits:

- *Donor*. Identify the person or entity that contributed the asset, along with contact information.
- *Restrictions*. Note any restrictions placed on use of the asset by the donor.

These two additional items may interact. For example, there may no longer be a need for an asset, and management wants to sell it to create space for another asset. If so, it may be necessary to contact the donor to have a restriction lifted, or to have the asset returned to the donor.

It is also useful to maintain a report that itemizes the restrictions on fixed assets, so that the entity does not deal with an asset in a manner that will violate a restriction. This report should be periodically updated and issued to the management team for review.

Fixed Asset Disclosures

The following accounting policies relating to fixed assets must be disclosed in the notes to the financial statements:

- Whether there is a time restriction imposed on the use of donated fixed assets that states the period over which the assets must be used
- The capitalization policy used
- The capitalization policy for collections
- Whether cost or fair value is used to derive the valuation of fixed assets

In the accompanying disclosures, also make separate note of all nondepreciable items, fixed assets not held for use in operations, and any improvements made to leased assets.

If there are liquidity issues with fixed assets or limitations on their use, these issues must be included in the financial statement disclosures. For example:

- Any fixed assets that are pledged as collateral in loan agreements
- Contracts which may result in the nonprofit gaining control of certain assets at the end of the contract
- Donor limitations placed on the use of any funds gained from the sale of donated assets

- Whether the title to donated assets may revert to a third party

If collections are capitalized, the amount must be stated in a separate collections line item in the statement of financial position. If there are other works of art, historical treasures, or similar items not considered to be collections, report their aggregate capitalized amount in a separate line item in the statement of financial position or in the accompanying notes.

If a nonprofit elects to not recognize its collections, or to only capitalize collections on a prospective basis, it must describe the collections, as well as their relative significance, and any policies it has regarding the stewardship of the collections. If collections have not been recognized, the entity must also describe or note the fair value of those items given away, damaged, destroyed, or lost during the reporting period. A reference to this information must be included in a line item in the statement of financial position.

If collections are not recognized, a nonprofit must separately report in the statement of activities the cost of any collection items purchased (thus, the treatment is as an expense, rather than a fixed asset). A possible line item description is:

Collection items purchased but not capitalized

If collections are not recognized or only recognized prospectively, the following items must be separately reported in the statement of activities:

- Proceeds from the sale of any collection items. A possible line item description is:

Gain on sale of art that is not held in a collection

- Proceeds from any insurance payments received that relate to lost or destroyed collection items. A possible line item description is:

Proceeds from insurance recoveries on destroyed collection items

Summary

A nonprofit entity must deal with several fixed asset decisions that a for-profit business never encounters – whether to record a contributed asset, at what value to record it, and whether to depreciate it at all. These decisions are only for *contributed* assets. For fixed assets that are directly purchased by a nonprofit, the fixed asset accounting follows essentially the same rules used by for-profit entities.

Chapter 9
Lease Accounting

Introduction

Nonprofits do not always have sufficient cash to purchase their own equipment or facilities, and so will enter into leases to obtain the use of these assets. A lease is an arrangement where the lessor agrees to allow the lessee to use an asset for a stated period of time in exchange for one or more payments.

The lease financing of assets is governed by a strict set of rules that require a lessee to either treat a leasing arrangement as a series of rental payments or as the purchase of an asset. In this chapter, we cover the accounting for the different types of leases, sale-leaseback transactions, and similar issues related to leases. We only present the accounting for leases from the perspective of the lessee, since nonprofits are rarely placed in the position of leasing assets to other entities.

The Nature of a Lease

A lease is an arrangement under which a lessor agrees to allow a lessee to control the use of identified property, plant, and equipment for a stated period of time in exchange for one or more payments. A lease arrangement is quite a useful opportunity, for the following reasons:

- The lessee reduces its exposure to asset ownership
- The lessee obtains financing from the lessor in order to pay for the asset
- The lessee now has access to the leased asset

An arrangement is considered to give control over the use of an asset when both of these conditions are present:

- The lessee obtains the right to substantially all of the economic benefits from using an asset; and
- The lessee obtains the right to direct the uses to which an asset is put.

EXAMPLE

The Rural Communications Consortium (RCC) obtains the rights to the entire output of an undersea cable for the next ten years, in order to benefit from an expected increase in traffic from new data centers in Sweden to users in the United States. Since RCC has the right to substantially all of the economic benefits from using the cable, the underlying contract is considered a lease. If the arrangement had instead been for only a certain proportion of the total capacity of the cable, where the cable operator could choose which fibers within the cable would carry RCC's data, the arrangement would not be considered a lease.

EXAMPLE

Teton Helicopter Rescue leases a helicopter for use in its personnel rescue operations. As part of the lease agreement, Teton is only allowed to operate the helicopter during daylight hours. This restriction is designed to reduce the risk of damage to the craft. This protective right limits the scope of Teton's usage of the helicopter, but does not actually prevent it from having the right to use the asset. Thus, the restriction does not prevent the contract from being designated as a lease.

The following additional points all apply to whether a lease exists:

- *Partial period.* If a leasing arrangement only lasts for a portion of the period spanned by a contract, a lease is still presumed to exist for the partial period specified within the contract.
- *Right of substitution.* If a contract allows the supplier to substitute an identified asset with another asset throughout the usage period, there is no lease. This situation only applies when the supplier has the practical ability to substitute alternative assets, and the supplier obtains a positive economic benefit from doing so. The evaluation of the ability to substitute assets does not include assets that are unlikely to occur.

EXAMPLE

Reef Bleaching Analysis (RBA) leases several submarines from Underwater Assets, for use in shallow-water research at nearby reefs. The lease agreement states that Underwater Assets can substitute a submarine for repairs or maintenance in the event that a submarine is not operating properly. This contract language still allows RBA to have the right to an identified asset, so the existence of the lease is not called into question.

EXAMPLE

Nova Asteroid Survey operates a deep field scanning telescope for sky survey work, which it leases from Alpha Centauri Leasing. If the contract language is interpreted in a certain way, it appears possible that Alpha could substitute the telescope at a later date. However, the telescope is located at Nova's observatory, and would be difficult to dismount and replace. The cost of substitution is therefore likely to be higher than any benefits that Alpha might gain from the substitution. In this case, it appears likely that there is a lease.

EXAMPLE

Feed the Poor Ministries stores corn and wheat along the Mississippi River. It enters into an agreement with a local transport firm to transport crops up and down the river. The volume of transport services indicated in the contract translates into the ongoing use of three barges. The transport firm has several hundred barges that it can use to fulfill the contract. When not in use, the barges are stored at one of the transport firm's riverside facilities. No specific barges are described in the contract. Given these conditions, it is apparent that Feed the Poor does not direct the use of the barges, nor does it have the right to obtain substantially all of the economic benefits from use of the barges. Consequently, this arrangement is not a lease.

Since the accounting for a lease only applies to property, plant, and equipment, it does not apply to the following types of assets that may also be leased:

- Assets under construction
- Biological assets (such as orchards)
- Exploration assets (such as oil and gas exploration rights)
- Intangible assets
- Inventory

Lease Components (Lessee)

Once it has been established that a contract contains a lease, it is necessary to separate the lease into its components (if any). This can result in a business tracking several different leases within one contract. A separate lease component exists when both of the following conditions are present:

- The lessee can benefit from the right of use of a single asset, or together with other readily available resources; and
- The right of use is separate from the rights to use other assets in the contract. This is not the case when the rights of use of the different assets significantly affect each other.

The right to use land is always considered a separate lease component, unless doing so would have an insignificant effect.

There may also be non-lease components to a contract. These components will not meet the criteria just stated for a lease component, but will transfer a good or service to the lessee. There may also be other activities that do not qualify as non-lease components, since there is no transfer of goods or services; for example, the reimbursement of lessor costs falls into this category.

A common charge associated with a lease is common area maintenance. The lessor typically performs maintenance and cleaning services for all common areas in a building, and then charges a portion of these costs through to the building tenants. The lessee would otherwise have to perform these services itself or pay a third party to do so. Common area maintenance costs are considered a non-lease component.

Once all lease and non-lease components have been identified, allocate the consideration in the contract to them. This allocation is derived as follows:

1. Determine the standalone price of each separate lease and non-lease component. This should be based on the observable standalone price. If this price is not available, it can be estimated.
2. Allocate the consideration in proportion to the standalone prices of the various components.
3. If there are any initial direct costs associated with the contract, allocate these costs on the same basis as the lease payments.

EXAMPLE

African Solar leases a stamping machine and a CNC (computer numerical control) machine for its solar powered washing machine production facility, along with periodic maintenance and repair services. The total consideration that African will pay over the five-year term of the lease is $800,000.

African's controller concludes that there are two separate leases, since the stamping and CNC machines are to be used separately, in different parts of the factory. The controller also decides to account for the maintenance and repair services as non-lease components of the contract. Further, these services are considered to be distinct for each machine, and so are separate non-lease performance obligations.

The controller needs to allocate the $800,000 of consideration to the various lease and non-lease components. She notes that there are a number of local suppliers that provide similar maintenance and repair services for each of the machines, and that standalone prices can be found to separately lease the two machines. These standalone prices are noted in the following table:

	Lease	Maintenance	Totals
Stamping machine	$200,000	$30,000	$230,000
CNC machine	570,000	100,000	670,000
Totals	$770,000	$130,000	$900,000

The controller allocates the $800,000 consideration in the contract to the lease and non-lease components on a relative basis, employing their standalone prices. This results in the following allocation:

	Lease	Maintenance	Totals
Stamping machine	$177,778	$26,667	$204,445
CNC machine	506,667	88,888	595,555
Totals	$684,445	$115,555	$800,000

The consideration in a lease should be remeasured and reallocated when either of the following events occurs:

- The lease liability is remeasured. This could be triggered by a change in the term of the lease, or a revision to the assessment of whether a lease option will be exercised.
- There is a contract modification that is not being accounted for as a separate contract.

Initial Direct Costs

Initial direct costs are those costs that are only incurred if a lease agreement occurs. This usually includes broker commissions and payments made to existing tenants to obtain a lease, because these costs are only incurred if a lease agreement is signed. Legal fees are usually not included, since the parties must pay their attorneys even if a lease arrangement falls through. Also, staff time spent working on a lease arrangement will be incurred irrespective of the lease agreement, and so is not considered part of initial direct costs.

Initial direct costs are capitalized at the inception of a lease, and are then amortized ratably over the term of the lease. Throughout the term of a lease, any unamortized initial direct costs are included in the measurement of the right-of-use asset (which is discussed later).

Lease Consideration

Consideration is defined as something of value that induces the parties to a contract to exchange mutual performances. The consideration in a leasing arrangement is most obviously the periodic fixed lease payments made by the lessee. Consideration can also include monthly service charges, as well as variable payments that are defined by an index or a rate. For example, a lease payment may be adjusted each year, based on changes in the consumer price index.

The Lease Term

One of the key components of a lease is the lease term. This is considered to be the noncancelable period of a lease, as well as the following additional periods that may apply:

- Lease extension options if it is reasonably certain that the lessee will exercise these options
- Lease termination options if it is reasonably certain that the lessee will not exercise these options
- Lease extension options where the lessor controls the options

An entity makes a judgment call as of the lease commencement date regarding which of the preceding factors will apply to the derivation of an estimated lease term. This judgment is based on those factors that create an economic incentive for the lessee. Examples of economic incentives are reduced lease payments in the optional period, the significance of any leasehold improvements, and the importance of the underlying asset to the lessee's operations.

EXAMPLE

Subatomic Research operates a laboratory in leased facilities. The laboratory has been designated as an airborne infection isolation room by the federal government, which is quite a difficult certification to obtain. The lease has an option for Subatomic to extend the lease term by five years. It is highly likely that Subatomic will renew the lease, given the high cost of moving elsewhere and then applying for recertification.

EXAMPLE

Newton Enterprises offers free science classes to high school students. These endeavors require Newton to lease training facilities. Its most recent lease is for 10 years, with a termination option after seven years. Annual lease payments are $100,000. If Newton terminates the lease, it must pay a $30,000 termination penalty. The managers of Newton conclude that it is not reasonably certain that Newton will need the facilities after seven years of use, especially considering the relatively small size of the termination penalty when compared to the amount of the annual lease payments. Consequently, Newton elects to measure the lease term as being seven years.

If the lessor provides a period of free rent, the lease term is considered to begin at the commencement date and to include all rent-free periods.

A lease term should not extend past the period when it is enforceable. A lease is no longer enforceable when both the lessee and the lessor can terminate the lease without permission from the other party, and by paying no more than an insignificant penalty.

Initial Measurement of Lease Payments

There are a number of possible payments by a lessee that can be associated with a lease component. All of the following payments relate to the use of the underlying asset in a lease:

- Fixed payments, minus any lease incentives payable to the lessee
- Variable lease payments that depend on an index or a rate (such as the consumer price index)
- The exercise price of an option to purchase the underlying asset, if it is reasonably certain that the lessee will exercise the option
- Penalty payments associated with an assumed exercise of an option to terminate the lease
- Fees paid to the owners of a special-purpose entity for creating the transaction
- Residual value guarantees, if it is probable that these amounts will be owed. Note that a lease provision requiring the lessee to pay for any deficiency in residual value that is caused by damage or excessive usage is not considered a guarantee of the residual value.

At the commencement of a lease, a number of direct costs may also have been incurred. Examples of these costs are commissions and payments made to incentivize a tenant to terminate a lease. Costs that would have been incurred even in the absence of a lease (such as general overhead and salaries) are not direct costs.

A lessor might pay a third party for a guarantee of the residual value of an underlying asset. This payment is considered an executory cost of the contract; it is not considered part of the lease payments.

If there is a requirement in a lease agreement that the lessee dismantle and remove an underlying asset following the end of a lease, this cost is considered a lease payment.

Subsequent Measurement of Lease Payments

It is only necessary to reassess a lessee's option to purchase an underlying asset or the length of the lease term when one of the following events occurs subsequent to the initial measurement of a lease:

- *Contractual requirement.* An event occurs that was addressed in the contract, requiring the lessee to exercise (or not exercise) an option or terminate the lease.
- *No option exercise.* The lessee does not exercise an option despite a previous determination that it was reasonably certain for the lessee to do so.
- *Option exercise.* The lessee exercises an option despite a previous determination that it was reasonably certain that the lessee would not do so.
- *Significant event.* A significant event has occurred that is within the control of the lessee, and which directly affects the lessee's decision to exercise or not exercise an option, or to purchase the underlying asset. Examples of significant events are the construction of significant leasehold improvements that will be of value to the lessee during the option period, and making significant modifications to the underlying asset.

It is only necessary to remeasure the lease payments associated with a lease when one of the following events occurs:

- *Lease modification.* The initial lease is modified, and the modification is not accounted for as a separate contract.
- *Resolved contingency.* A contingency that had resulted in variable lease payments has now been resolved, so that the payments become fixed for the remainder of the lease term.
- *Other changes.* There is a change in the lease term, a change in the assessment of whether an option will be exercised, or a change in the probable amount that will be owed by the lessee under a residual value guarantee.

Types of Leases

There are several types of lease designations, which differ if an entity is the lessee or the lessor. It is critical to determine the type of a lease, since the accounting varies by lease type. The choices for a **lessee** are that a lease can be designated as either a finance lease or an operating lease. In essence, a *finance lease* designation implies that the lessee has purchased the underlying asset (even though this may not actually be the case), while an *operating lease* designation implies that the lessee has obtained the use of the underlying asset for only a period of time. A lessee should classify a lease as a finance lease when <u>any</u> of the following criteria are met:

- *Ownership transfer*. Ownership of the underlying asset is shifted to the lessee by the end of the lease term.
- *Ownership option*. The lessee has a purchase option to buy the leased asset, and is reasonably certain to use it.
- *Lease term*. The lease term covers the major part of the underlying asset's remaining economic life. This is considered to be 75% or more of the remaining economic life of the underlying asset. This criterion is not valid if the lease commencement date is near the end of the asset's economic life, which is considered to be a date that falls within the last 25% of the underlying asset's total economic life.
- *Present value*. The present value of the sum of all lease payments and any lessee-guaranteed residual value matches or exceeds the fair value of the underlying asset. The present value is based on the interest rate implicit in the lease.
- *Specialization*. The asset is so specialized that it has no alternative use for the lessor following the lease term. In this situation, there are essentially no remaining benefits that revert to the lessor.

When none of the preceding criteria are met, the lessee must classify a lease as an operating lease.

Asset and Liability Recognition (Lessee)

A central concept of the accounting for leases is that the lessee should recognize the assets and liabilities that underlie each leasing arrangement. This concept results in the following recognition in the balance sheet of the lessee as of the lease commencement date:

- Recognize a liability to make lease payments to the lessor
- Recognize a right-of-use asset that represents the right of the lessee to use the leased asset during the lease term

There are a number of sub-topics related to asset and liability recognition, which are stated in the following sub-sections.

Initial Measurement

As of the commencement date of a lease, the lessee measures the liability and the right-of-use asset associated with the lease. These measurements are derived as follows:

- *Lease liability*. The present value of the lease payments, discounted at the discount rate for the lease. This rate is the rate implicit in the lease when that rate is readily determinable. If not, the lessee instead uses its incremental borrowing rate.

- *Right-of-use asset.* The initial amount of the lease liability, plus any lease payments made to the lessor before the lease commencement date, plus any initial direct costs incurred, minus any lease incentives received.

EXAMPLE

Deciduous Research Labs enters into a five-year lease, where the lease payments are $35,000 per year, payable at the end of each year. Deciduous incurs initial direct costs of $8,000. The rate implicit in the lease is 8%.

At the commencement of the lease, the lease liability is $139,745, which is calculated as $35,000 multiplied by the 3.9927 rate for the five-period present value of an ordinary annuity. The right-of-use asset is calculated as the lease liability plus the amount of the initial direct costs, for a total of $147,745.

Short-Term Leases

When a lease has a term of 12 months or less, the lessee can elect not to recognize lease-related assets and liabilities in the balance sheet. This election is made by class of asset. When a lessee makes this election, it should usually recognize the expense related to a lease on a straight-line basis over the term of the lease.

If the lease term changes so that the remaining term now extends more than 12 months beyond the end of the previously determined lease term or the lessee will likely purchase the underlying asset, the arrangement is no longer considered a short-term lease. In this situation, account for the lease as a longer-term lease as of the date when there was a change in circumstances.

Finance Leases

When a lessee has designated a lease as a finance lease, it should recognize the following over the term of the lease:

- The ongoing amortization of the right-of-use asset
- The ongoing amortization of the interest on the lease liability
- Any variable lease payments that are not included in the lease liability
- Any impairment of the right-of-use asset

The amortization period for the right-of-use asset is from the lease commencement date to the earlier of the end of the lease term or the end of the useful life of the asset. An exception is when it is reasonably certain that the lessee will exercise an option to purchase the asset, in which case the amortization period is through the end of the asset's useful life.

After the commencement date, the lessee increases the carrying amount of the lease liability to include the interest expense on the lease liability, while reducing the carrying amount by the amount of all lease payments made during the period. The interest on the lease liability is the amount that generates a constant periodic discount rate on the remaining liability balance.

After the commencement date, the lessee reduces the right-of-use asset by the amount of accumulated amortization and accumulated impairment (if any).

EXAMPLE

Deciduous Research Labs agrees to a five-year lease of equipment that requires an annual $20,000 payment, due at the end of each year. At the end of the lease period, Deciduous has the option to buy the equipment for $1,000. Since the expected residual value of the equipment at that time is expected to be $25,000, the large discount makes it reasonably certain that the purchase option will be exercised. At the commencement date of the lease, the fair value of the equipment is $120,000, with an economic life of eight years. The discount rate for the lease is 6%.

Deciduous classifies the lease as a finance lease, since it is reasonably certain to exercise the purchase option.

The lease liability at the commencement date is $84,995, which is calculated as the present value of five payments of $20,000, plus the present value of the $1,000 purchase option payment, discounted at 6%. Deciduous recognizes the right-of-use asset as the same amount, since there are no initial direct costs, lease incentives, or other types of payments made by Deciduous, either at or before the commencement date.

Deciduous amortizes the right-of-use asset over the eight-year expected useful life of the equipment, under the assumption that it will exercise the purchase option and therefore keep the equipment for the eight-year period.

As an example of the subsequent accounting for the lease, Deciduous recognizes a first-year interest expense of $5,100 (calculated as 6% × $84,995 lease liability), and recognizes the amortization of the right-of-use asset in the amount of $10,624 (calculated as $84,995 ÷ 8 years). This results in a lease liability at the end of Year 1 that has been reduced to $70,095 (calculated as $84,995 + $5,100 interest - $20,000 lease payment) and a right-of-use asset that has been reduced to $74,371 (calculated as $84,995 - $10,624 amortization).

By the end of Year 5, which is when the lease terminates, the lease liability has been reduced to $1,000, which is the amount of the purchase option. Deciduous exercises the option, which settles the remaining liability. At that time, the carrying amount of the right-of-use asset has declined to $31,875 (reflecting five years of amortization at $10,624 per year). Deciduous shifts this amount into a fixed asset account and depreciates it over the remaining three years of its useful life.

Operating Leases

When a lessee has designated a lease as an operating lease, the lessee should recognize the following over the term of the lease:

- A lease cost in each period, where the total cost of the lease is allocated over the lease term on a straight-line basis. This can be altered if there is another systematic and rational basis of allocation that more closely follows the benefit usage pattern to be derived from the underlying asset.
- Any variable lease payments that are not included in the lease liability
- Any impairment of the right-of-use asset

EXAMPLE

Deciduous Research Labs enters into an operating lease in which the lease payment is $25,000 per year for the first five years and $30,000 per year for the next five years. These payments sum to $275,000 over ten years. Deciduous will therefore recognize a lease expense of $27,500 per year for all of the years in the lease term.

At any point in the life of an operating lease, the remaining cost of the lease is considered to be the total lease payments, plus all initial direct costs associated with the lease, minus the lease cost already recognized in previous periods.

After the commencement date, the lessee measures the lease liability at the present value of the lease payments that have not yet been made, using the same discount rate that was established at the commencement date.

After the commencement date, the lessee measures the right-of-use asset at the amount of the lease liability, adjusted for the following items:

- Any impairment of the asset
- Prepaid or accrued lease payments
- Any remaining balance of lease incentives received
- Any unamortized initial direct costs

EXAMPLE

Nova Asteroid Survey enters into a 10-year operating lease for its corporate offices. The annual lease payment is $40,000 to be paid at the end of each year. The company incurs initial direct costs of $8,000, and receives $15,000 from the lessor as a lease incentive. Nova's incremental borrowing rate is 6%. The initial direct costs and lease incentive will be amortized over the 10 years of the lease term.

Nova measures the lease liability as the present value of the 10 lease payments at a 6% discount rate, which is $294,404. The right-of-use asset is measured at $287,404, which is the initial $294,404 measurement, plus the initial direct costs of $8,000, minus the lease incentive of $15,000.

After one year, the carrying amount of the lease liability is $272,068, which is the present value of the remaining nine lease payments at a 6% discount rate. The carrying amount of the right-of-use asset is $265,768, which is the amount of the liability, plus the unamortized initial direct costs of $7,200, minus the remaining balance of the lease incentive of $13,500.

Right-of-Use Asset Impairment

If a right-of-use asset is determined to be impaired, the impairment is immediately recorded, thereby reducing the carrying amount of the asset. Its subsequent measurement is calculated as the carrying amount immediately after the impairment transaction, minus any subsequent accumulated amortization.

EXAMPLE

Nova Asteroid Survey enters into a five-year equipment lease that is classified as an operating lease. At the end of Year 2, when the carrying amount of the lease liability and the right-of-use asset are both $100,000, the controller determines that the asset is impaired, and recognizes an impairment loss of $70,000. This reduces the carrying amount of the asset to $30,000.

Beginning in Year 3 and continuing through the remainder of the lease term, Nova amortizes the right-of-use asset at a rate of $10,000 per year, which will bring the carrying amount of the asset to zero by the end of the lease term.

Leasehold Improvement Amortization

A leasehold improvement is a customization of rented property, such as the addition of carpeting, cabinetry, lighting, and walls. This asset should be amortized over the shorter of the remaining lease term and its useful life. The one exception is when it is reasonably certain that the lessee will take possession of the underlying asset at the end of the lease, in which case the amortization period is through the end of the asset's useful life.

Subleases

A sublease occurs when a lessee leases the underlying asset to a third party. A sublease agreement typically arises when the original tenant no longer needs to use leased space or can no longer afford to make the lease payments. This situation is most common for commercial properties, but can arise for residential properties as well. The following accounting can apply to this situation:

- *Operating lease.* If a lease is classified as an operating lease, the original lessee continues to account for it in the same manner that it did before the commencement of the sublease.
- *Conversion from finance lease.* If the original lease was classified as a finance lease and the sublease is classified as either a sales-type or direct

financing lease, then the original lessee must derecognize the right-of-use asset on its books. The accounting for the original lease liability remains the same.

- *Conversion from operating lease.* If the original lease was classified as an operating lease and the sublease is classified as either a sales-type lease or a direct financing lease, then the original lessee must derecognize the right-of-use asset on its books, and account for the original lease liability as of the sublease commencement date as though it were a finance lease (see the preceding Finance Leases sub-section).

Maintenance Deposits

A lessee may be required to pay the lessor a maintenance deposit, which the lessor retains if the lessee damages the property during the lease term. If it is probable that the lessor will retain this deposit at the end of the lease, the lessee should recognize the payment as a variable lease expense.

Derecognition

At the termination of a lease, the right-of-use asset and associated lease liability are removed from the books. The difference between the two amounts is accounted for as a profit or loss at that time. If the lessee purchases the underlying asset at the termination of a lease, then any difference between the purchase price and the lease liability is recorded as an adjustment to the asset's carrying amount.

   If a lessee subleases an underlying asset and the terms of the original agreement then relieve the lessee of the primary lease obligation, this is considered a termination of the original lease.

Elections

There are several elections that an organization can use to simplify the accounting for leases. One option is to use a risk-free discount rate for present value calculations, rather than having to justify some other rate. Another election is to include non-leasing components in a leasing arrangement, thereby reducing the number of elements within a contract to which costs may be assigned. These two options are explained within this section. In addition, a lessee can elect not to recognize lease-related assets and liabilities in the balance sheet when a lease has a term of 12 months or less. This option was explained earlier in the Asset and Liability Recognition section.

Discount Rate

A business that is not publicly-held can elect to use a risk-free discount rate when deriving the present value of a lease. If so, this discount rate should be determined using a period comparable to that of the lease term. This election will apply to all of the entity's leases; it is not available for just a single lease or class of asset.

Separation of Non-Lease Components

A leasing arrangement may contain non-leasing components. For example, a lease contract might include a maintenance contract under which the lessor provides ongoing servicing of the leased asset. In this case, the consideration stated in the contract is to be allocated by the lessee to these separate parts based on their relative standalone prices. The accounting for non-leasing contract components will vary depending on their nature; it is not covered by the leasing standard.

A lessee can choose to not separate non-lease components from lease components. Instead, it can account for a lease component and any non-lease components associated with that lease component as a single lease component. This election must be made by class of asset; it is not available for just a single lease.

EXHIBIT

Home Food Delivery (HFD) leases two trucks from Grinder International, along with maintenance services, for a total of $80,000. The two trucks are of different types, and so will be accounted for as separate leases. HFD has made an accounting policy election to combine non-lease and lease components for its slot machines. This means that there are only two lease components in the contract, with no non-lease components.

The controller of HFD can easily find standalone prices for combinations of trucks and maintenance services. These amounts are noted in the following table, along with the allocation of the $80,000 total contract price that is based on their standalone prices:

	Standalone Price	Allocated Price
Flatbed truck lease & maintenance	$40,000	$36,364
Air ride truck lease & maintenance	48,000	43,636
Totals	$88,000	$80,000

Sale and Leaseback Transactions

A sale and leaseback transaction occurs when the seller transfers an asset to the buyer, and then leases the asset from the buyer. This arrangement most commonly occurs when the seller needs the funds associated with the asset being sold, despite still needing to occupy the space.

When such a transaction occurs, the first accounting step is to determine whether the transaction was at fair value. This can be judged from either of the following comparisons:

- Compare the difference between the sale price of the asset and its fair value.
- Compare the present value of the lease payments and the present value of market rental payments. This can include an estimation of any variable lease payments reasonably expected to be made.

If this comparison results in the determination that a sale and leaseback transaction is not at fair value, the entity must adjust the sale price on the same basis just used to determine whether the transaction was at fair value. This can result in the following adjustments:

- Any increase to the asset's sale price is accounted for as a rent prepayment
- Any reduction of the asset's sale price is accounted for as additional financing provided to the seller-lessee by the buyer-lessor. The seller-lessee should adjust the interest rate on this liability to ensure that:
  - Interest on the liability is not greater than the principal payments over the shorter of the lease term and the financing term; and
  - The carrying amount of the asset is not greater than the carrying amount of the liability at the earlier of the termination date of the lease or the date when asset control switches to the buyer-lessor.

In this arrangement, the consideration paid for the asset is accounted for as a financing transaction by both parties. However, if there is a repurchase option under which the seller can later buy back the asset, then the initial transaction cannot be considered a sale. The only exceptions are when:

- There are alternative assets readily available in the marketplace, and
- The price at which the option can be exercised is the fair value of the asset on the option exercise date.

If a sale and leaseback transaction is not considered a sale, then the seller-lessee cannot derecognize the asset, and accounts for any amounts received as a liability. Also, the buyer-lessor does not recognize the transferred asset, and accounts for any amount paid as a receivable.

EXAMPLE

Charities International sells one of its properties to Capital Inc. The sale price is a cash payment of $7 million. At the same time as the sale, Charities enters into a contract with Capital for the right to use the property for the next 10 years, in exchange for annual payments of $800,000, payable in arrears. Additional facts are:

- Immediately prior to the transaction, the property had a carrying amount on Charities' books of $6 million
- The fair value of the property is $7 million
- Capital obtains legal title to the property
- Capital has significant risks and rewards of ownership, such as the risk of loss if the property value declines
- The transaction is classified as an operating lease

As of the transaction commencement date, Charities derecognizes the $6 million carrying amount of the property, recognizes the $7 million cash receipt, and recognizes a $1 million gain on the sale. Also as of this date, Capital recognizes the property at a cost of $7 million.

Lease Disclosures

There are a considerable number of required disclosures for leases. In this section, we provide descriptions of these disclosures for the lessee, as well as a few additional disclosures related to sale and leaseback transactions.

Lessee Disclosures

The following disclosure requirements related to leases must be followed by the *lessee* in its financial statements:

Nature of the Leases

- General description of the leases
- The basis upon which variable lease payments are calculated
- The nature of any lease extension or termination options
- The nature of any residual value guarantees
- The nature of any restrictions imposed by leases
- The nature of any leases that have not yet commenced, that will create significant rights and obligations for the lessee
- The significant assumptions and judgments made, including whether a lease exists, the allocation of consideration to leases, and the determination of the lease discount rate

Lease Costs

- The finance lease cost, separately reporting the amortization of right-of-use assets and the interest expense on lease liabilities
- The operating lease cost
- The short-term lease cost, not including leases with a term of one month or less
- The variable lease cost
- The income from subleases
- The net gain or loss on sale and leaseback transactions

Other Information

- Cash paid for items included in the measurement of lease liabilities
- Non-cash information regarding lease liabilities caused by securing right-of-use assets
- The weighted-average remaining lease term
- The weighted-average discount rate
- A maturity analysis of finance lease liabilities and operating lease liabilities, which reveals undiscounted cash flows for each of the first five years and the total for all subsequent years

- A reconciliation of undiscounted cash flows to the finance lease liabilities and operating lease liabilities recognized in the balance sheet
- All lease transactions between related parties
- Disclosure of a policy to account for short-term leases without the recognition of a lease liability or right-of-use asset
- Disclosure of a policy to not separate lease components from non-lease components, and the classes of underlying assets to which it applies

SAMPLE LESSEE DISCLOSURE

(000s)	Year Ending December 31,	
	20X4	20X3
Lease cost		
Finance lease cost:		
Amortization of right-of-use assets	$1,320	$1,295
Interest on lease liabilities	475	463
Operating lease cost	280	240
Short-term lease cost	72	65
Variable lease cost	11	9
Sublease income	40	10
Total lease cost	$2,198	$2,082
Other Information		
(Gains) and losses on sale and leaseback transactions	$--	$400
Cash paid for amounts included in the measurement of lease liabilities		
Operating cash flows from finance leases	810	615
Operating cash flows from operating leases	275	228
Financing cash flows from finance leases	460	420
Weighted-average remaining lease term – finance leases	4.7 years	4.3 years
Weighted-average remaining lease term – operating leases	3.0 years	2.9 years
Weighted-average discount rate – finance leases	6.9%	6.5%
Weighted-average discount rate – operating leases	7.2%	7.0%

Sale and Leaseback Transactions

A seller-lessee in a sale and leaseback transaction should disclose the primary terms and conditions of the transaction. In addition, it should separately disclose any gains or losses from the transaction, so that they are not aggregated into the gains or losses derived from the disposal of other assets.

Summary

A key element of the accounting for leases is that an organization must now recognize assets and liabilities for the rights and obligations created by leases that have terms of more than 12 months. This level of disclosure gives a substantial amount of transparency regarding a lessee's financial leverage and its leasing activities. Unfortunately, it also introduces a greater degree of complexity to the accounting for leases. Consequently, it may be useful to create a procedure for the leasing transactions that an entity engages in most frequently, along with accompanying examples, and rigidly adhere to that procedure when accounting for leases. It may also be useful to structure leasing transactions in the future so that the procedure can be applied to them. Doing so reduces the potential variability in the accounting that may be applied to leasing transactions, which in turn reduces the risk of having errors creep into the financial statements.

Chapter 10
Pension Plan Accounting

Introduction

This chapter addresses the accounting for two types of pension plans, called defined benefit plans and defined contribution plans. Nearly all of the discussion is concentrated on defined benefit plans, which require ongoing estimations of and accounting for future costs that may be incurred, as well as changes to existing benefits. Nonprofits are fairly likely to use one or the other of these plan types. By offering these pension plans, they can reduce the risk that employees will be tempted to leave the organization in search of higher pay in the for-profit sector.

Some of the complexity of this topic is caused by a rare circumstance in GAAP – where provisions are made to allow an organization to defer costs and recognize them in later periods through amortization. This approach contravenes the vastly more common approach of charging all costs to expense as incurred. While this type of modified accounting undoubtedly allows an entity to defer expense recognition, it causes ongoing headaches for accountants, and likely increases the profits of the actuarial industry.

Overview of Retirement Benefits

A retirement benefit is one in which the employer promises to deliver a fixed benefit to its employees at some point in the future. Examples of these benefits are pensions and health benefits to be paid following the retirement of employees. Employees qualify for retirement benefits either through the passage of time, by attaining a certain age, or a combination of both. Retirement benefits paid to employees may begin as soon as they retire, or the benefits may be delayed until a certain age is reached, or even when employees elect to begin accepting benefits.

Retirement benefits are a form of deferred compensation, so the employer must estimate the amount of future expenditure that will be made, and recognize a portion of it in the current period. Expense recognition occurs before the benefits are paid, because employees are earning these future benefits via their services in earlier periods.

Defined Benefit Plans

In a defined benefit retirement plan, the employer provides a pre-determined periodic payment to employees after they retire. The amount of this future payment depends upon a number of future events, such as estimates of employee lifespan, how long current employees will continue to work for the organization, and the pay level of employees just prior to their retirement. In essence, the accounting for defined benefit plans revolves around the estimation of the future payments to be made, and recognizing the related expense in the periods in which employees are rendering the services that qualify them to receive payments in the future under the terms of the plan.

There are a number of costs associated with defined benefit plans that may at first appear arcane. Here is a summary of the relevant costs, which sum to the net periodic pension cost that is recognized in each accounting period:

Cost	Explanation
+ Service cost	This is the actuarial present value of benefits related to services rendered during the current reporting period. The cost includes an estimate of the future compensation levels of employees from which benefit payments will be derived.
+ Interest cost	This is the interest on the projected benefit obligation. It is a financial item, rather than a cost related to employee compensation.
+ Actual return on plan assets	This is the difference between the fair values of beginning and ending plan assets, adjusted for contributions and benefit payments. It is a financial item, rather than a cost related to employee compensation.
+ Amortization of prior service costs	When an employer issues a plan amendment, it may contain increases in benefits that are based on services rendered by employees in prior periods. If so, the cost of these additional benefits is amortized over the future periods in which those employees active on the amendment date are expected to receive benefits.
+ Gain or loss	This is the gain or loss resulting from a change in the value of a projected benefit obligation from changes in assumptions, or changes in the value of plan assets.
= Net periodic pension cost	

The accounting for the relevant defined benefit plan costs is as follows:

- *Service cost.* The amount of service cost recognized in earnings in each period is the incremental change in the actuarial present value of benefits related to services rendered during the current reporting period.
- *Interest cost.* The interest cost associated with the projected benefit obligation is recognized as incurred.
- *Amortization of prior service costs.* These costs are charged to other comprehensive income on the date of the amendment, and then amortized to earnings over time. The amount to be amortized is derived by assigning an equal amount of expense to each future period of service for each employee who is expected to receive benefits. If most of the employees are inactive, the amortization period is instead the remaining life expectancy of the employees. Straight-line amortization of the cost over the average remaining

service period is also acceptable. Once established, this amortization schedule is not usually revised, unless there is a plan curtailment or if events indicate that a shorter amortization period is warranted.

Each of these costs represents a change in the net assets without donor restrictions of the nonprofit sponsoring the plan.

EXAMPLE

Archimedes Education creates a pension plan amendment that grants $90,000 of prior service costs to the 200 employees in its Mississippi facility. The organization expects the employees at this location to retire in accordance with the following schedule:

Group	Number of Staff	Expected Year of Retirement
A	20	Year 1
B	40	Year 2
C	80	Year 3
D	40	Year 4
E	20	Year 5
Total	200	

The entity uses the following grid to calculate the service years for each of the employee groups:

	Service Years					
Year	Group A	Group B	Group C	Group D	Group E	Total
1	20	40	80	40	20	200
2		40	80	40	20	180
3			80	40	20	140
4				40	20	60
5					20	20
Totals	20	80	240	160	100	600

There are 600 service years listed in the preceding table, over which the $90,000 prior service cost is to be allocated, which is $150 of cost per service year. Archimedes inserts the $150 per year figure into the following table to determine the amount of prior service cost amortization to recognize in each year.

Year	Total of Service Years	×	Cost per Service Year	=	Amortization per Year
1	200		$150		$30,000
2	180		150		27,000
3	140		150		21,000
4	60		150		9,000
5	20		150		3,000
Totals	600				$90,000

- *Prior service credits.* If a plan amendment reduces plan benefits, record it as a change in net assets without donor restrictions on the date of the amendment. This amount is then offset against any prior service cost remaining in net assets without donor restrictions that have not yet been reclassified as components of net periodic pension cost. Any residual amount of the credit is then amortized using the same methodology just noted for prior service costs.
- *Gains and losses.* Gains and losses can be recognized immediately if the method is applied consistently. If the election is not made to recognize them immediately, it is also possible to account for them as changes in net assets without donor restrictions that have not yet been reclassified as components of net periodic pension cost as they occur. If there is a gain or loss on the difference between the expected and actual amount of return on plan assets, recognize the difference in net assets without donor restrictions in the period in which it occurs, and then reclassify it over time as a component of net periodic pension cost using the following calculation:

  1. Include the gain or loss in net pension cost for a year in which, as of the beginning of that year, the gain or loss is greater than 10% of the greater of the projected benefit obligation or the market-related value of plan assets.
  2. If this test is positive, amortize the excess just noted over the average remaining service period of those active employees who are expected to receive benefits. If most of the plan participants are inactive, amortize the excess over their remaining life expectancy.

A key additional term that arises in the accounting for defined benefit plans is the *projected benefit obligation.* This is the actuarial present value of future benefits attributed to service already rendered by employees. The "actuarial" part of the definition refers to *expected* payments, since some payments will never be made, due to the turnover of employees before they vest, the death of employees who would otherwise have been entitled to payments, and so forth. The projected benefit obligation also incorporates assumptions regarding the future pay levels and service periods of existing employees, which tends to increase the amount of the benefit obligation in comparison to what the obligation would be based on current employee compensation levels and periods of service.

When a business incurs obligations for future pension payments, it should presumably begin accumulating assets into a pension plan that will be available to pay the pension benefits in the future. If the projected benefit obligation is greater than the fair value of the plan assets on the statement of financial position date, the employer should recognize a liability for the difference (known as the *unfunded projected benefit obligation*). In those rare cases where plan assets exceed the projected benefit obligation, the employer recognizes an asset in the amount of the difference. If there are multiple plans, all overfunded plans should be aggregated for reporting purposes, and all underfunded plans should be aggregated for reporting purposes.

If there are adjustments to the funded status of a pension plan, net gains or losses, prior service costs, and so forth, the offset to these entries is net assets without donor restrictions.

When the employer buys annuity contracts to cover the cost of future employee benefits, the cost of the benefits should be the same as the cost of acquiring the annuity contracts.

Expense Attribution for Delayed Vesting

There are a number of methods available for assigning benefits to employees, usually with the intent of delaying the vesting of benefits. For example, a plan may provide no benefits after nine years of service, and then vests employees in a future benefit payment following the tenth year of service (known as *cliff vesting*). In these situations, do not defer the recognition of a benefit expense until the delayed vesting occurs. Instead, assume that the benefit accumulates over time in proportion to the number of completed periods of service, which means that there should be an ongoing accrual of the related benefit expense over time.

EXAMPLE

Suture Indigent Medical Care has a defined benefit pension plan, under which it pays a pension benefit of $60 per month for the remainder of each employee's life for each year of service completed, up to a maximum of ten years of service. The actuary employed by Suture calculates that the average employee will have 210 months of life expectancy following their retirement from Suture, and will have the full 10 years of service completed as of their retirement. The actuarial present value discount is set at 0.35. Based on this information, the actuary calculates the following pension benefits attributable to each of Suture's employees:

Years of service period completed	10
× Pension benefit per month	× $60
= Payment to be made per month to each employee	= $600
× Average life expectancy (in months)	× 210
= Gross pension payment	= $126,000
× Actuarial present value discount rate	× 0.35
= Present value of pension benefit	$44,100

Discount Rates

Service costs are based on the actuarial present value of benefits to be paid in the future. A discount rate must be employed to arrive at this actuarial present value. The discount rate should be one that reflects the rate at which benefits can actually be settled. A good source of information for this discount rate is the rate implicit in the current prices of annuity contracts that an employer could purchase to settle a future benefit obligation. Another source of information is the rate of return on high-quality fixed income investments that are expected to be available through the period during which the pension benefits will be paid.

Interest rates vary, depending upon the time period of investments. Thus, the discount rate used for benefits to be paid to a group of 50-year old employees will likely be different from the discount rate used for benefits to be paid to a group of 30-year olds.

Settlements and Curtailments

A benefit plan may be adjusted or terminated at some point. Variations that may be encountered include:

- *Curtailments.* Employee services or the benefit plan itself may be terminated earlier than expected, which reduces or eliminates the accrual of additional benefits.
- *Settlements.* Lump-sum cash payments may be made to plan participants in exchange for their rights to receive pension benefits.

When benefit obligations are settled, curtailed, or terminated, net gains or losses and prior service costs are shifted from net assets without donor restrictions to earnings. This transfer occurs in the period in which all pension obligations are settled, benefits are no longer accrued, no plan assets remain, employees are terminated, *and* the plan ceases to exist. Also, the plan cannot be replaced by another plan.

If only a portion of the projected benefit obligation is settled, recognize in net assets without donor restrictions that portion of the settlement that represents the reduction in the projected benefit obligation.

If the cost of the settlements completed in a year is greater than the sum of the service and interest cost components of the net periodic pension cost for that period, record a gain or loss in the amount of the difference. If the cost is lower than the sum of the service and interest cost components, recognition as a change in net assets without donor restrictions is permitted, but not required. The manner in which management chooses to deal with a lower-cost situation should be followed consistently.

If there is a curtailment of a benefit plan, the associated amount of prior service cost already recorded in net assets without donor restrictions that is related to future years of service should be recognized as a loss. Also, the projected benefit obligation may be increased or decreased by a curtailment. This is a curtailment gain in the amount by which it exceeds any loss included in net assets without donor restrictions. This is a curtailment loss in the amount by which it exceeds any net gain included in net assets without donor restrictions. A curtailment loss should be recognized in earnings when the amount can be reasonably estimated and the curtailment is probable. A curtailment gain should be recognized in earnings when the plan is formally suspended or the impacted employees are terminated.

EXAMPLE

Following the devastation of a major earthquake, Senior Care Home Supplies (SCHS) closes down its California facility. The employees located there will no longer earn any benefits. As of the plan curtailment date, the actuarial assumptions associated with the plan are:

- Defined benefit obligation = $300,000
- Plan assets fair value = $275,000
- Net cumulative unrecognized actuarial gains = $15,000

The curtailment event shrinks the present value of the benefit obligation by $20,000, to $280,000. Also, 20% of the net cumulative unrecognized actuarial gains are associated with that portion of the obligation that was eliminated by the curtailment. These alterations are incorporated into the following table:

	Before Curtailment	Gain on Curtailment	After Curtailment
Present value of obligation	$300,000	-$20,000	$280,000
Fair value of plan assets	-275,000	--	-275,000
	25,000	-20,000	5,000
Unrecognized actuarial gains	15,000	3,000	18,000
Net liability	$40,000	-$17,000	$23,000

Based on the preceding information, SCHS' controller records the following entry to record the gain on curtailment:

	Debit	Credit
Accrued pension cost	17,000	
Curtailment gain		17,000

Termination Benefits

An employer may provide a certain set of benefits to employees that it terminates. Examples of termination benefits are lump-sum cash payments and a series of periodic payments in the future. The employer should recognize a liability and expense for the full amount of these benefits as soon as terminated employees accept the termination offer to which the benefits are linked. This expense should include the present value of any future payments to be made. To determine the amount of termination expense to recognize, use the following calculation:

+	Actuarial present value of accumulated pension benefits, including termination benefits
+	Actuarial present value of accumulated pension benefits, without termination benefits
=	Termination benefits to charge to expense

Combined Pension Plans

An organization may elect to combine several of its pension plans, which means that the assets of each predecessor plan can now be used to satisfy the obligations of the combined plan. The entity should create a single amortization schedule for each of the pension costs that must be amortized. The amortization periods incorporated into these schedules shall be based on a weighted average of the remaining amortization periods used by the individual pension plans before they were combined. However, the prior service cost associated with each individual pension plan shall continue to be amortized under the old amortization schedules formulated prior to the combination of plans.

Defined Contribution Plans

Under a defined contribution plan, the employer's entire obligation is complete once it has made a contribution payment into the plan, as long as no associated costs are being deferred for recognition in later periods. Thus, the employer commits to pay a specific amount of funds into a plan, but does not commit to the amount of benefits subsequently distributed by that plan.

The accounting for a defined contribution plan is simplicity itself (as opposed to the accounting just described for a defined benefit plan). The employer charges its contributions to expense as incurred. If such a plan calls for additional payments to be made after an employee leaves the organization, the estimated cost of these additional payments shall be accrued during the service period of the applicable employee.

In those cases where an employer terminates a defined benefit plan and shifts the assets in the plan to a defined contribution plan that is a replacement plan, there may be an excess of assets in the replacement plan over the required annual contribution to the plan. If so, the employer should maintain the excess assets in a suspense account until such time as they are needed to fund the replacement account. Until the assets in the suspense account are used to fund the replacement account, the employer continues to retain the risks and rewards of ownership associated with those assets, and so shall account for the assets within its own statement of financial position.

Presentation of Retirement Benefit Information

If an employer has a defined benefit pension or other postretirement plan, it should provide line items in the financial statements for the following information:

- The funding status of each plan in the financial statements.
- The recognized amounts of related assets, current liabilities, and noncurrent liabilities.
- Classify any underfunded plan liabilities as being current or noncurrent liabilities, or both. For the purposes of this classification, a current plan liability is the excess amount of the actuarial present value of the longer of the benefits payable in the next 12 months or the operating cycle, over the fair value of plan assets.
- If a plan is overfunded, classify the overfunding as a noncurrent asset.

Retirement Benefit Disclosures

The bulk of the disclosures associated with pension plans only pertain to defined benefit plans. There is also a discussion of the much more abbreviated disclosures for defined contribution plans.

Defined Benefit Plan Disclosures

The following disclosures must be attached to the financial statements when an entity sponsors a defined benefit plan:

- *Benefit obligation.* The benefit obligation, funded status, and fair value of plan assets.
- *Contributions.* Employer and participant contributions, and the amount of benefits paid.
- *Plan asset information.* Investment policies and strategies, target allocation percentages, the fair value of each class of plan assets as of each statement of financial position date, the approach used to estimate the long-term rate of return on assets assumption, and enough information for users to assess the inputs and valuation techniques used to develop fair value measurements.
- *Accumulated benefit obligation.* The amount of this obligation.
- *Benefit payments.* The expected benefits to be paid in each of the next five years, and in aggregate for the five years thereafter.
- *Contributions paid.* The estimated amount of contribution payments expected during the next fiscal year, aggregating required, discretionary, and noncash contributions.

- *Assets and liabilities.* The postretirement benefit assets, and both current and noncurrent postretirement benefit liabilities.
- *Net assets without donor restrictions.* The net gain or loss, the net prior service cost or credit, and reclassification adjustments recognized for the period in net assets without donor restrictions. Also, any amounts in net assets without donor restrictions that have not been reclassified as components of net periodic benefit cost, along with the net gain or loss, net prior service cost or credit, and net transition asset or obligation.
- *Assumptions.* In tabular format, the assumptions for assumed discount rates, rates of compensation increase, and expected long-term rates of return on plan assets that were used to calculate the benefit obligation and net benefit cost.
- *Cost trends.* The projected trends in health care costs for the next year, as well as the pattern of change thereafter, the ultimate trend rate, and when the ultimate rate is expected.
- *Asset contents.* The types and amounts of securities issued by the employer and related parties that are part of plan assets, significant transactions between the plan and the employer and related parties in the period, and the amount of future annual benefits covered by insurance contracts.
- *Nonroutine events.* The nature of significant nonroutine events, including divestitures, combinations, amendments, curtailments, and settlements.
- *Recognition of net assets without donor restrictions.* Any amounts in net assets without donor restrictions to be recognized in the next year as net periodic benefit cost, showing the net gain or loss, net prior service cost or credit, and net transition asset or obligation.
- *Assets returned to employer.* The amount of any plan assets to be returned to the employer in the next year, and the timing of the return.
- *Net periodic benefit.* The amount of net periodic benefit cost recognized in the period.

EXAMPLE

Newton Education discloses the following information about its retirement plans in the notes accompanying its financial statements:

The entity has a funded defined benefit pension plan that covers substantially all of its employees. The plan provides defined benefits based on years of service and the average salary of employees over their final five years of service.

Obligations and Funded Status of Pension Benefits

(000s)	20X3	20X2
Change in benefit obligation:		
Benefit obligation at beginning of year	$2,190	$2,200
Service cost	110	120
Interest cost	65	50
Amendments	25	10
Actuarial loss	15	
Benefits paid	-205	-190
Benefit obligation at end of year	$2,200	$2,190

Change in Plan Assets

(000s)	20X3	20X2
Change in plan assets:		
Fair value of plan assets at beginning of year	$1,845	$1,860
Actual return on plan assets	65	50
Employer contributions	180	125
Benefits paid	-205	-190
Fair value of plan assets at end of year	$1,885	$1,845
Funded status at end of year	-$315	-$345

The estimated net loss and prior service cost that will be amortized from net assets without donor restrictions into net periodic benefit cost over the next fiscal year are $3,000 and $12,000, respectively.

Weighted-Average Assumptions used to Determine Pension Obligations at December 31

	20X3	20X2
Discount rate	4.50%	3.75%
Rate of compensation increase	4.25%	4.00%

Weighted-Average Assumptions used to Determine Net Periodic Benefit Cost at December 31

	20X3	20X2
Discount rate	4.75%	4.00%
Expected long-term return on plan assets	5.50%	5.00%
Rate of compensation increase	4.75%	4.25%

Plan Assets

The entity follows an investment strategy of 60 percent in long-term growth investments and 40 percent in short-term investments from which benefits can be paid. Target allocations are 70 percent in large cap equities and 20 percent in corporate bonds, in all cases with issuers located in the United States and Europe. Ten percent of the target allocation is to other investments approved in advance by the board of directors. The fair value of Newton's pension plan assets at December 31, 20X3 is as follows:

Fair Value of Pension Plan Assets

(000s)	Total	Fair Value Measurements at 12/31/X3		
		Quoted Prices in Active Markets for Identical Assets (Level 1)	Significant Observable Inputs (Level 2)	Significant Unobservable Inputs (Level 3)
Cash	$90	$90		
Equity securities				
U.S. large-cap	750	750		
Europe large-cap	480	480		
Corporate bonds	375		$375	
Hedge funds	120			$120
Real estate	70			70
	$1,885	$1,320	$375	$190

The organization expects to contribute $200,000 to its pension plan in 20X4.

Defined Contribution Plan Disclosures

If an entity has one or more defined contribution plans, it should disclose the amount of cost recognized for these plans for all periods presented in the financial statements. These costs should be disclosed separately from the costs disclosed for any defined benefit plans. Also, describe the nature of any significant changes during the presented periods that affect the comparability of the information from period to period. Examples of such comparability events are the effects of an acquisition or divestiture.

Summary

When a nonprofit has a defined benefit plan, the number of variables impacting the amount of future payments makes it extremely difficult to recognize expenses that actually approximate the amounts that are later paid. In many cases, the variance between actual and estimated pension costs can have a profound impact on the financial results reported by an organization, to the extent that users of this information may decide that the financial statements cannot be relied upon to reveal the actual results and condition of the entity.

The level of confusion engendered by defined benefit plans bolsters the case for not entering into such plans. As an alternative, the accounting for defined contribution plans is neat, simple, and highly predictable, and results in more reliable financial statements. While the complaints of accountants are hardly likely to convince management to avoid using defined benefit plans, these issues can be considered alongside other factors, such as the massive long-term liabilities associated with defined benefit plans, to hopefully reduce their use.

Chapter 11
Joint Costs and Allocations

Introduction

Perhaps the most closely-watched metrics in a nonprofit are the proportion of fundraising expenses and management and administration expenses to total expenses. Donors are more willing to contribute to organizations that spend the bulk of their funding on programs, so nonprofits have an ongoing interest in allocating expenses away from these two areas. In this chapter, we discuss the accounting rules for the cost of activities that include fundraising, as well as the methods available for allocating management and administration expenses.

Costs of Activities that Include Fundraising

There are rules in GAAP that govern how costs that are at least partially expended on fundraising activities are to be allocated. These rules only govern situations in which there is a joint activity. Under GAAP, a *joint activity* is considered to be an activity that is part of the fundraising function and which has elements of other functions used by a nonprofit. A joint activity may incur a variety of costs that are not specifically identifiable with a single activity, which are referred to as *joint costs*. Examples of these costs are:

Compensation	Event advertising	Postage
Consultants	Facility rentals	Professional fees
Contract labor	Paper and printing	Radio airtime
E-mail marketing		Telephones

Joint costs are to be allocated between the fundraising activity and programs or the management and administration area, as may be appropriate. This allocation can only be performed if a specific set of criteria are met. If not, the costs are not considered joint costs, and so must be assigned entirely to the fundraising area. In order to qualify for allocation, joint costs must meet the following criteria:

- *Purpose criterion.* When the purpose of a joint activity includes the accomplishment of program or management and administration functions. The following guidance can assist in determining whether the purpose criterion is being met:

  - *When program functions are combined with fundraising activities.* The activity asks for specific actions by the audience that helps accomplish the mission of the nonprofit. It is not sufficient to just inform the audience about causes. It is also not sufficient if the audience merely has the potential to learn from information presented, or has the ability to assist in meeting program goals. In short, there must be a call for specific action to help accomplish the nonprofit's mission.

EXAMPLE

Obesity Alert assists parents in identifying the causes of obesity in their children. An activity that motivates the intended audience to take specific action to improve the health of their children is to mail a brochure that urges them to examine the eating and exercise habits of their children, and which contains specific instructions for doing so.

o *When program functions, management and administration functions, or both are combined with fundraising activities.* Consider the following tests, in the order presented, to see if the purpose criterion is being met:

1. *Compensation or fees test.* This is the preeminent joint cost allocation test. The test fails if a majority of the compensation or fees paid to a third party for their performance of a joint activity is based on the amount of contributions raised. If an activity fails this test, the purpose criterion is not met under any circumstances. If an activity does not fail this test, go on to the next test.

EXAMPLE

Archimedes Education pays a consultant to develop a brochure, and agrees to pay the consultant 25% of all contributions received as a result of mailing the brochure to a mailing list. This arrangement fails the compensation or fees test, because the majority of the fee earned by the consultant is based on the amount of contributions received. All costs of this arrangement should be charged to fundraising.

2. *Separate and similar activities test.* The program component of the joint activity calls for a specific action by the recipient that will help the nonprofit to accomplish its mission. Also, there must be a similar program component that is conducted in the absence of the fundraising component and on the same scale or larger, and which uses the same means of mass communication. If this test is met, there is no need to proceed to the other evidence test.

EXAMPLE

Newton Education manages a program that creates training videos that cover the basics of physics theory, and distributes them through various on-line video posting services. The program has been running for the past five years, and now includes more than 100 videos. Newton decides to issue another series of these videos that contains training information, but which also includes a request for donations. Since Newton already conducts a program component that is conducted in the absence of fundraising, and on a larger scale than the fundraising activity, and does so using the same means of communication, it passes the separate and similar activities test.

3. *Other evidence test*. Other evidence may be assembled to consider whether the preponderance of evidence indicates that the purpose criterion has been met. Examples of favorable relevant evidence are:

- Measuring the results and accomplishments of the activity.
- The nonprofit conducts the program or management and administration component of the joint activity without a significant fundraising component through a different means of mass communication.
- Where the bulk of employee job duties are performed in program or management and administration activities, rather than fundraising.
- There is tangible evidence of intent regarding the intended purpose of a joint activity that favors programs or management and administration, such as board minutes, long-range plans, and internal memos.

EXAMPLE

Obesity Alert trains a group of physical therapists in the key causes of childhood obesity, and sends them through local neighborhoods to distribute flyers to residents, as well as to provide counseling if asked. Neighborhoods are targeted based on the percentage of overweight students in local schools. The flyer also contains a request for donations. Since the bulk of employee job duties are targeted at meeting the goals of the childhood obesity program, rather than fundraising, the entity passes the other evidence test, and can allocate the cost of the neighborhood access program.

- *Audience criterion*. This criterion is not met if the target audience has been selected based on its ability or likelihood to contribute to the nonprofit. The criterion is met if the audience is largely selected for any of the following reasons:

- o The audience has a need to use the action called for by the program element of the joint activity.
- o The audience has the ability to take specific action to assist the non-profit in the program element of the joint activity.
- o The audience has reasonable potential to use the management and administration component of the joint activity, or the nonprofit is required to direct this component of the joint activity to the audience in question.

EXAMPLE

Archimedes Education purchases a mailing list from an institute of higher education. Since the seller has similar programs to those of Archimedes, the target audience represented by the mailing list is likely to need to use the action called for by the program element of Archimedes' joint activity. This mailing list passes the audience criterion.

Archimedes also purchases a mailing list from the investment bank owned by a member of its board of directors. This list is entirely comprised of high net-worth individuals, so the target audience is being selected based on its ability to contribute to Archimedes. This mailing list does not pass the audience criterion.

- *Content criterion.* This criterion is met if the joint activity supports either program or management and administration functions as noted next:
  - o *Program.* The joint activity calls for specific action by the recipient that helps to accomplish a program's mission. Examples are reducing calorie intake, cutting back on driving low-mileage vehicles, contacting legislators about a conservation issue, and boycotting the manufacturers of products that are environmentally unfriendly.
  - o *Management and administration.* The joint activity fulfills at least one of the responsibilities of the management and administration area.

The general thrust of these criteria is to make it fairly difficult to allocate joint costs away from the fundraising function. A joint activity must meet such tightly-defined criteria that the presumption in most cases is that costs are more likely to be assigned just to the fundraising function.

When assigning joint costs, it is essential to do so in a rational and systematic manner. This means documenting the reasons why assignments are made, and following the same reasoning through multiple reporting periods. The accounting standards recommend that one of the following allocation methods be followed:

- *Physical units method.* Under this approach, joint costs are allocated in proportion to the number of units of output that can be attributed to each activity. This allocation only works if the units of output can be clearly ascribed to the fundraising, program, or management and administration areas.

EXAMPLE

Newton Education conducts a direct mail campaign that jointly conducts activities on behalf of its physics education program and also raises money for the organization. The fundraising letter contains 80 lines of text. Of this amount, 35 lines relate to the physics education program and 45 to the fundraising appeal. Newton spends $10,000 on the mailing. Based on these text proportions, Newton assigns $4,375 of the total cost to the physics education program and $5,625 to the fundraising activity.

- *Relative direct cost method.* Under this approach, joint costs are allocated based on the aggregate amount of direct costs associated with the underlying programs and activities. A direct cost is one that is incurred in connection with a specific program or activity; if the program or activity were to be terminated, the direct cost would also disappear. This allocation only works if joint costs are incurred in roughly the same proportion as direct costs.

EXAMPLE

Suture Indigent Medical Care conducts a direct mail campaign that jointly conducts activities on behalf of its in-house medical training program and also raises money for the organization. Suture incurs $15,000 of direct costs to create and print a medical training manual for its in-house medical training program. The organization also incurs $5,000 to craft and print a fundraising letter. Thus, the proportion of direct costs incurred for the direct mail campaign is 75% for the program and 25% for fundraising. Joint costs associated with the mailing are $8,000. The joint costs are allocated based on these proportions, so $6,000 of joint costs are assigned to the program and $2,000 to fundraising.

- *Standalone joint cost allocation method.* This method uses as the basis of allocation estimates of the costs that would have been incurred if the joint activities had instead been conducted independently. The allocation is derived from a ratio that divides the cost of conducting the activity independently by the total cost of conducting all components of the activity independently. This approach may not work well if the underlying estimates are inaccurate.

EXAMPLE

The executive director of Obesity Alert concludes that the mail campaigns independently run by its obesity education program and fundraising staff can save on postage costs if they are combined into a joint activity. The controller estimates that the cost of independent campaigns would be $18,000 for the program and $12,000 for fundraising, which represents a 60/40 ratio of costs. When a joint campaign is conducted, the total cost is $26,000. This cost is allocated based on the 60/40 ratio, which means that $15,600 is allocated to the program and $10,400 to fundraising.

In essence, joint cost allocations are to be based on the degree to which direct costs or other bases of allocation are incurred for each function to which the costs are to be assigned.

There may be instances in which the fundraising portion of joint activities is incidental to the overall activities being conducted. If so, it is permissible to allocate no joint costs at all to fundraising activities.

EXAMPLE

Obesity Alert routinely mails brochures to the parents of overweight children to educate them about the causes of obesity. In the lower right corner of the back page of these 20-page brochures is a brief notice to call Obesity Alert at a certain phone number if the recipient wishes to make a donation. This minor inclusion is considered incidental to the general thrust of the message, which clearly falls into a program. Consequently, the cost of the mailing is not apportioned to fundraising.

Allocations

In the last section, we addressed the allocation of costs that are at least partially expended on fundraising activities; that type of allocation is governed by GAAP rules. A nonprofit may also find it necessary to allocate to programs certain expenses that would otherwise be recorded as part of the management and administration function. Doing so reduces the total amount of management and administration expense, which shows donors that the organization operates in a lean manner, not wasting their contributions on profligate administrative spending.

The only type of expense that can be allocated is an *indirect expense*. This is any expense that is incurred to operate a business as a whole or a segment of a business, and so cannot be directly associated with a specific product or service. Examples of indirect costs are accounting fees, legal fees, business permits, office expenses, rent, supervisor salaries, and utilities.

Cost allocations that do not involve fundraising activities are not governed by GAAP at all. Instead, a nonprofit should derive a standard allocation methodology using the following steps:

1. *Identify indirect expenses.* Go through the chart of accounts and make note of all expenses that are not directly traceable to specific programs or other functions. These expenses are tagged as indirect expenses.
2. *Define basis of allocation.* Determine how indirect expenses are to be allocated. For example, indirect expenses might be allocated based on the total costs incurred by each program. Alternatively, expenses could be allocated based on just a specific cost within a program, such as compensation. Allocations may also be made based on a non-monetary basis, such as hours worked by the management and administrative staff on program-related activities.

3. *Calculate allocations*. Aggregate all indirect costs into a cost pool, and then use the basis of allocation to charge these costs out to the various programs and other functions. The following example illustrates the concept.

When engaging in expense allocations, be sure to document the reasoning for why certain proportions of an expense are allocated in a certain way, in case these allocations are later questioned. Also, it is best to be consistent and use the same allocations from period to period, unless there is a significant change in expense usage that mandates a different allocation. Here are several additional thoughts regarding the use of allocations:

- *Emphasis on direct costs*. The amount of costs identified as indirect costs can be reduced with additional tracking effort by converting them into direct costs that can be specifically applied to particular programs or other functions. For example, the telephone expense could be treated as an indirect cost that is to be allocated, or specific phone charges can be traced to individuals working for a particular program, and then charged to that program. The latter approach requires more accounting effort, so only use it when fairly substantial costs can be removed from the indirect expenses classification.

- *Survey-based allocations*. If allocations are based on time worked by the staff, it can be burdensome to have them continually track their time for years. Realistically, the time spent by employees on various activities does not change much from month to month. Consequently, it is easier to conduct a survey of hours worked at relatively long intervals, and apply the results of that survey to all allocations for subsequent months.

- *Multiple cost pools*. If there is a need for more allocation precision, it could make sense to divide indirect expenses into several cost pools, and apply a different basis of allocation to each one. For example, compensation and benefits costs could be aggregated into one cost pool and assigned based on hours worked, while utilities are aggregated into a different cost pool and allocated based on square footage used.

EXAMPLE

First Aid Educators provides basic medical response training to middle school students. The management and administration function of the organization incurs $30,000 of expenses in the current month. Of this amount, $20,000 relates to compensation and benefits costs, and the remainder involves rent, utilities, facility maintenance, and other costs of running the organization.

First Aid uses two methods to allocate these costs. It conducts a time study once a year to determine how staff time is spent. For the current year, the analysis shows that 20% of the management and administration's staff time is spent on fundraising, and 10% on programs. Accordingly, $6,000 of this cost is allocated to fundraising, and $3,000 to programs.

The remaining $10,000 is allocated based on the total costs incurred by each program and functional area. In the current month, the allocation calculation is:

	Costs Incurred	Proportion	Overhead Allocation
Management and administration	$30,000	8%	$800
Fundraising	20,000	5%	500
Program A	180,000	47%	4,700
Program B	150,000	40%	4,000
Totals	$380,000	100%	$10,000

Larger donors may impose their own allocation systems on a nonprofit. These systems may specify exactly which expenses are considered direct or indirect, and how they are to be allocated. If there are several donors who impose these systems, a nonprofit may find itself allocating expenses several different ways, which imposes an administrative burden. See the Government Grants chapter for a discussion of the allocation methods imposed by the federal government.

The simplest method by which a nonprofit keeps track of program-specific revenues and expenses is to set up separate accounts in the chart of accounts for each area to which these items must be assigned. Doing so means that fewer expenses are considered indirect, so that fewer expenses are subject to allocation. To track information at this level of detail, a nonprofit can use a five-digit chart of accounts. This format associates a three-digit account number with each revenue and expense account, and then adds a two-digit code to the left, which indicates specific programs. The three-digit codes for revenues and expenses are then duplicated for each program or function for which management wants to record information. A selection of accounts from a five-digit chart of accounts follows, using the management and administration department and the elderly housing program to show how the account codes are duplicated.

Sample Chart of Accounts

Account Number	Department/ Program	Description
10-600	Management and administration	Donor contributions
10-610	Management and administration	Fundraising events
10-620	Management and administration	Grants
10-630	Management and administration	Investment income
10-640	Management and administration	Membership fees
10-650	Management and administration	Program revenue
20-600	Elderly housing	Donor contributions
20-610	Elderly housing	Fundraising events

Account Number	Department/ Program	Description
20-620	Elderly housing	Grants
20-630	Elderly housing	Investment income
20-640	Elderly housing	Membership fees
20-650	Elderly housing	Program revenue
10-800	Management and administration	Compensation expense
10-810	Management and administration	Depreciation expense
10-820	Management and administration	Payroll tax expense
10-830	Management and administration	Rent expense
10-840	Management and administration	Supplies expense
10-850	Management and administration	Utilities expense
10-860	Management and administration	Other expenses
10-800	Elderly housing	Compensation expense
10-810	Elderly housing	Depreciation expense
10-820	Elderly housing	Payroll expense
10-830	Elderly housing	Rent expense
10-840	Elderly housing	Supplies expense
10-850	Elderly housing	Utilities expense
10-860	Elderly housing	Other expenses

The preceding chart of accounts sample shows an exact duplication of accounts for each department or program listed. This is not necessarily the case in reality, since some departments or programs have accounts for which they are the only probable users. For example, the management and administration department is assigned a program revenue account that it is unlikely to use. The accountant would likely flag this account as inactive in the accounting software, so that it does not appear in the formal chart of accounts.

There are situations where it is allowable for more than one government grant to fund an expense. For example, an expenditure must be made that is needed for the purposes of two different grants, such as a cancer researcher who is working on the analysis of two related types of cancer. In this situation, there must be an allocation of the cost between the multiple funding sources. This allocation should be on a reasonable basis, consistently applied. Also, it is useful to document the reasoning behind the allocation, in the likely event that a government auditor questions the allocation.

Tip: When it is likely that there will be allocable expenses before entering into a contract for a government grant, negotiate the terms of the cost allocation into the contract, so there is no uncertainty about cost reimbursement at a later date.

Disclosures

When a nonprofit allocates joint costs, it must disclose the following information in the notes accompanying its financial statements:

- *Activity types.* The types of activities for which the entity has incurred joint costs.
- *Statement.* A statement that joint costs have been allocated.
- *Allocation amount.* The total expense amount allocated in the period, and amounts apportioned to each functional expense category.

It is encouraged, but not required, that a nonprofit also disclose the amount of joint costs for each kind of joint activity. For example:

Note J. Allocation of Joint Costs

In 20X4, Archimedes Education conducted activities that included appeals for contributions, which incurred $200,000 of joint costs. These activities included special events, direct mail campaigns, and e-mail campaigns. The joint costs were allocated among these activities as follows:

	Special Events	Direct Mail Campaigns	E-mail Campaigns	Totals
Fundraising	5,000	$80,000	$35,000	$120,000
Management and administration	2,000	--	8,000	10,000
Program A	13,000	20,000	17,000	50,000
Program B	20,000	--	--	20,000
Totals	$40,000	$100,000	$60,000	$200,000

Summary

Nonprofits are usually quite sensitive to the amount of costs recognized as fundraising expenses. To reduce the amount of this expense, the development manager, controller, and executive director should have a keen understanding of the GAAP requirements related to joint cost allocations. By doing so, fundraising activities can be tailored to create joint costs and apportion them elsewhere within an organization.

The amount of costs allocated among a nonprofit's programs and other functions can be considerable. If these allocations are not dealt with consistently, the result is likely to be constant (and noticeable) swings in the amounts of recognized expenses among the various programs and functions on an ongoing basis, which confuses donors. To avoid this problem, compile a detailed set of allocation procedures, and ensure that they are adhered to by the accounting staff.

Chapter 12
Accounting Changes and Error Corrections

Introduction

From time to time, a nonprofit will find that it must change its accounting to reflect a change in accounting principle or estimate, or it may locate an accounting error that must be corrected. In this chapter, we address the rules for both situations and how to disclose them, as well as for several related situations.

Changes in Accounting Principle

There is an assumption in GAAP that, once an accounting principle has been adopted by an organization, the principle shall be consistently applied in recording transactions and events from that point forward. Consistent application is a cornerstone of accounting, since it allows the readers of financial statements to compare the results of multiple accounting periods. Given how important it is to maintain consistency in the application of accounting principles, an entity should only change an accounting principle in one of the two following situations:

- The change is required by an update to GAAP
- The use of an alternative principle is preferable

> **Tip:** Thoroughly document the reason for any change in accounting principle, since it will likely be reviewed by the nonprofit's auditors.

Whenever there is a change in accounting principle, retrospective application of the new principle to prior accounting periods is required, unless it is impracticable to do so. If it is impracticable to retroactively apply changes to prior interim periods of the current fiscal year, then the change in accounting principle can only be made as of the start of a subsequent fiscal year.

> **Tip:** Where possible, organizations are encouraged to adopt changes in accounting principle as of the first interim period of a fiscal year.

The activities required for retrospective application are:

1. Alter the carrying amounts of assets and liabilities for the cumulative effect of the change in principle as of the beginning of the first accounting period presented.
2. Adjust the beginning balance of net assets to offset the change noted in the first step.

3. Adjust the financial statements for each prior period presented to reflect the impact of the new accounting principle.

If it is impracticable to make these changes, then do so as of the earliest reported periods for which it is practicable to do so. It is considered impracticable to make a retrospective change when any of the following conditions apply:

-   *Assumptions.* Making a retrospective application calls for assumptions about what management intended to do in prior periods, and those assumptions cannot be independently substantiated.
-   *Efforts made.* The organization has made every reasonable effort to do so.
-   *Estimates.* Estimates are required, which are impossible to provide due to the lack of information about the circumstances in the earlier periods.

When making prior period adjustments due to a change in accounting principle, do so only for the direct effects of the change. A direct effect is one that is *required* to switch accounting principles.

EXAMPLE

Suture Indigent Medical Care changes from the last in, first out method of inventory accounting to the first in, first out method. Doing so calls for an increase in the ending inventory in the preceding period, which in turn increases net assets for that period. Altering the inventory balance is a direct effect of the change in principle.

An indirect effect of the change in principle would be a change in the accrual for bonus payments in the prior period. Since it is an indirect effect, Suture does not record the change.

Changes in Accounting Estimate

A change in accounting estimate occurs when there is an adjustment to the carrying amount of an asset or liability, or the subsequent accounting for it. Examples of changes in accounting estimate are changes in:

-   The allowance for doubtful accounts
-   The reserve for obsolete inventory
-   Changes in the useful life of depreciable assets
-   Changes in the salvage values of depreciable assets

Changes in accounting estimate occur relatively frequently, and so would require a significant effort to make an ongoing series of retroactive changes to prior financial statements. Instead, GAAP only requires that changes in accounting estimate be accounted for in the period of change and thereafter. Thus, no retrospective change is required or allowed.

Changes in Reporting Entity

There are situations where a change in the entities included in consolidated financial statements effectively means that there is a change in reporting entity. If so, apply the change retrospectively to all of the periods being reported. The result should be the consistent presentation of financial information for the same reporting entity for all periods, including interim periods.

Correction of an Error in Previously Issued Financial Statements

From time to time, financial statements will be inadvertently issued that contain one or more errors. When such an error is discovered, the prior period financial statements to which the error applies must be restated. Restatement requires the following steps:

1. Alter the carrying amounts of assets and liabilities for the cumulative effect of the error as of the beginning of the first accounting period presented.
2. Adjust the beginning balance of net assets to offset the change noted in the first step.
3. Adjust the financial statements for each prior period presented to reflect the impact of the error.

Corrections Related to Prior Interim Periods

GAAP specifies several situations in which the financial statements of prior interim periods of the current fiscal year should be adjusted. These adjustments are for the following:

- Adjustment or settlement of litigation
- Income taxes (only applicable to any unrelated business income of a nonprofit)
- Renegotiation proceedings
- Utility revenue under rate-making processes (not applicable to a nonprofit)

Adjustments for these items are only necessary if all of the following criteria apply:

- The effect of the change is material to the statement of activities, or its trend
- The adjustments are directly related to the prior interim periods
- The adjustment amount could not be reasonably estimated prior to the current interim period, but can now be estimated

If an adjustment occurs in any interim period other than the first period, use the following steps to account for it:

1. Include any portion of the adjustment that relates to current business activities in the current interim period.

2. Restate prior interim periods of the current fiscal year to include that portion of the item that relates to the business activities in those periods.
3. Restate the first interim period of the current fiscal year to include that portion of the item that relates to the business activities in prior fiscal years.

Summary

Retrospective changes can require a large amount of detective accounting work, judgment, and thorough documentation of the changes made. Given the amount of labor involved, it is cost-effective to find justifiable reasons for not making retrospective changes. Two valid methods for doing so are to question the materiality of the necessary changes, or to find reasons to instead treat issues as changes in accounting estimate.

If retrospective application is completely unavoidable, it may make sense to have the nonprofit's auditors review proposed retrospective changes in advance. Doing so minimizes the risk that an error in handling an issue will be discovered by the auditors during the annual audit, which will require additional retrospective changes.

Chapter 13
Fair Value

Introduction

A nonprofit may have certain assets or liabilities that are to be recorded at their fair values, rather than their historical costs. A classic example is marketable securities, for which the recognized costs of certain classes of securities are to be adjusted at the end of each reporting period. The adjustment to fair value is based on a theoretical price at which an asset may be sold or a liability settled – there is no need to actually sell off assets or obtain bids in order to derive fair value. In this chapter, we discuss the fair value concept, how fair values are derived, and the option to use fair value.

The Fair Value Concept

Fair value is the estimated price at which an asset can be sold or a liability settled in an orderly transaction to a third party under current market conditions. This definition includes the following concepts:

- *Current market conditions.* The derivation of fair value should be based on market conditions on the measurement date, rather than a transaction that occurred at some earlier date.
- *Intent.* The intention of the holder of an asset or liability to continue to hold it is irrelevant to the measurement of fair value. Such intent might otherwise alter the measured fair value. For example, if the intent is to immediately sell an asset, this could be inferred to trigger a rushed sale, which may result in a lower sale price.
- *Orderly transaction.* Fair value is to be derived based on an orderly transaction, which infers a transaction where there is no undue pressure to sell, as may be the case in a corporate liquidation.
- *Third party.* Fair value is to be derived based on a presumed sale to an entity that is not an insider or related in any way to the seller. Otherwise, a related-party transaction might skew the price paid.

The ideal determination of fair value is based on prices offered in an active market. An active market is one in which there is a sufficiently high volume of transactions to provide ongoing pricing information. Also, the market from which a fair value is derived should be the principal market for the asset or liability, since the greater transaction volume associated with such a market should presumably lead to the best prices for the seller. The market in which a business normally sells the asset type in question or settles liabilities is assumed to be the principal market.

> **Tip:** If there is no principal market for the assets or liabilities being valued, the alternative is to obtain a fair value from the most advantageous market, which is the market in which the best price can be obtained, net of transaction costs.

It is possible to derive a price from a quote issued by a broker. In this case, the resulting price is considered more reliable when it is associated with a binding offer. Conversely, the mere issuance of an indicative price by a broker does not indicate much pricing research by the broker or a commitment to sell, and so is considered less reliable.

In addition, the determination of fair value should be based on the condition and location of the asset, as well as any restrictions on the use of the asset. For example, shares in a company that are restricted will have a substantially lower fair value than unrestricted shares. Also, machinery that has been used more than the average number of hours will have a lower fair value.

> **Tip:** If an asset or liability is location-dependent, include in the fair value determination the cost required to transport the item to the market in which its fair value is to be estimated.

An additional consideration when determining fair value is the concept of highest and best use. Under this concept, fair value is determined based on the price at which an asset could theoretically be employed in its highest and best use, rather than the use in which an asset is currently employed.

EXAMPLE

Creekside Research buys a patent for $1,000,000 that would allow the nonprofit to develop a technologically-advanced lithium-ion battery. However, Creekside simply sits on the patent, thereby preventing any competitors from using the technology. The fair value of the patent should be based on licensing the patent to competitors, since doing so would yield substantially higher profits than not using the patent, as is currently the case.

Depending on the applicable GAAP standards, it may be necessary to update fair values in the accounting records at regular intervals. If so, account for these changes as changes in accounting estimate (see the Accounting Changes and Error Corrections chapter).

Fair Value Differences from Actual Prices Paid

There are a number of reasons why the price at which an asset is sold or a liability is settled can vary from its fair value. Consider the following situations:

- *Duress.* The seller may be in a position where it must liquidate assets at once, and so cannot engage in a more prolonged and detailed sales process to achieve a better price. The most common case is the seller's bankruptcy, but it is also possible that the seller was required to sell in order to meet new regulatory requirements.

- *Market.* The asset or liability may be sold or settled in a market that is not the most advantageous one in which to handle such a transaction, resulting in a less-than-favorable price. For example, securities may be sold in a local market, where there are fewer bidders than on a national exchange.
- *Related parties.* The buyer and seller may be related, which introduces the possibility that there are insider reasons for skewing the price paid.
- *Unusual elements.* The seller may be including additional warranties or bundling other products or services with the item being sold, which makes it difficult to compare prices.

In these situations, do not place reliance on the information for deriving fair values, for these results could vary significantly from actual fair market values. Conversely, if these factors are not present, *and* the volume of market transactions is large, *and* the comparison transactions are close to the measurement date, the derived fair values can probably be relied upon.

Fair Value Measurement Approaches

There are several general approaches that are permitted for deriving fair values. These approaches are outlined below:

- *Market approach.* Uses the prices associated with actual market transactions for similar or identical assets and liabilities to derive a fair value. For example, the prices of securities held can be obtained from a national exchange on which these securities are routinely bought and sold.
- *Income approach.* Uses estimated future cash flows or earnings, adjusted by a discount rate that represents the time value of money and the risk of cash flows not being achieved, to derive a discounted present value. An alternative way to incorporate risk into this approach is to develop a probability-weighted-average set of possible future cash flows. Option pricing models can also be used under the income approach.
- *Cost approach.* Uses the estimated cost to replace an asset (or the capabilities of the asset), adjusted for the obsolescence of the existing asset.

EXAMPLE

There are several possible cash flows expected from the use of an asset. Management assigns the following probabilities to each scenario:

Cash Flow Scenario	Probability	Probability-Weighted Cash Flows
$800,000	10%	$80,000
1,500,000	70%	1,050,000
3,000,000	20%	600,000
	100%	$1,730,000

The risk-free interest rate is 3%, and the estimated risk premium for the variability of cash flows is 4%, for a combined discount rate of 7%. The discounted cash flows of these probability-weighted cash flows are therefore $1,730,000 ÷ 1.07, or $1,616,822. This is the fair value of the asset, using the income approach.

EXAMPLE

A nonprofit recently purchased a machine and heavily customized it to meet the needs of the organization's unique production line for solar-powered light bulbs to be distributed in poor countries. Since the machine has been so heavily customized, there are no comparable market transactions that relate to it. Also, since the machine is part of a production line, there is no way to associate any cash flows specifically to it. These concerns leave management with no alternative other than to use the cost approach to derive fair value. The organization determines that it would require a $380,000 expenditure to replace the capabilities of this asset, adjusted for the amount of existing wear and tear on the equipment.

Ideally, the valuation method chosen should maximize the use of observable inputs to the valuation process. Observable inputs are derived from market data that properly reflect the assumptions that third parties would use when setting prices for assets and liabilities. Examples of markets that are considered to provide observable inputs are stock exchanges and dealer markets.

No matter which method is chosen, it may be necessary to include a risk adjustment in the formulation of fair value. This risk adjustment may be a premium that a counterparty would require in order to take on any uncertainties in the cash flows associated with an asset or liability.

The ideal conditions are not always available for obtaining the fair value of an asset or liability. Consequently, GAAP provides a hierarchy of information sources that range from Level 1 (best) to Level 3 (worst). The general intent of these levels of information is to step the accountant through a series of valuation alternatives, where solutions closer to Level 1 are preferred over Level 3. The characteristics of the three levels are as follows:

- *Level 1.* This is a quoted price for an identical item in an active market on the measurement date. This is the most reliable evidence of fair value, and should be used whenever this information is available. When there is a bid-ask price spread, use the price most representative of the fair value of the asset or liability. This may mean using a bid price for an asset valuation and an ask price for a liability. When a quoted Level 1 price is adjusted, doing so automatically shifts the result into a lower level. Also, do not alter a Level 1 price just because the organization's holdings of a security are quite large in comparison to the normal daily trading volume of the relevant market.
- *Level 2.* This is directly or indirectly observable inputs other than quoted prices. An example of a Level 2 input is a valuation multiple for a business unit that is based on the sale of comparable entities. This definition includes prices for assets or liabilities that are (with key items noted in bold):
  - For **similar** items in active markets; or
  - For identical or similar items in **inactive** markets; or
  - For inputs **other than** quoted prices, such as credit risks, default rates, and interest rates; or
  - For inputs **derived from** correlation with observable market data.

  It may be necessary to adjust the information derived from Level 2 inputs, since it does not exactly match the assets or liabilities for which fair values are being derived. Adjustments may be needed for such factors as the condition of assets and the transaction volume of the markets from which information is derived.
- *Level 3.* This is an unobservable input. It may include the organization's own data, adjusted for other reasonably available information. Examples of a Level 3 input are an internally-generated financial forecast and the prices contained within an offered quote from a distributor.

These three levels are known as the *fair value hierarchy*. Please note that these three levels are only used to select inputs to valuation techniques (such as the market approach). The three levels are not used to directly create fair values.

A nonprofit may rely upon the prices obtained in a particular market to derive its fair value calculations. These prices can require significant adjustment if the volume of activity in the market has declined. Evidence of such a decline includes a reduced number of recent transactions, large swings in price quotations over time, wide bid-ask spreads, and a decline in new issuances.

If the accountant is using information in a higher category of the fair value hierarchy and adjusting it with information from a lower level of the hierarchy, it may be necessary to designate the outcome as being from the lower level of the hierarchy. This happens when the adjustment results in a significantly higher or lower fair value measurement.

When adjusting fair values from period to period, use the same valuation technique(s) each time. Doing so introduces consistency into the derivation process.

However, it is permissible to switch to alternative valuation technique(s) if the resulting change will be equally or more representative of the fair value of the asset or liability in question. Such a change may be necessary, for example, when a new market develops for the sale of an asset that yields enhanced pricing. If there is a change in fair value that is triggered by a change in measurement method, account for the change as a change in accounting estimate.

Fair Value Option

A nonprofit has the option to record its financial instruments at their fair values. GAAP allows this treatment for the following items:

- A financial asset or financial liability
- A firm commitment that only involves financial instruments
- A loan commitment
- An insurance contract where the insurer can pay a third party to provide goods or services in settlement, and where the contract is not a financial instrument (i.e., requires payment in goods or services)
- A warranty in which the warrantor can pay a third party to provide goods or services in settlement, and where the contract is not a financial instrument (i.e., requires payment in goods or services)

The fair value option cannot be applied to the following items:

- An investment in a subsidiary that will be consolidated
- Deposit liabilities of depository institutions
- Financial assets or financial leases recognized under lease arrangements
- Obligations or assets related to pension plans, postemployment benefits, and other types of deferred compensation

When the election is made to measure an item at its fair value, do so on an instrument-by-instrument basis. Once the election is made to follow the fair value option for an instrument, the change in reporting is irrevocable. The fair value election can be made on either of the following dates:

- The election date, which can be when an item is first recognized, when there is a firm commitment, when qualification for specialized accounting treatment ceases, or there is a change in the accounting treatment for an investment in another entity.
- In accordance with an organization policy for certain types of eligible items.

In most cases, it is acceptable to choose the fair value option for an eligible item, while not electing to use it for other items that are essentially identical.

If the fair value option is taken, report unrealized gains and losses on the elected items at each subsequent reporting date.

Summary

The information imparted in this chapter was at a greater level of detail than a smaller nonprofit really needs; for these entities, it is usually sufficient to understand that the recorded amount of any securities held as investments should probably be stated at their fair values. The more in-depth explanations in this chapter are intended for larger nonprofits that carry substantial amounts of assets and liabilities on their statements of financial position; in this latter case, it is more likely that a nonprofit accountant will run into situations where a detailed knowledge of the fair value rules and alternatives is needed. When there is any uncertainty about how to employ fair value concepts, discuss the matter with the nonprofit's auditors.

Chapter 14
Other Accounting Topics

Introduction

There are a number of accounting topics that do not include a sufficient amount of material to deserve standalone chapters. However, they are commonly found within a nonprofit, and so should be included within the overall nonprofit accounting topic. Consequently, this chapter addresses an array of disparate topics, including petty cash, interests in perpetual trusts, receivables, contingent liabilities, lines of credit, and the disclosures related to these topics.

Petty Cash

Petty cash is a small amount of cash that is kept on a nonprofit's premises to pay for minor cash needs, such as office supplies, cards, flowers, and so forth. Petty cash is stored in a petty cash drawer or box near where it is most needed. There may be several petty cash locations in a larger organization, probably one per building or even one per department. A separate accounting system is used to track petty cash transactions.

To set up a petty cash fund, the cashier creates a check in the amount of the funding assigned to a particular petty cash fund (usually a few hundred dollars). Alternatively, the cashier could simply count out the cash for the petty cash fund, if there are enough bills and coins on the premises. The initial petty cash journal entry is a debit to the petty cash account and a credit to the cash account.

The petty cash custodian then disburses petty cash from the fund in exchange for receipts related to whatever the expense may be. There is no journal entry at this point; instead, the cash balance in the petty cash fund continues to decline, while the number of receipts continues to increase. The total of the receipts and remaining cash should equal the initial amount of petty cash funding at all times, though recordation errors and theft may result in a variance.

When the cash balance in the petty cash fund drops to a sufficiently minimal level, the petty cash custodian applies for more cash from the cashier. This takes the form of a summarization of all the receipts that the custodian has accumulated. The cashier creates a new check in the amount of the receipts, and swaps the check for the receipts. The petty cash journal entry is a debit to the petty cash account and a credit to the cash account.

The petty cash custodian refills the petty cash drawer or box, which should now contain the original amount of cash that was designated for the fund. The cashier creates a journal entry to record the petty cash receipts. This is a credit to the petty cash account, and probably debits to several different expense accounts, such as the office supplies account (depending upon what was purchased with the cash). The balance in the petty cash account should now be the same as the amount at which it started.

In reality, the balance in the petty cash account is higher than the amount of cash actually in the petty cash box, since the cash in the box is continually being paid out. However, the difference is so minor that it is completely immaterial to the results in the financial statements. Thus, the difference is only reconciled when the petty cash box must be replenished.

EXAMPLE

Archimedes Education sets up a petty cash fund and initially funds it with $300. The entry is:

	Debit	Credit
Petty cash	$300	
Cash		$300

The petty cash custodian lets the cash balance in the petty cash box decline to $20 before applying for replenishment. The cashier issues a replenishment check for $280. The entry is:

	Debit	Credit
Petty cash	$280	
Cash		$280

The cashier records the expenses associated with the petty cash receipts that were submitted. The entry is:

	Debit	Credit
Office expenses	$280	
Petty cash		$280

The balance in the petty cash account is now $300, which is where it was originally authorized to be.

A petty cash reconciliation is a formal review of petty cash records, to see if there have been any undocumented disbursements. Such disbursements are a common problem in petty cash, where there is a high risk of fraud. Also, since most petty cash custodians are not trained as accountants, they may incorrectly record disbursements. For these reasons, a petty cash reconciliation should be conducted at regular intervals.

The review can be treated as an audit, which means not warning the petty cash custodian of the reviewer's arrival. This lack of warning is useful for detecting any personal withdrawals from the petty cash fund by the custodian. The petty cash reconciliation follows:

1. *Ascertain stated balance.* Review the nonprofit's petty cash policy and determine the stated petty cash balance for the fund to be reviewed. Petty cash funds can have different stated balances, since some experience higher transaction volumes than others.
2. *Calculate withdrawn cash.* Count the cash remaining in the petty cash fund and subtract it from the stated balance for the fund. The result is the amount of cash withdrawn from the fund.
3. *Summarize vouchers.* Add up the total expenditure listed on each petty cash voucher in the petty cash fund. Subtract this amount from the calculated amount of cash withdrawn. The result should be zero. If there is a residual balance, there is a cash overage in the fund. If there is a negative balance, there is a cash shortage in the fund.
4. *Investigate variances.* Investigate any differences between the stated amount of the petty cash fund and the actual total of cash and vouchers. If the difference is unexplained, complete a voucher stating the unexplained amount, and charge it to a predetermined departmental or program account in the general ledger.

It is useful to charge unexplained differences to an expense account set aside for that purpose. By doing so, it is much easier to track the cumulative amount of undocumented losses over time. Also, consider having a policy that requires the controller to be notified if the amount of an unexplained shortage in a petty cash fund exceeds a certain amount.

Finally, flag petty cash funds for more frequent reconciliations if an ongoing pattern of errors is detected. Increased review frequency can uncover problems before material losses accumulate.

Interest in a Perpetual Trust

When a beneficiary receives a contribution of a perpetual interest in a trust held by a third party, it should be classified as donor-restricted support, since the trust is similar to a donor-restricted endowment that is essentially perpetual, rather than a multi-year promise to give. Any distributions from the trust that are free of restrictions should be reported as net assets without donor restrictions. Any distributions that are restricted are to be reported as net assets with donor restrictions, and can later be reclassified as the restrictions lapse.

Receivables

When a nonprofit has receivables outstanding, it can elect to record them at their fair value (see the Fair Value Option in the Fair Value chapter). If it takes this option, the receivables are to be initially and subsequently recorded at their fair value. A possible method for determining fair value is to calculate the present value of expected cash flows from a receivable. At each subsequent measurement date, the organization must review the present value assumptions, and revise the expected cash flow amounts and timing, discount rate assumptions, and other factors. These assumptions are especially likely to change when the receivables are for unconditional promises to give, since there may be unexpected variations in the timing and amounts to be contributed.

> **Note:** When a present value calculation is used for a promise to give that is donor restricted, the nonprofit should report the subsequent accrual of the interest element as an increase in net assets with donor restrictions.

When there is a contribution receivable that is comprised of a promise to give equity securities, it is possible that the value of those securities will increase or decline between the time when they are promised (and recorded as a receivable) and when they are paid to the nonprofit. If there is such a change, and the receiving nonprofit has chosen to measure the receivable at its fair value, the receivable is to be recognized as an increase or decrease in contribution revenue in the periods in which the change occurs.

When there is a contribution receivable that is comprised of a promise to give noncash assets that are not debt or equity securities, it is possible that their future fair values will change before they are received. If there is such a change, and the receiving nonprofit has chosen to measure the receivable at its fair value, subsequent measurements are to use the same measurement technique used to originally derive the value of the asset. If the future fair value decreases, recognize the change as a reduction in contribution revenue when the change occurs. If the future fair value increases, do not recognize any additional revenue.

When there is an expectation of a decline in a contribution receivable, this is to be accounted for as a bad debt in the period in which the expectation first arises. If, following the recognition of a bad debt, the expectation of a decline is reversed, the bad debt can be reversed up to the amount of the cumulative bad debt that had previously been charged to expense. If contributions are collected that exceed the amount of the related receivable, the difference is to be recognized as additional contribution revenue.

Contingent Liabilities

A contingent liability is a potential loss that may occur at some point in the future, once various uncertainties have been resolved. A contingent liability is not yet an actual, confirmed liability. The exact status of a contingent liability is important when determining which liabilities to present in the statement of financial position.

There are three scenarios for contingent liabilities, all involving different accounting treatments. They are:

- Record a contingent liability when it is probable that the loss will occur, and the amount of the loss can be reasonably estimated. If only a range of possible amounts can be estimated, record that amount in the range that appears to be a better estimate than any other amount; if no amount is better, record the lowest amount in the range. Also describe the liability in the footnotes that accompany the financial statements.
- Disclose the existence of the contingent liability in the notes accompanying the financial statements if the liability is reasonably possible but not probable, or if the liability is probable, but the amount cannot be estimated. "Reasonably possible" means that the chance of the event occurring is more than remote but less than likely.
- Do not record or disclose the contingent liability if the probability of its occurrence is remote.

Examples of contingent liabilities are the outcome of a lawsuit, a government investigation, or the threat of expropriation.

EXAMPLE

A user of the services of Newton Education files a lawsuit against Newton for $500,000. Newton's attorney feels that the suit is without merit, so Newton merely discloses the existence of the lawsuit in the notes accompanying its financial statements. Several months later, the attorney recommends that Newton should settle out of court for $75,000; at this point, the liability is both probable and can be estimated, so Newton records a $75,000 liability. A possible entry for this transaction might be:

	Debit	Credit
Legal expense	75,000	
Accrued liabilities		75,000

When Newton later pays the user the settlement, the final entry is:

	Debit	Credit
Accrued liabilities	75,000	
Cash		75,000

Line of Credit

A line of credit is an agreement between a lender and a borrower to issue cash to the borrower as needed, not to exceed a certain predetermined amount. A line of credit is commonly secured by selected assets of an organization, such as its accounts receivable. Since the line is secured, the lender typically allows a relatively low interest rate that does not greatly exceed the prime rate.

A line of credit is intended for the funding of short-term cash shortfalls caused by periodic (possibly seasonal) changes in a nonprofit's ongoing cash flows. Thus, it should be paid off at some point each year. If not, the line of credit is being used to fund long-term operations, and so should be supplemented by long-term debt.

Several aspects of a line of credit are:

- *Audit.* The lender will likely require the borrower to undergo an audit of certain asset balances, which the lender needs to assure itself that the borrower has correctly represented its financial position and financial results.
- *Balance pay down.* The lender may require that the outstanding balance for a line of credit be completely paid off at some point during each year, or else it can cancel the line.
- *Compensated balance.* If the lender is a bank, it may require the borrower to maintain a certain minimum cash balance in accounts at the bank. By doing so, the lender increases the effective interest rate paid by the borrower, since the borrower earns little or no return on cash kept in a checking account.
- *Maintenance fee.* The lender charges the borrower an annual maintenance fee in exchange for keeping the line of credit open. This fee is payable even if the borrower never uses the line of credit. The reason given for this fee is that the lender must still invest a certain amount of administrative time in loan-related paperwork, and must have funds available if required by the borrower.

In short, the line of credit is a necessary part of the financing structure of a business, but is only intended to fund short-term cash shortfalls that are not expected to continue over the long term.

A current balance due on a line of credit is almost always classified in the statement of financial position as a current liability, since these arrangements are typically payable within one year.

Disclosures

When a nonprofit will receive unconditional promises to give, it should disclose the following information in the notes accompanying the financial statements:

- The aggregate amounts of these receivables due in less than one year, in one to five years, and in more than five years.
- The total amount of the allowance for uncollectible promises receivable.
- The discount derived from the measurement of promises to give at their present value.

When a nonprofit will receive conditional promises to give, disclose the aggregate dollar amount of these promises, as well as the description and promise amount for each group of these promises that have similar characteristics. Examples of groups of conditional promises are those conditioned on the creation of a new facility, or the raising of a certain amount of matching funds.

If a nonprofit has made any unconditional promises to give to other entities, it should present a schedule of these promises that shows the amount payable in each of the next five years, as well as the aggregate amount due in more than five years. If these promises are presented at their present values, also disclose the unamortized discount.

The primary disclosures related to contingent liabilities are noted within the text of the Contingent Liabilities section. In addition, if a nonprofit is not in compliance with donor-imposed restrictions, the situation is to be disclosed in either of the following situations:

- There is a reasonable possibility that the entity has incurred a material contingent liability; or
- There is a reasonable possibility that noncompliance with the restrictions could result in either a material loss of revenue or endanger the entity's ability to continue in business.

Further, if the nonprofit is not in compliance with donor-imposed restrictions because the organization has not maintained an appropriate mix or amount of assets, disclose the nature of the situation.

Summary

Of the accounting topics noted in this chapter, the one most deserving of attention is contingent liabilities. These liabilities may not be overly frequent, but should be monitored closely and reported as necessary, since they can result in the acknowledgment of significant problems. Conversely, if a nonprofit were *not* to report a probable contingent liability, it could be seriously misstating its financial statements.

Chapter 15
Split-Interest Agreements

Introduction

A donor may decide to contribute funds to a nonprofit under an arrangement where both the donor and the nonprofit retain an interest in the underlying assets and liabilities. These arrangements, known as split-interest agreements, come in many shapes and sizes. Unfortunately, the accounting varies by type of agreement, making this one of the more time-consuming transactions for an accountant to deal with. In this chapter, we discuss the nature and types of split-interest agreements, how they are measured and accounted for, and the types of disclosures required for them.

Split-Interest Agreements

A split-interest agreement is an arrangement under which a nonprofit splits the benefits of assets with other entities. These other entities are typically not nonprofits. A common example of a split-interest agreement is when a donor gives a nonprofit the right to receive all interest income from a portfolio of investments held by a bank. Conversely, a donor might want to retain that interest to support her living expenses for the rest of her life, after which the underlying investments become the property of a designated nonprofit.

A split-interest agreement is comprised of a *lead interest* and a *remainder interest*. The lead interest is the right to receive the benefits of assets during the term of the agreement, while the remainder interest is the right to receive any remaining benefits of the assets after the term of the agreement expires. For example, one beneficiary (the lead interest) may be paid an annuity from the donated funds for the next ten years, after which any funds remaining are paid to another beneficiary (the remainder interest).

EXAMPLE

Ms. Marcy Dawes sets aside $1,000,000 in an investment fund, and stipulates that her favorite charity, Dogs without Homes, receives all interest earned on these funds for the earlier of the next ten years or her death. Once either triggering event occurs, the remaining balance in the investment fund will be given to the Advanced Diabetes Care Institute (ADCI). Under the terms of this arrangement, Dogs without Homes has the lead interest, and ADCI has the remainder interest.

Under a split-interest agreement, funds may be given to an independent third party, such as a bank, that acts as the trustee. The trustee follows the directions of the donor in investing the funds and paying beneficiaries. Alternatively, the funds may be sent straight to a nonprofit, which takes on the trustee role.

A split-interest agreement may allow a donor to back out of the arrangement under certain circumstances. This is called a *revocable* split-interest agreement. Or, if the donor has no right to cancel the agreement, the arrangement is called an *irrevocable* split-interest agreement.

Types of Split-Interest Agreements

The following are all examples of split-interest agreements:

- *Charitable lead annuity trust.* This is a trust in which a nonprofit receives a fixed amount of distributions during the term of the arrangement. Once the trust terminates, remaining trust assets are paid to the donor or any stated beneficiaries of the donor.
- *Charitable lead unitrust.* This is a trust in which a nonprofit receives a fixed percentage of the fair value of the assets in the trust during the term of the trust. Once the trust terminates, remaining trust assets are paid to the donor or any stated beneficiaries of the donor.
- *Charitable remainder annuity trust.* This arrangement is the reverse of a charitable lead annuity trust. Under this arrangement, a nonprofit receives any assets remaining when a trust is terminated, while the donor or its beneficiaries receive a fixed amount of distributions during the term of the trust.
- *Charitable remainder unitrust.* This arrangement is the reverse of a charitable lead unitrust. Under this arrangement, a nonprofit receives any assets remaining when a trust is terminated, while the donor or its beneficiaries receive a fixed percentage of the fair value of the assets in the trust during the term of the trust.
- *Charitable gift annuity.* This arrangement calls for a donor to transfer assets to a nonprofit, after which the nonprofit is obligated to make certain periodic payments to the donor or its beneficiaries for a period of time. The nonprofit retains all residual assets.
- *Pooled income fund.* This is a trust arrangement under which donors contribute assets to a pooled fund, and are assigned a certain number of units based on the proportion of their contribution to the total size of the pool. The donor is paid the income on these units until the person's death, after which the value of these units are assigned to a nonprofit.
- *Net income unitrust.* This is a trust arrangement where the donor or a designated beneficiary receives distributions from the trust based on the lower of earned net income or a fixed percentage of the fair value of the assets in the trust. A nonprofit retains all residual assets.

There are a multitude of variations on the basic split-interest types just noted. For accounting purposes, it is easiest to associate a specific agreement with one of these types, since the accounting standards assign specific accounting treatments to each one. When in doubt about the proper accounting treatment, the accountant should confer with a nonprofit's auditors.

Tip: Have a small number of pre-written split-interest agreements available for any potential donors inquiring about making contributions. Doing so funnels these contributions into predetermined agreement types for which the relevant accounting can be more easily determined.

Accounting for Split-Interest Agreements

The accounting for a split-interest agreement varies, depending on the underlying structure of the arrangement. Here are several possible agreements and their related accounting:

- *Revocable agreement.* This is considered an intention to give, but not a finalized arrangement. When a nonprofit receives funds under a revocable split-interest agreement, the received funds are recognized as a refundable advance, which is a liability. The advance is then recognized as contribution revenue when the agreement becomes irrevocable, or when the assets are unconditionally distributed to the nonprofit.

- *Irrevocable agreement – assets held by nonprofit.* If there are no conditions imposed by a donor, a nonprofit can recognize contributed assets as contribution revenue as soon as a split-interest agreement is executed. When the arrangement is a charitable gift annuity, charitable lead trust, charitable remainder trust or similar arrangement where the transferred assets are held by the nonprofit for the benefit of the donor or its beneficiaries, it is also necessary to recognize a liability for the payments due to these other parties. The liability is recorded at its fair value on the initial recognition date.

- *Irrevocable agreement – assets held by third party.* If there are no conditions imposed by a donor but the assets are held by an independent trustee, the nonprofit recognizes its beneficial interest in the contributed assets as contribution revenue. This recognition relates to the nonprofit's entitlement to either the lead interest or the remainder interest in the arrangement. Recognition can occur as soon as the nonprofit is made aware of the existence of the arrangement. However, recognition of contribution revenue is not allowed for as long as the third party has the ability to redirect the assets or their benefits elsewhere.

- *Pooled income fund or net income unitrust.* Under these arrangements, the nonprofit is given the remainder interest in assets. The nonprofit recognizes assets as they are received, and recognizes its remainder interest as contribution revenue as those assets are received from the donor. The difference between the assets received and the remainder interest is recorded as deferred revenue (a liability).

EXAMPLE

Mr. Euclid establishes a charitable lead annuity trust agreement. Euclid transfers $150,000 of assets to a bank that acts as the trustee. The agreement authorizes the bank to pay Archimedes Education $8,000 per year until the death of Euclid. The use of these annuity payments is unrestricted. When Euclid eventually dies, the remainder interest shall be transferred back into the estate of Euclid, and will be distributed in accordance with the provisions of his will.

Archimedes estimates that the present value of the annuity payments is $65,000 and so records contribution revenue of $65,000 and a receivable in the same amount. Each year, when Archimedes receives an $8,000 payment, the entry is an increase in cash and an $8,000 reduction of the receivable. In each year, Archimedes also amortizes the discount on the present value calculation, which increases the value of the split-interest agreement.

EXAMPLE

Newton Education receives $200,000 from a donor under a charitable remainder annuity trust agreement. Newton is the designated trustee, as well as the remainder beneficiary. Newton is required to invest the funds and pay a $12,000 annuity back to the donor for the remainder of her life, after which Newton is entitled to all remaining assets.

Newton accounts for this transaction by initially recognizing the contribution portion of the $250,000 as contribution revenue. The amount of revenue is the $250,000 fair value of the trust assets, less the fair value of the estimated annuity payments (which is calculated by an actuary as $172,000). Thus, Newton recognizes $78,000 of contribution revenue, which is classified as a net asset with donor restrictions. Once the donor dies, the annuity restriction is lifted, and the net assets are then reclassified as net assets without donor restrictions.

Initial Measurement

The initial measurement of assets received under a revocable split-interest agreement is to do so at the fair value of the assets. The accounting for assets received under an irrevocable agreement has more alternatives, which are as follows:

- *If the assets are held by the nonprofit.* If the assets are under the control of the nonprofit or it acts as trustee, assets are initially recognized at their fair value. In addition:
  - If the assets are being held for the benefit of a third party, the fair value of the liability may be measured at the fair value of the future payments to be made to that party.
  - Under a lead interest arrangement, the nonprofit measures the asset fair value based on the present value of future distributions to be received as the beneficiary.
  - Under a remainder interest arrangement, the nonprofit measures the asset fair value based on the difference between the fair value of the

contributed assets and the fair value of the payments to be made to the beneficiary of the lead interest.

- o Under a pooled income fund or net income unitrust arrangement, the nonprofit measures assets at their fair value. Fair value can be derived from present value techniques; if so, calculate present value based on the estimated time period until the death of the donor.

- *If assets are held by a third party.* If a nonprofit is the unconditional beneficiary of a split-interest agreement that is held by a third party, the nonprofit measures its interest in the assets at their fair value.

Ongoing Measurement

The subsequent measurement of split-interest agreements must be at their fair value if a nonprofit elects to take the fair value option (see the Fair Value chapter) or if the funds are held by independent trustees.

If a split-interest agreement is irrevocable and the assets are held by the nonprofit, their subsequent measurement is the same as outlined for investments in the Investment Accounting chapter. In addition, if assets are held under any split-interest agreement other than a pooled income fund or a net income unitrust, report the following information in the financial statements of the nonprofit:

- Any income earned on the assets
- Gains and losses on the assets
- Distributions made to other beneficiaries, as per the terms of the agreement

When a nonprofit holds assets in trust for other beneficiaries, the nonprofit measures its liabilities to the beneficiaries at fair value, if it chose the fair value option (see the Fair Value chapter). If the nonprofit did not select the fair value option, ongoing remeasurement of the liability includes any revisions of expectations regarding future payments to beneficiaries under various actuarial assumptions, as well as the amortization of any present value discount associated with the original contribution (which gradually increases the amount of the liability). If the fair value option is not taken, the present value discount rate used to calculate the initial fair value shall not be revised in later periods.

If assets are held by a nonprofit under a pooled income fund or a net income unitrust, any periodic income associated with these assets is recognized as a change in the liability owed to the beneficiary. Any amortization of the discount associated with future interest is to be recognized as a reduction in the deferred revenue account, as well as a change in the value of the split-interest agreement.

If assets are instead held by a third party under a split-interest agreement and the nonprofit has an unconditional right to receive funds as a beneficiary, the nonprofit must measure its beneficial interest in the assets at their fair value. Any change in this fair value is to be recognized in the statement of activities. The fair value valuation method used shall be the same one used to derive the initial value of the assets. Any distribution to the nonprofit from the trust is to be accounted for as a reduction in the remaining balance of the beneficial interest.

If the assets held by a nonprofit are revocable under a split-interest agreement, the nonprofit shall recognize their value in accordance with the guidance noted in the Investment Accounting chapter for the subsequent measurement of invested assets.

Termination

When a split-interest agreement is closed out, the asset and liability accounts linked to the agreement are also closed. If there are any residual balances in these accounts at the closing date, they are recognized as changes in the value of the agreement.

Classification of Net Assets

Under GAAP, there are rules for how to classify net assets under split-interest agreements, with different specifications for the initial recognition of net assets, their subsequent measurement, and net asset derecognition.

When net assets are initial recognized under a split-interest agreement, the basic rule is to do so as an increase in net assets with donor restrictions. Or, if a donor gives the nonprofit an immediate right of use without restrictions, this is classified as an increase in net assets without donor restrictions.

Another initial recognition concept is when assets are received under a charitable gift annuity. Under this arrangement, the nonprofit makes certain payments back to the donor or its beneficiaries for a period of time, after which the nonprofit retains all residual assets. The contribution portion of this agreement is treated as unrestricted, if the donor does not restrict use of the assets, and there is no stipulation to invest the assets until the death of the income beneficiary. If these criteria are *not* met, the contribution is classified as a net asset with donor restrictions.

Following the initial recognition of net assets, amounts may be reclassified into net assets without donor restrictions when the underlying restrictions expire.

If assets are made available to a nonprofit once a split-interest agreement expires, these amounts are then reclassified as net assets without donor restrictions.

Disclosures

Any assets and liabilities associated with split-interest agreements are to be reported separately in the statement of financial position. Alternatively, they can be separately disclosed in the notes accompanying the financial statements. Similarly, any revenues or changes in the value of split-interest agreements are to be recognized separately in the statement of activities, or else within the notes accompanying the financial statements.

Besides the presentation of information just noted, there are also a number of disclosures that must be made regarding split-interest agreements. They are:

- *Terms*. Describe the terms of the existing agreements.
- *Recognition*. Note the assets and liabilities recognized under split-interest agreements, if not separately reported within the statement of financial position.
- *Basis*. State the basis used for recognizing assets, such as fair market value or cost.
- *Present value assumptions*. If present value techniques were used to derive fair values, note the discount rates and actuarial assumptions used.
- *Contribution revenues*. Note the amount of contribution revenue recognized under these agreements, if not separately reported in the statement of activities.
- *Changes in value*. State any changes in the recognized value of split-interest agreements, if not separately reported in the statement of activities.
- *Reserves*. If state law imposes restrictions on how net assets can be used, or requires additional annuity reserves, disclose this information. If the nonprofit voluntarily sets aside reserves for unexpected actuarial losses, it can also disclose this set-aside as a board-designated net asset without donor restrictions.

Summary

At some point, a nonprofit is likely to encounter a donor who proposes a split-interest agreement. The asset amounts underlying these agreements can be quite large, so most nonprofits will eagerly agree to such an arrangement. However, it makes sense to review the terms of each proposed split-interest agreement to see how the related accounting must be configured, and propose changes to make the accounting more efficient. Where possible, propose a standardized split-interest agreement format to donors, so that the accounting staff can apply a standardized accounting procedure to each one.

Chapter 16
Affiliated Organizations

Introduction

Nonprofit organizations may be related to each other in several ways. For example, their economic interests may be closely aligned, or one entity may exercise a certain degree of control over another organization. Also, since there are a variety of legal forms that a nonprofit may take, it is possible to have an ownership interest in some nonprofits. Depending on the type of relationship, it may be necessary to consolidate the financial statements of two or more entities, or at least require additional disclosure of the extent of the relationship. In this chapter, we explore the types of relationships between nonprofit organizations, and the related accounting and disclosure rules.

Affiliated Organizations

A nonprofit may have a number of relationships with other entities. Here are several examples:

- A ballet auxiliary provides education classes to young students for a fee, and forwards all proceeds to the regional ballet company.
- A women's scholarship organization conducts fundraising events, and uses the proceeds to fund a scholarship program at a local college; it also grants scholarships directly to worthy candidates.
- A wetlands protection nonprofit shifts several endowment funds into a separate legal entity, which is empowered to purchase threatened wetlands.
- A senior citizens support nonprofit creates a separate legal entity for each of its programs, which deal with senior transportation, in-home care, and meals.
- A nonprofit creates a for-profit subsidiary to market a variety of merchandise that bears the logo of the organization.

Under GAAP rules, there is considered to be a relationship with another nonprofit in any of the following four situations:

- *Ownership.* There is a controlling financial interest caused by either direct or indirect ownership of a majority voting interest or sole corporate membership in the other nonprofit.
- *Control and economic interest.* There is control of a related nonprofit via a majority voting interest in the board of directors of the other nonprofit by some means other than ownership or sole corporate membership; there is

also an economic interest in the other entity. An *economic interest* exists in either of the following situations:

- One nonprofit has significant resources that must be used for the purposes of the other entity. This use can either be directly for the other entity, or indirectly by generating income or providing services to the other entity.
- One nonprofit is responsible for the liabilities of the other organization.

- *Economic interest and other means of control.* There is an economic interest in the other entity, combined with some other means of control than was described in the last two bullet points.
- *Economic interest or control.* There is an economic interest in or control of the other entity, but not both.

The reporting for interrelated organizations varies, depending upon which of the preceding four conditions exists. The types of reporting are noted in the following table.

Types of Accounting for Affiliated Organizations

Type of Relationship	Reporting Required
Ownership	Consolidate the financial statements of the entities. However, if the majority owner or sole corporate member does not have control, do not consolidate. This can happen when supermajority voting is required to such an extent that control does not exist, or when the other entity is in bankruptcy.
Control and economic interest	Consolidate the financial statements of the entities, unless the holder of the majority voting interest does not have control. A majority voting interest exists when a nonprofit has the direct or indirect ability to appoint a sufficient number of individuals to constitute a majority of the votes of a board of directors.
Economic interest and other means of control	Consolidation is permitted, but not required. Other means of control include an affiliation agreement. Consolidation is encouraged if doing so would be meaningful.
Economic interest or control	Do not consolidate the financial statements of the entities.

When the required reporting refers to a consolidation, this means that the financial statements of the entities are merged, net of any transactions there may be between the organizations. This usually means that all inter-entity receivables and payables are eliminated from the consolidated financial statements, since an organization cannot be liable to itself for any receivables. Also, if one of the consolidating entities contributes funds to the other entity, the inter-entity contribution revenue and expense must be eliminated in the consolidated financial statements; otherwise, the consolidated statement of activities would be counting revenues that the entity has paid to itself.

> **Note:** Consolidated financial statements should report all asset and net asset restrictions that were reported in the financial statements of the individual entities. Thus, if a subsidiary reports $25,000 of net assets with donor restrictions, this same designation should carry forward into the statement of financial position of the consolidated entity.

> **Tip:** A significant concern for a nonprofit is whether the financial statements of another entity with which its financial statements are being consolidated have been audited. If not, the nonprofit's auditors will be unable to render an opinion on the consolidated financial statements, which could be a major issue if those statements are needed for fundraising or grant reporting purposes.

A nonprofit that is a general partner of a for-profit limited partnership is presumed to control a for-profit limited partnership, irrespective of the extent of that ownership interest, unless the presumption of control is overcome. As such, the nonprofit should consolidate its results with those of the limited partnership. The presumption of control can be overcome if the limited partners either have substantive kick-out rights or substantive participating rights. The kick-out rights must be exercisable via a simple majority vote of the limited partners.

Special Purpose Entities

A nonprofit may engage in leasing transactions with a special purpose entity (SPE). An SPE is a legal entity created to fulfill a specific objective, which is usually to separate an organization from a certain type of risk. Thus, a nonprofit might create an SPE to own a large asset, such as a building, which the nonprofit then leases from the SPE. When a nonprofit is engaged in leasing transactions with an SPE, it may be necessary to consolidate the financial statements of the two entities. If all of the following conditions exist, consolidation is mandated:

- *Asset usage.* Substantially all SPE assets are leased to a single entity.
- *Risks.* Expected residual risks and rewards associated with the leased assets, as well as the obligation imposed by the underlying SPE debt reside with the lessee through the lease agreements, residual value guarantees, a guarantee of the SPE's debt, or an option to grant the lessee the right to either purchase leased assets at non-fair value prices or receive sale proceeds over a certain amount.
- *Investment.* The owner of record of the SPE has not made a substantive equity investment that has been at risk during the lease term. If this owner is not an independent third party, the condition is considered to have been met.

The preceding conditions are intended to prove that the nonprofit and the SPE are essentially the same entity for consolidation purposes. If these conditions are met, consolidation shall aggregate the assets, liabilities, results of operations, and cash flows of the SPE into those of the nonprofit.

Noncontrolling Interests

When combining the financial statements of a subsidiary with its parent organization, report noncontrolling interests (also known as a minority interest) in the net assets section of the statement of financial position of the consolidated entity. A noncontrolling interest is that portion of net assets in a subsidiary that cannot be attributed to the parent entity. This interest is to be clearly identified and described sufficiently to distinguish it from the ownership interest of the parent entity. An example of the presentation of a noncontrolling interest appears in the following statement of financial position:

Archimedes Education
Statement of Financial Position
As of April 30, 20X1

ASSETS		LIABILITIES AND NET ASSETS	
Cash and cash equivalents	$25,000	Accounts payable	$12,000
Accounts and pledges receivable	63,000	Accrued expenses	5,000
Prepaid expenses	5,000	Grants payable	14,000
Investments	10,000	Deferred revenue	8,000
Fixed assets	180,000	Debt	10,000
		Net assets:	
		Net assets without donor restrictions	214,000
		Noncontrolling interests in Subsidiary ABC	20,000
Total assets	$283,000	Total liabilities and net assets	$283,000

Related Parties

A nonprofit may do business with a variety of parties with which it has a close association, where these parties can exercise control over or at least significantly influence the decisions made by the nonprofit. These individuals or organizations are known as related parties. Examples of related parties are:

- Affiliates
- Other subsidiaries under common control
- Owners of the business, its managers, and their families
- The parent entity

- Trusts for the benefit of employees

There are many types of transactions that can be conducted between related parties, such as sales, asset transfers, leases, lending arrangements, guarantees, allocations of common costs, and the filing of consolidated tax returns. For example:

- The executive director personally owns office space, and leases it to the nonprofit at a below-market lease rate.
- An affiliate raises money on behalf of the nonprofit.
- An affiliate shares many of the same members of the nonprofit's board of directors.

The reimbursement of expenses is not considered a related party transaction. For example, members of the board of directors are routinely reimbursed for the cost of their travel to board meetings. This is not a related party event. Similarly, the payment of compensation to an employee of a nonprofit is not considered a related party transaction.

The disclosure of related party information (as noted in the following section) is considered useful to the readers of a nonprofit's financial statements, particularly in regard to the examination of changes in financial results and financial position over time, and in comparison to the same information for other organizations.

Disclosures

This section describes a number of disclosures that a nonprofit may have to include in the notes accompanying its financial statements, depending on the circumstances.

Revenue Sharing

Nonprofits may agree to share their revenues. If so, the entity collecting the revenue will have a liability to pay over some portion of the revenues to the other nonprofit. This liability should be disclosed.

Consolidated Financial Statements

When it is necessary to present consolidated financial statements, disclose any restrictions made by third parties on distributions from the subsidiary to the parent, as well as the amount of assets affected by the restriction.

A nonprofit may control another entity through a form other than majority ownership and has an economic interest in the entity. If the nonprofit does not present consolidated financial statements, it must disclose the following:

- Identify the other entity and state the nature of the relationship between the two entities that results in control by the nonprofit.
- Summarize financial information for the controlled entity, including its total assets, liabilities, net assets, revenues, and expenses, as well as any re-

sources held for the benefit of the reporting entity or which are under its control.

- Disclose all of the items noted later in this section for related party transactions.

Noncontrolling Interests

If there is a noncontrolling interest in a consolidated subsidiary, include in the financial statements a schedule of changes in consolidated net assets that are attributable to the parent and the noncontrolling interest. This schedule reconciles the beginning and ending balances of the controlling and noncontrolling interests for each class of net assets. The schedule should at least include the following line items, if they exist:

- Amounts of discontinued operations
- Changes in ownership interests in the subsidiary, which includes incoming investments and outgoing distributions associated with noncontrolling interests
- The aggregate amount of all other changes in net assets without donor restrictions and with donor restrictions during the period

An example of such a disclosure is:

Archimedes Education
Notes to Consolidated Financial Statements
Changes in Consolidated Net Assets without Donor Restrictions Attributable to Archimedes
and Transfers (to) from the Noncontrolling Interest
Year Ended December 31, 20X2

	Total	Controlling Interest	Noncontrolling Interest
Balance January 1, 20X2	$1,000,000	$1,000,000	$0
Excess of revenues over expenses from continuing operations	42,000	37,800	4,200
Discontinued operations, net of tax	-20,000	-18,000	-2,000
Sale of subsidiary shares to noncontrolling shareholders	110,000	--	110,000
Change in net assets	132,000	19,800	112,200
Balance December 31, 20X2	$1,132,000	$1,019,800	$112,200

Related Party Transactions

In general, any related party transaction should be disclosed that would impact the decision making of the users of a nonprofit's financial statements. This involves the following disclosures:

- *General.* Disclose all material related party transactions, including the nature of the relationship, the nature of the transactions, the dollar amounts of the transactions, the amounts due to or from related parties and the settlement terms (including tax-related balances), and the method by which any current and deferred tax expense is allocated to the members of a group.
- *Control relationship.* Disclose the nature of any control relationship where the organization and other entities are under common ownership or management control, and this control could yield results different from what would be the case if the other entities were not under similar control, even if there are no transactions between the organizations.
- *Receivables.* Separately disclose any receivables from officers, employees, or affiliated entities.

Depending on the transactions, it may be acceptable to aggregate some related party information by type of transaction. Also, it may be necessary to disclose the name of a related party, if doing so is required to understand the relationship.

When disclosing related party information, do not state or imply that the transactions were on an arm's-length basis, unless the claim can be substantiated.

Note: It is not necessary to report related party transactions when those transactions were eliminated as part of the consolidation of the financial statements of a nonprofit and another entity.

Summary

The main point of this chapter was to define those circumstances under which organizations are so closely affiliated that their financial statements should be consolidated. There are other circumstances where consolidation is not necessary, but the entities have a close working relationship where one entity raises funds on behalf of another organization. See the Revenue Accounting chapter for more information about these pass-through funding arrangements.

There may be situations in which a nonprofit has a more modest financial interest in another entity, while exercising some level of control over it. If so, the appropriate accounting may involve use of the equity method, which is described in the Investment Accounting chapter.

The concept of related parties is not a minor one, for it is extremely common in the nonprofit arena. It is quite likely that there will be several related parties that interact with a nonprofit on a regular basis. If so, the accountant must identify these situations and be sure to disclose them properly in the notes accompanying the financial statements.

Chapter 17
Mergers and Acquisitions

Introduction

A nonprofit may elect to engage in a merger or acquisition transaction, where it combines operations with or entirely takes over another entity. The accounting for a merger is not especially complex, while there are substantially more rules governing how to account for an acquisition. In addition, there are a large number of disclosures required, particularly for an acquisition. In this chapter, we define mergers and acquisitions, describe how to account for them, present the outcome in the financial statements, and make a number of related disclosures. We also describe how to test for the impairment of goodwill; goodwill is a result of some acquisition transactions.

The Nonprofit Merger

When there is a merger of nonprofit entities, a new nonprofit entity is created. A merger occurs when the existing entities cede control to a new nonprofit. The *carryover method* is used to account for this event. Under the carryover method, the assets and liabilities of the merged entities are combined as of the merger date; this is the date on which the merger transaction becomes effective.

There are several adjustments required to the combination of the assets and liabilities of the merging entities in order to create properly merged financial statements. The adjustments are:

- *Contract modifications.* If a merger transaction will alter the terms of a contract, adjust the classification of the impacted asset or liability to match the state of the altered contract.
- *Reclassifications.* If the entities are using different methods to account for their assets and liabilities, adjust the impacted items to reflect a consistent method of accounting. This does not mean that the merged entity can revise accounting options that were restricted to the initial acquisition or recognition of an item. For example, if the fair value option (see the Fair Value chapter) was originally taken for an asset, this option cannot be revoked by the merged entity.
- *Intra-entity transactions.* If there were any transactions between the merging entities prior to the merger transaction, remove these intra-entity transactions from the merged assets, liabilities, and net assets.

When accounting for a merger, it is not permissible to recognize any new assets or liabilities, such as internally-developed intangible assets, which may be allowed under an acquisition transaction (see the next section).

A merged entity is considered a new entity, so it does not report any activities prior to the merger date. The beginning financial statements of the entity incorporate the adjustments just noted for the effects of contract modifications, reclassifications, and intra-entity transactions.

The Nonprofit Acquisition

An acquisition occurs when one entity obtains control over another entity. When there is an acquisition of an entity by a nonprofit, the *acquisition method* is used to account for the event. This method requires the following steps:

1. *Identify the acquirer.* The entity that gains control of the acquiree is the acquirer. Control refers to the ability to determine the direction of the management and policies of an entity through ownership, contracts, or other means. Several indicators of control are:

   - The ability to dominate the process of selecting the management team of the resulting entity.
   - The ability to dominate the process of selecting the governing body of the resulting entity.
   - When the resulting entity continues to use the mission statement and legal name of the acquirer.

2. *Determine the acquisition date.* The acquisition date is when the acquirer gains control of the acquiree, which is typically the closing date. When a nonprofit is gaining control of another entity with sole corporate membership, the acquisition date is the date on which the acquiring nonprofit becomes the sole corporate member of the acquiree.

3. *Recognize and measure all assets acquired and liabilities assumed.* These measurements should be at the fair values of the acquired assets and liabilities as of the acquisition date.

4. *Recognize any noncontrolling interest in the acquiree.* The amount recognized should be the fair value of the noncontrolling interest.

5. *Recognize and measure any goodwill or contribution received.* See the Goodwill Calculation and Contribution Received sub-sections for a discussion of goodwill and inherent contributions received. However, if the operations of the acquiree are predominantly supported by contributions and returns on investment, record a separate charge in the statement of activities, rather than recording goodwill.

EXAMPLE

Polio Containment acquires African Helicopter for consideration of $2,500,000. On the acquisition date, the net identifiable assets of African Helicopter total $2,100,000. Polio acquires African with the intent of using its helicopters to transport doctors to distant locations to administer polio vaccinations. The operating costs of African are expected to be predominantly supported by contributions from donors. The following statement of activities shows how Polio Containment might record the excess of consideration transferred over net assets acquired.

Polio Containment
Statement of Activities
August 31, 20X4

	Net Assets without Donor Restrictions	Net Assets with Donor Restrictions	Totals
Revenue	$10,000,000	$2,500,000	$12,500,000
Net assets released from restrictions	3,250,000	-3,250,000	--
Total revenue	$13,250,000	-$750,000	$12,500,000
Expenses	-12,200,000	--	-12,200,000
Excess of consideration transferred over net assets acquired	-400,000	--	-400,000
Change in net assets	$650,000	-$750,000	-$100,000

Note: The use of a separate charge in the statement of activities rather than the recognition of a goodwill asset is quite likely in nonprofits, where many organizations rely upon contributions as their principal form of revenue.

One scenario that can result in some modification of the preceding accounting treatment is the step acquisition. In this situation, a nonprofit may already own a minority interest in another entity, and then acquires an additional equity interest at a later date that results in an acquisition event. In this situation, the acquirer measures the fair value of its existing equity interest in the acquiree at the acquisition date, and recognizes a gain or loss at that time.

There are a number of additional issues that can affect the accounting for an acquisition, as outlined below:

- *Consideration transferred.* There may be situations in which the nonprofit acquirer transfers consideration to either the former owner of the acquiree, or to another party designated by the former owner. If the consideration transferred has a carrying amount different from its fair value, the acquirer is to recognize a gain or loss based on the difference between the carrying amount and fair value. However, if the transferred assets remain within the control of the combined organization after the acquisition, no gain or loss is to be recognized.

- *Contingent consideration.* Some portion of the consideration paid to the owners of the acquiree may be contingent upon future events or circumstances. If the consideration paid is with assets or liabilities, remeasure these items at their fair values until such time as the related consideration has been fully resolved, and recognize the related changes in the statement of activities.
- *Provisional accounting.* If the accounting for an acquisition is incomplete at the end of a reporting period, report provisional amounts, and later adjust these amounts to reflect information that existed as of the acquisition date.
- *New information.* If new information becomes available about issues that existed at the acquisition date concerning the acquiree, adjust the recordation of assets and liabilities, as appropriate.

EXAMPLE

Polio Containment acquires Sub-Saharan Doctors on December 31, 20X3. Polio hires an independent appraiser to value Sub-Saharan, but does not expect a valuation report for three months. In the meantime, Polio issues its December 31 financial statements with a provisional fair value of $4,500,000 for the acquisition. Three months later, the appraiser reports a valuation of $4,750,000 as of the acquisition date, based on an unexpectedly high valuation for a number of fixed assets.

In Polio's March 31 financial statements, it retrospectively adjusts the prior-year information to increase the carrying amount of fixed assets by $250,000, as well as to reduce the amount of goodwill by the same amount.

Any changes to the initial accounting for an acquisition must be offset against the recorded amount of goodwill. These changes to the initial provisional amounts should be recorded retrospectively, as though all accounting for the acquisition had been finalized at the acquisition date.

The measurement period during which the recordation of an acquisition may be adjusted ends as soon as the acquirer receives all remaining information concerning issues existing as of the acquisition date, not to exceed one year from the acquisition date.

The acquirer will probably incur a number of costs related to an acquisition, such as fees for valuations, legal advice, accounting services, and finder's fees. These costs are to be charged to expense as incurred.

Identifiable Assets and Liabilities, and Noncontrolling Interests

When the acquirer recognizes an acquisition transaction, it should recognize identifiable assets and liabilities separately from goodwill, and at their fair values as of the acquisition date. The following special situations also apply:

- No asset or liability is recognized in relation to an acquired operating lease in which the acquiree is the lessee, except to the extent of any favorable or unfavorable lease feature relative to market terms, or the willingness of third parties to acquire a lease even at market rates.

- Do not include any costs that the acquirer expects to incur in the future, but is not obligated to incur in relation to the acquiree, such as possible employee relocation costs.

It is entirely possible that the acquirer will recognize assets and liabilities that the acquiree had never recorded in its own accounting records. In particular, the acquirer will likely assign value to a variety of intangible assets that the acquiree may have developed internally, and so was constrained by GAAP from recognizing as assets. Examples of intangible assets are:

Broadcast rights	Internet domain names	Noncompetition agreements
Computer software	Lease agreements	Order backlog
Customer lists	Licensing agreements	Patented technology
Customer relationships	Literary works	Pictures
Employment contracts	Motion pictures	Service contracts
Franchise agreements	Musical works	Trademarks

A key intangible asset for which GAAP does not allow separate recognition is the concept of the assembled workforce, which is the collected knowledge and experience of an organization's employees. It is also not allowable to recognize an intangible asset for donor relationships. These intangibles must be included in the goodwill asset.

The accounting treatment for special cases related to the recognition of assets and liabilities is as follows:

- *Collections.* When the acquiring nonprofit has a policy of not recognizing collections as fixed assets, it cannot recognize the fair value of the collections of the acquiree. Instead, the acquirer must recognize the cost of the collection items purchased as a reduction in the related class of net assets, as well as a cash outflow for investing activities in the statement of cash flows.
- *Conditional promises to give.* A conditional promise to give is not recognized as of the acquisition date unless the conditions associated with the promise have been substantially met. If the conditions have not been met but assets have been transferred to the nonprofit, the assets are treated as a refundable advance (which is a liability).
- *Contingency fair value not determinable.* It is quite common for a contingent asset or liability to not be measurable on the acquisition date, since these items have not yet been resolved. If so, only recognize them if the amount can be reasonably estimated, and events during the measurement period confirm that an asset or liability existed at the acquisition date.

- *Defined benefit pension plan*. If the acquiree sponsored a defined benefit pension plan, the acquirer should recognize an asset or liability that reflects the funding status of that plan.
- *Indemnification clause*. The seller of the acquiree may agree to an indemnification clause in the acquisition agreement, whereby it will indemnify the acquirer for changes in the value of certain assets or liabilities, such as for unusual bad debt losses from receivables in existence at the acquisition date. In these cases, the seller recognizes an indemnification asset when it recognizes a loss on an item to be indemnified; this should be retrospectively applied as of the acquisition date.

Tip: Realistically, if the accountant is still attempting to establish a valuation for assets and liabilities more than a few months after an acquisition, they probably had no value at the acquisition date, and so should not be recognized as part of the acquisition.

Acquired assets and liabilities are supposed to be measured at their fair values as of the acquisition date. Fair value measurement can be quite difficult, and may call for different valuation approaches, as noted below:

- *Alternative use assets*. Even if the acquirer does not intend to apply an asset to its best use (or use the asset at all), the fair value of the asset should still be derived as though it were being applied to its best use.
- *Assets where acquiree is the lessor*. If the acquiree owns assets that it leases to a third party (such as a building lease), derive fair values for these assets in the normal manner, irrespective of the existence of the lease.
- *Fair value exceptions*. There are exceptions to the general rule of recognizing acquired assets and liabilities at their fair values. The GAAP related to the recognition of income taxes, employee benefits, indemnification assets, reacquired rights, share-based awards, assets held for sale, and certain contingency situations override the use of fair value.
- *Valuation allowances*. Some assets, such as receivables and inventory, are normally paired with a valuation allowance. The valuation allowance is not used when deriving fair values for these assets, since the fair value should already incorporate a valuation allowance.

A few assets and liabilities that are initially measured as part of an acquisition require special accounting during subsequent periods. These items are:

- *Contingencies*. If an asset or liability was originally recognized as part of an acquisition, derive a systematic and consistently-applied approach to measuring it in future periods.
- *Indemnifications*. Reassess all indemnification assets and the loss items with which they are paired in each subsequent reporting period, and adjust the recorded amounts as necessary until the indemnifications are resolved.

- *Reacquired rights.* An acquirer may regain control over a legal right that it had extended to the acquiree prior to the acquisition date. If these reacquired rights were initially recognized as an intangible asset as part of the acquisition accounting, amortize the asset over the remaining period of the contract that the acquiree had with the acquirer.
- *Leasehold improvements.* If the acquirer acquires leasehold improvement assets as part of an acquisition, amortize them over the lesser of the useful life of the assets or the remaining reasonably assured lease periods and renewals.

> **Tip:** The amortization period for leasehold improvements may be a significant issue for the acquirer, if it intends to shut down acquiree leases as soon as practicable. Doing so may accelerate the recognition of leasehold improvement assets.

Goodwill Calculation

Goodwill is an intangible asset that represents the future benefits arising from assets acquired in a business combination that are not otherwise identified. Goodwill is a common element in acquisition transactions, since the owners of acquirees generally do not part with their businesses unless they are paid a premium.

The acquirer must recognize goodwill as an asset as of the acquisition date. The goodwill calculation is as follows:

Goodwill = (Consideration paid + Fair value of noncontrolling interest + Fair value of acquirer's previously held equity interest in the acquiree) – (Assets acquired – Liabilities assumed)

If no consideration is transferred in an acquisition transaction, use a valuation method to determine the fair value of the acquirer's interest in the acquiree as a replacement value.

When the acquirer transfers its assets to the owners of the acquiree as payment for the acquiree, measure this consideration at its fair value. If there is a difference between the fair value and carrying amount of these assets as of the acquisition date, record a gain or loss to reflect the difference. However, if these assets are simply being transferred to the acquiree entity (which the acquirer now controls), do not restate these assets to their fair value; this means there is no recognition of a gain or loss.

Contribution Received

When an acquirer gains control of an acquiree whose fair value is greater than the consideration paid for it, the acquirer is said to have received an *inherent contribution*; this would be known as a bargain purchase if the acquirer had instead been a for-profit entity. The amount of the inherent contribution received is derived from the same calculation already noted for goodwill in the last sub-section.

A contribution received transaction most commonly arises when an entity must be sold due to a liquidity crisis, where the short-term nature of the sale tends to result in a less-than-optimum sale price from the perspective of the owners of the acquiree. An inherent contribution received is accounted for as the excess of assets acquired over liabilities assumed, but only if all of the following criteria are met:

- There is no noncontrolling interest in the acquiree.
- The acquisition was achieved in a single stage; it was not a multi-stage transaction.
- No consideration was transferred.

Presentation Issues

The acquirer includes the financial statements of an acquiree as of the period in which the acquisition takes place. Any acquiree revenues and expenses from prior periods are not included in the acquirer's financial statements.

If the circumstances of the acquisition mandate that goodwill cannot be recognized, goodwill is instead recorded in the statement of activities in a separate line item, such as "excess of consideration paid over net assets acquired in acquisition of [entity name]". If the liabilities acquired are greater than the assets acquired, then the line item name might instead be "excess of liabilities assumed over assets acquired in acquisition of [entity name]".

If there is an inherent contribution received as a result of an acquisition, this amount is reported in a separate line item in the statement of activities. Possible names for the line item are "contribution received in donation of [entity name]" or "excess of fair value of net assets acquired over consideration paid in acquisition of [entity name]". The inherent contribution received may increase the balance in either of the net asset line items (with or without donor restrictions), depending on the restrictions imposed on the net assets of the acquiree by donors.

The acquirer should report as an investing activity in the statement of cash flows the aggregate amount of any net cash flow related to an acquisition, which shall be comprised of any cash consideration paid, less any cash acquired. An example of the text that might be used in the statement of cash flows is:

Payment for acquisition of [acquiree name], net of cash acquired $xxxx,xxx

Goodwill Testing

After goodwill has initially been recorded as an asset, do not amortize it. Instead, test it for impairment at the reporting unit level. Impairment exists when the carrying amount of the goodwill is greater than its implied fair value.

A *reporting unit* is defined as an operating segment or one level below an operating segment. At a more practical level, a reporting unit is a separate business for which the parent compiles financial information, and for which management reviews the results. If several components of an operating segment have similar economic characteristics, they can be combined into a reporting unit. In a smaller organization, it is entirely possible that one reporting unit could be an entire operating segment, or even the entire entity.

The examination of goodwill for the possible existence of impairment involves a multi-step process, which is:

1. *Assess qualitative factors.* Review the situation to see if it is necessary to conduct further impairment testing, which is considered to be a likelihood of more than 50% that impairment has occurred, based on an assessment of relevant events and circumstances. Examples of relevant events and circumstances that make it more likely that impairment is present are the deterioration of macroeconomic conditions, increased costs, declining cash flows, possible bankruptcy, and a change in management. If impairment appears to be likely, continue with the impairment testing process. It is possible to bypass this step and proceed straight to the next step.

2. *Identify potential impairment.* Compare the fair value of the reporting unit to its carrying amount. Be sure to include goodwill in the carrying amount of the reporting unit, and also consider the presence of any significant unrecognized intangible assets. If the fair value is greater than the carrying amount of the reporting unit, there is no goodwill impairment, and there is no need to proceed to the next step. If the carrying amount exceeds the fair value of the reporting unit, proceed to the next step to calculate the amount of the impairment loss.

3. *Calculate impairment loss.* Compare the implied fair value of the goodwill associated with the reporting unit to the carrying amount of that goodwill. If the carrying amount is greater than the implied fair value, recognize an impairment loss in the amount of the difference, up to a maximum of the entire carrying amount (i.e., the carrying amount of goodwill can only be reduced to zero).

These steps are illustrated in the following flowchart.

Goodwill Impairment Decision Steps

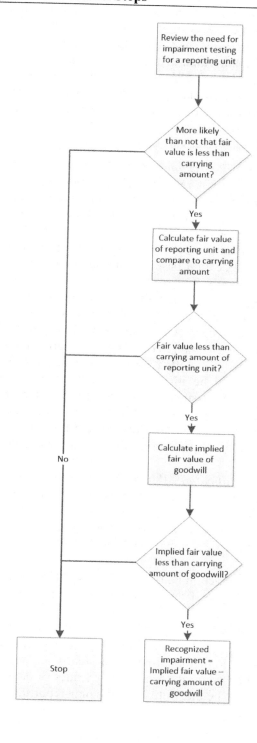

To calculate the implied fair value of goodwill, assign the fair value of the reporting unit with which it is associated to all of the assets and liabilities of that reporting unit. The excess amount (if any) of the fair value of the reporting unit over the amounts assigned to its assets and liabilities is the implied fair value of the associated goodwill. The fair value of the reporting unit is assumed to be the price that the organization would receive if it were to sell the unit in an orderly transaction (i.e., not a rushed sale) between market participants. Other alternatives to the quoted market price for a reporting unit may be acceptable, such as a valuation based on multiples of revenue.

The following additional issues are associated with goodwill impairment testing:

- *Asset and liability assignment*. Assign acquired assets and liabilities to a reporting unit if they relate to the operations of the unit *and* they will be considered in the determination of reporting unit fair value. If these criteria can be met, even corporate-level assets and liabilities can be assigned to a reporting unit. If some assets and liabilities could be assigned to multiple reporting units, assign them in a reasonable manner (such as an allocation based on the relative fair values of the reporting units), consistently applied.

- *Asset recognition*. It is not allowable to recognize an additional intangible asset as part of the process of evaluating goodwill impairment.

- *Goodwill assignment*. All of the goodwill acquired in a business combination must be assigned to one or several reporting units as of the acquisition date, and not shifted among the reporting units thereafter. The assignment should be in a reasonable manner, consistently applied. If goodwill is to be assigned to a reporting unit that has not been assigned any acquired assets or liabilities, the assignment could be based on the difference between the fair value of the reporting unit before and after the acquisition, which represents the improvement in value caused by goodwill.

- *Impairment estimation*. If it is probable that there is goodwill impairment and the amount can be reasonably estimated, despite the testing process not being complete when financial statements are issued, recognize the estimated amount of the impairment. The estimate should be adjusted to the final impairment amount in the following reporting period.

- *No reversal*. Once impairment of goodwill has been recorded, it cannot be reversed, even if the condition originally causing the impairment is no longer present.

- *Reporting structure reorganization*. If a nonprofit reorganizes its reporting units, reassign assets and liabilities to the new reporting units based on a reasonable methodology, consistently applied. Goodwill should be reassigned based on the relative fair values of the portions of the old reporting unit to be integrated into the new reporting units.

- *Reporting unit disposal.* If a reporting unit is disposed of, include the goodwill associated with that unit in determining any gain or loss on the transaction. If only a portion of a reporting unit is disposed of, associate some of the goodwill linked to the reporting unit to the portion being disposed of, based on the relative fair values of the portions being disposed of and retained. Then test the remaining amount of goodwill assigned to the residual portion of the reporting unit for impairment.

EXAMPLE

Polio Containment is selling off a portion of a reporting unit for $500,000. The remaining portion of the unit, which Polio is retaining, has a fair value of $1,500,000. Based on these values, 25% of the goodwill associated with the reporting unit should be included in the carrying amount of the portion being sold.

- *Reporting unit disposal, minority owner.* If a nonprofit has less than complete ownership of a reporting unit, attribute any impairment losses to the parent entity and the noncontrolling interest in the reporting unit on a rational basis. However, if the reporting unit includes goodwill that is attributable to the parent entity, attribute the loss entirely to the parent, not the noncontrolling interest.
- *Subsidiary goodwill impairment testing.* Any goodwill recognized by a subsidiary should be dealt with in the same manner described elsewhere in this section for the impairment of goodwill. If there is a goodwill impairment loss at the subsidiary level, also test the reporting unit of which that subsidiary is a part for goodwill impairment, if the triggering event is more likely than not to have also reduced the fair value of that reporting unit below its carrying amount.
- *Taxable transaction.* As part of the fair value estimation, determine whether the reporting unit could be bought or sold in a taxable or non-taxable transaction, since this affects its fair value.

Impairment testing is to be conducted at annual intervals. The impairment test may be conducted at any time of the year, provided that the test is conducted thereafter at the same time of the year. If the nonprofit is comprised of different reporting units, there is no need to test them all at the same time.

Tip: Each reporting unit is probably subject to a certain amount of seasonal activity. If so, select a period when activity levels are at their lowest to conduct impairment testing, so it does not conflict with other activities. Impairment testing should not coincide with the annual audit.

It may be necessary to conduct more frequent impairment testing if there is an event that makes it more likely than not that the fair value of a reporting unit has been reduced below its carrying amount. Examples of triggering events are a lawsuit, regulatory changes, the loss of key employees, and the expectation that a reporting unit will be sold.

The information used for an impairment test can be quite detailed. To improve the efficiency of the testing process, it is permissible to carry forward this information to the next year, as long as the following criteria have been met:

- There has been no significant change in the assets and liabilities comprising the reporting unit.
- There was a substantial excess of fair value over the carrying amount in the last impairment test.
- The likelihood of the fair value being less than the carrying amount is remote.

Disclosures

The disclosures for merger transactions vary from those required for acquisition transactions, so we have separated their respective disclosure requirements into two sub-sections.

Merger Disclosures

In general, the new entity resulting from a merger transaction shall disclose information in its financial statements that allow readers to evaluate the nature and financial effect of the transaction. To do so, the following disclosures are needed:

- The name and description of the entities that were merged
- The date of the merger
- The reasons for the merger
- For each merged entity, the amounts on the merger date of each major class of assets, liabilities, and net assets, as well as the nature and amounts of any other significant assets or liabilities not recognized; examples are conditional promises receivable and payable. For example:

Major Classes of Assets
September 1, 20X3

	Entity A	Entity B	Merged Entity
Assets			
Cash	$150,000	$75,000	$225,000
Contributions receivable	320,000	190,000	510,000
Fixed assets	95,000	62,000	157,000
Long-term investments	400,000	275,000	675,000
Total assets	$965,000	$602,000	$1,567,000
Liabilities			
Accounts payable	$120,000	$85,000	$205,000
Grants payable	200,000	--	200,000
Long-term debt	--	50,000	50,000
Net assets			
Without donor restrictions	445,000	200,000	645,000
With donor restrictions	200,000	267,000	467,000
Total liabilities and net assets	$965,000	$602,000	$1,567,000

- The nature and amount of any significant adjustments made to eliminate intra-entity transactions or to standardize accounting policies.
- If the new entity is publicly-held, and the merger does not occur at the beginning of its fiscal year, disclose revenue and changes in all types of net assets as though the merger had taken place at the beginning of the year. If the entity is also providing comparative information for prior years, this additional information is to be provided for the prior years. If it is impracticable to provide this additional information, explain why.

An example containing the first three of these disclosures is:

Armonk Training was formed on September 1, 20X3, as the result of the merger of two nonprofit entities – Armonk Specialized Education and Armonk Rural Training. Both entities shared similar missions, to provide trade school training to minors. Through their merger, the entities expect to expand upon their similar missions by increasing the region over which they provide services. They also expect to reduce management and administration costs by combining their overhead structures.

Acquisition Disclosures

The acquisitions topic is one of the areas in which GAAP requires unusually thorough disclosures. Disclosures are as follows:

- The name and description of the acquiree
- The date of the acquisition
- The percentage of voting equity interests acquired by the acquirer
- The main reasons for the transaction, as well as how the acquirer obtained control over the acquiree
- If there were any transactions recognized separately from the acquisition of assets and assumption of liabilities, describe each transaction, note how it was accounted for, the amounts recognized, and the line items in which the amounts are recognized. If the transaction settles a preexisting relationship, describe how the settlement amount was derived. Also note the amount of any acquisition-related costs, the amount of this cost recognized as expense, and the statement of activities line items in which the expenses are recognized. Also note any issuance costs not recognized as expense, and how they were treated.
- If the acquisition was achieved in stages, disclose the following:
  - The fair value of the acquirer's equity interest in the acquiree just before the acquisition date.
  - Any gain or loss recognized on the fair value remeasurement of the acquirer's equity interest in the acquiree immediately before the acquisition, and the line item in the statement of activities where this gain or loss is recognized.
  - The valuation method used to determine the fair value of the acquirer's equity interest in the acquiree immediately before the acquisition.
  - Additional information that enables readers to assess the inputs used to calculate the fair value of the acquirer's equity interest in the acquiree immediately before the acquisition.
- If the acquirer is publicly-held, disclose the following additional information:
  - The revenue amount attributable to the acquiree since the acquisition date.
  - Changes in all types of net assets since the acquisition date.
  - The revenues of the combined entity as though the acquisition had taken place on the first day of the acquirer's fiscal year.
  - Changes in all types of net assets as though the acquisition had taken place on the first day of the acquirer's fiscal year.
  - The nature and amount of any material and nonrecurring pro forma adjustments that were attributable to the acquisition that impacted pro forma revenues or any types of net assets.

- o If the entity is also providing comparative information for prior years, the preceding disclosures for a publicly-held entity are to be provided for the prior years.
- o If it is impracticable to provide any of these disclosures, explain why.

- A number of descriptive disclosures are also required that deal with the reasons why an acquisition was completed. These disclosures are:
  - o A description of the elements that comprise recognized goodwill or the separate charge in the statement of activities that takes the place of goodwill. Examples are expected synergies from the combination and intangible assets that could not be separately recognized.
  - o The fair value on the acquisition date of the total consideration paid, by asset class. For example, this may include cash, liabilities incurred, and intangible assets transferred.
  - o If there is contingent consideration that may be paid, disclose the amount recognized on the acquisition date, describe the arrangement and the calculation method, and note the range of undiscounted possible outcomes or the reason why no range can be calculated.
  - o The total amount of goodwill that the acquirer expects will be tax-deductible.
  - o If there is an inherent contribution received resulting from the transaction, note the reasons for this situation.
  - o The amount of collection items acquired that have been recognized as a decrease in the acquirer's net assets.
  - o The undiscounted amount of any acquired conditional promises to give, including a description and aggregate amount for every similar group of promises.

- In those situations where the acquisition date falls after the reporting date but before the issuance of financial statements, the acquirer shall disclose all of the preceding information, unless the transaction accounting is not yet complete when the financial statements are issued. If the disclosures cannot be provided, note the reason why.

- If there are any contingent consideration assets or liabilities, continue to disclose the following information until settlement of these items is achieved:
  - o Any changes in the recognized amounts.
  - o Any changes in the undiscounted range of possible outcomes, as well as the reasons for the changes.
  - o Information that allows readers to assess the fair values of the contingent items.

- Provide a reconciliation of the beginning and ending carrying amounts of goodwill for each acquisition.

Summary

Clearly, the accounting and related disclosures for an acquisition transaction are quite detailed and complex. Since the typical nonprofit's accounting staff may have only occasionally engaged in acquisition transactions, they are likely to have a rusty knowledge of these requirements. Consequently, it can be useful to engage outside counsel and accounting specialists to assist in the recordation and reporting of acquisitions. In addition, keep the nonprofit's auditors apprised of the entries being made, in order to trigger discussions over any treatments with which the auditors are uncomfortable. Doing so improves the odds of achieving a fault-free acquisition recordation.

Chapter 18
Nonprofit Tax Reporting

Introduction

Most nonprofits are required to file a tax return with the federal government. At a minimum, this return simply requires the filing of a large amount of information about the entity. In some cases, the filing may also require a nonprofit to pay income taxes. In addition, tax reporting to the government is also required when a nonprofit pays its employees. In this chapter, we cover the annual tax reporting and ongoing payroll reporting required for the United States federal government.

Overview of the Form 990

Nonprofits are required to file some variation on the Form 990 with the IRS each year. The available variations on the form and the applicability guidelines are as follows:

Form Type	Form Name	Applicability
Form 990	Return of Organizations Exempt from Income Tax	When gross receipts are greater than or equal to $200,000 or total assets are greater than or equal to $500,000 at the end of the tax year
Form 990-EZ	Short Form Return of Organizations Exempt from Income Tax	When gross receipts are less than $200,000 and total assets are less than $500,000 at the end of the tax year
Form 990-N	e-Postcard	When gross receipts are $50,000 or less
Form 990-T	Exempt Organization Business Income Tax Return	When there is gross income of $1,000 or more from a regularly conducted unrelated trade or business

Please note that the information in the applicability column in the preceding table is updated by the IRS on a regular basis, so check the IRS website for the most recent changes.

Several terms were noted in the preceding table that should be clarified. According to the IRS, *gross receipts* are the total amounts an organization receives from all sources during its tax year, without subtracting any expenses. *Gross income* is gross receipts minus the cost of goods sold.

Whenever possible, a nonprofit should use the easier versions of the Form 990, since the filing requirements are far less onerous. However, a nonprofit can choose to escalate its reporting to a more comprehensive report. For example, an entity that files a Form 990-N could choose to file a Form 990-EZ or a Form 990. Or, an entity that qualifies to file a Form 990-EZ could choose to file a Form 990. This option might be taken when a nonprofit wants to provide copies of a more complete tax form to its donors.

It can be quite difficult to complete the financial information in a Form 990 or Form 990-EZ if the accounting records do not compile information in the manner needed by the IRS. Accordingly, it can make sense to structure the chart of accounts to closely adhere to the filing requirements of a Form 990. By doing so, information can be directly transferred from the general ledger to the form. If the IRS subsequently changes the information needed in the form, this may call for a corresponding change in the chart of accounts.

> **Tip:** If there are differences between the information stated in a Form 990 and the accounting records (known as reconciling items), be sure to fully document the amounts of these items and the reasons for them. Store the documentation with the organization's copy of the Form 990, so that the backup information is readily available for examination at a later date.

No matter what type of form is filed, it must be filed no later than the 15th day of the fifth month after the fiscal year-end of a nonprofit. If a nonprofit is using a calendar year as its fiscal year, this means that the filing due date is May 15th. A nonprofit can file for an extension of this date by submitting Form 8868, *Application for Extension of Time to File an Exempt Organization Return*. Upon receipt of this filing, the IRS automatically grants a six-month filing extension. The first part of this form appears in the following exhibit, noting the automatic time extension.

Some version of the Form 990 must be completed, except as noted in the next paragraph. If a nonprofit neglects to do so for three consecutive tax years, its tax-exempt status will be automatically revoked. Monetary penalties for non-filing may also apply.

There are few instances in which a nonprofit is *not* required to file any version of a Form 990. The most common exclusions are for:

- Churches and church-affiliated organizations
- Political organizations

The amount of work required to complete a Form 990 can be substantial, and may leave one wondering why so much information must be reported. One reason is that the IRS is using the form to affirm whether a nonprofit deserves its tax exempt status. Another reason is that these forms are made available to the public, and so provide a major source of information to people interested in a nonprofit. Consequently, when filling out this form, the second reason may lead a nonprofit to provide a more complete set of information, especially if the form might be perused by a potential donor.

Form 8868 Application for Filing Extension

Form **8868** (Rev. January 2017) Department of the Treasury Internal Revenue Service	**Application for Automatic Extension of Time To File an Exempt Organization Return** ▶ File a separate application for each return. ▶ Information about Form 8868 and its instructions is at www.irs.gov/form8868.	OMB No. 1545-1709

Electronic filing (e-file). You can electronically file Form 8868 to request a 6-month automatic extension of time to file any of the forms listed below with the exception of Form 8870, Information Return for Transfers Associated With Certain Personal Benefit Contracts, for which an extension request must be sent to the IRS in paper format (see instructions). For more details on the electronic filing of this form, visit www.irs.gov/efile, click on Charities & Non-Profits, and click on e-file for Charities and Non-Profits.

Automatic 6-Month Extension of Time. Only submit original (no copies needed).

All corporations required to file an income tax return other than Form 990-T (including 1120-C filers), partnerships, REMICs, and trusts must use Form 7004 to request an extension of time to file income tax returns.

Type or print File by the due date for filing your return. See instructions.	Name of exempt organization or other filer, see instructions.	Enter filer's identifying number, see instructions Employer identification number (EIN) or
	Number, street, and room or suite no. If a P.O. box, see instructions.	Social security number (SSN)
	City, town or post office, state, and ZIP code. For a foreign address, see instructions.	

Enter the Return Code for the return that this application is for (file a separate application for each return) . . . . . . ☐☐

Application Is For	Return Code	Application Is For	Return Code
Form 990 or Form 990-EZ	01	Form 990-T (corporation)	07
Form 990-BL	02	Form 1041-A	08
Form 4720 (individual)	03	Form 4720 (other than individual)	09
Form 990-PF	04	Form 5227	10
Form 990-T (sec. 401(a) or 408(a) trust)	05	Form 6069	11
Form 990-T (trust other than above)	06	Form 8870	12

• The books are in the care of ▶ ------------------------------

Telephone No. ▶ ---------------- Fax No. ▶ ----------------
• If the organization does not have an office or place of business in the United States, check this box . . . . ▶ ☐
• If this is for a Group Return, enter the organization's four digit Group Exemption Number (GEN) _____. If this is for the whole group, check this box . . . ▶ ☐. If it is for part of the group, check this box . . . . ▶ ☐ and attach a list with the names and EINs of all members the extension is for.

1 I request an automatic 6-month extension of time until _____, 20 ____, to file the exempt organization return for the organization named above. The extension is for the organization's return for:
▶ ☐ calendar year 20 ____ or
▶ ☐ tax year beginning _____, 20 ____, and ending _____, 20 ____.

2 If the tax year entered in line 1 is for less than 12 months, check reason: ☐ Initial return ☐ Final return ☐ Change in accounting period

3a	If this application is for Forms 990-BL, 990-PF, 990-T, 4720, or 6069, enter the tentative tax, less any nonrefundable credits. See instructions.	**3a**	$
b	If this application is for Forms 990-PF, 990-T, 4720, or 6069, enter any refundable credits and estimated tax payments made. Include any prior year overpayment allowed as a credit.	**3b**	$
c	**Balance due.** Subtract line 3b from line 3a. Include your payment with this form, if required, by using EFTPS (Electronic Federal Tax Payment System). See instructions.	**3c**	$

Caution: If you are going to make an electronic funds withdrawal (direct debit) with this Form 8868, see Form 8453-EO and Form 8879-EO for payment instructions.

For Privacy Act and Paperwork Reduction Act Notice, see instructions.	Cat. No. 27916D	Form **8868** (Rev. 1-2017)

The Form 990

The Form 990 is an oppressively long and detailed form that must be filed by any nonprofit that has gross receipts greater than or equal to $200,000 or total assets greater than or equal to $500,000 at the end of the tax year. The form contains a mix of reporting requirements, ranging from financial results to a checklist of operational information. The main sections of the form are summarized as follows:

- *Header*. Notes the name, address, employer identification number, contact information, and tax-exempt status of the entity.
- *Part I, Summary*. Describes the activities of the organization, as well as summaries of its revenue, expenses, and net assets.
- *Part II, Signature block*. An officer signs the form, declaring that he or she has examined the return and asserts that its contents are correct and complete.
- *Part III, Statement of Program Service Accomplishments*. This section requires an organizational mission statement, as well as program service accomplishments. The intent of this requirement is to spot any organizations that gained tax-exempt status under a different mission statement, and then altered their missions.
- *Part IV, Checklist of Required Schedules*. This is a checklist of required schedules, which is essentially a reminder list of which additional schedules to complete, based on the circumstances and organizational structure of the nonprofit.
- *Part V, Statements Regarding Other IRS Filings and Tax Compliance*. The nonprofit must affirm that it met a number of tax filing requirements, such as backup withholding rules, and the use of tax shelters.
- *Part VI, Governance, Management, and Disclosure*. Note the number of directors, their independence, any changes to governing documents, and so forth.
- *Part VII, Compensation*. Note the compensation paid to officers, directors, trustees, key employees, and highly compensated employees, as well as separate reporting for independent contractors.
- *Part VIII, Statement of Revenue*. This is a detailed report of all sources of revenue during the reporting period.
- *Part IX, Statement of Functional Expenses*. This is a detailed report of all expenses incurred, broken down by program services, management and administration expenses, and fundraising expenses.
- *Part X, Balance Sheet*. This is a detailed report of all assets, liabilities, and net assets as of the reporting date.
- *Part XI, Reconciliation of Net Assets*. This is a brief reconciliation that subtracts expenses from revenues and factors in other reconciling items to arrive at the change in net assets.
- *Part XII, Financial Statements and Reporting*. The nonprofit clarifies the basis of accounting used, notes whether the financial statements were audited, describes whether it has an audit committee, and so forth.

The first page of the form is shown in the next exhibit. This page summarizes a large amount of the information required by the form, as noted by the multitude of references in the page to information contained in other parts of the form.

Form 990, Page 1

Form **990**	**Return of Organization Exempt From Income Tax**	OMB No. 1545-0047

Under section 501(c), 527, or 4947(a)(1) of the Internal Revenue Code (except private foundations)

2016

Department of the Treasury
Internal Revenue Service

▶ Do not enter social security numbers on this form as it may be made public.
▶ Information about Form 990 and its instructions is at www.irs.gov/form990.

**Open to Public
Inspection**

A For the 2016 calendar year, or tax year beginning _____ , 2016, and ending _____ , 20 ____

B Check if applicable:	**C** Name of organization		**D** Employer identification number
☐ Address change	Doing business as		
☐ Name change	Number and street (or P.O. box if mail is not delivered to street address)	Room/suite	**E** Telephone number
☐ Initial return	City or town, state or province, country, and ZIP or foreign postal code		
☐ Final return/terminated			**G** Gross receipts $
☐ Amended return			
☐ Application pending	**F** Name and address of principal officer:		H(a) Is this a group return for subordinates? ☐ Yes ☐ No

H(b) Are all subordinates included? ☐ Yes ☐ No
If "No," attach a list. (see instructions)

I Tax-exempt status: ☐ 501(c)(3) ☐ 501(c) ( ) ◀ (insert no.) ☐ 4947(a)(1) or ☐ 527

J Website: ▶

H(c) Group exemption number ▶

K Form of organization: ☐ Corporation ☐ Trust ☐ Association ☐ Other ▶   **L** Year of formation: **M** State of legal domicile:

Part I Summary

Activities & Governance

1 Briefly describe the organization's mission or most significant activities: _____

2 Check this box ▶ ☐ if the organization discontinued its operations or disposed of more than 25% of its net assets.

3	Number of voting members of the governing body (Part VI, line 1a)	3
4	Number of independent voting members of the governing body (Part VI, line 1b)	4
5	Total number of individuals employed in calendar year 2016 (Part V, line 2a)	5
6	Total number of volunteers (estimate if necessary)	6
7a	Total unrelated business revenue from Part VIII, column (C), line 12	7a
b	Net unrelated business taxable income from Form 990-T, line 34	7b

Revenue

		Prior Year	Current Year
8	Contributions and grants (Part VIII, line 1h)		
9	Program service revenue (Part VIII, line 2g)		
10	Investment income (Part VIII, column (A), lines 3, 4, and 7d)		
11	Other revenue (Part VIII, column (A), lines 5, 6d, 8c, 9c, 10c, and 11e)		
12	Total revenue—add lines 8 through 11 (must equal Part VIII, column (A), line 12)		

Expenses

13	Grants and similar amounts paid (Part IX, column (A), lines 1–3)		
14	Benefits paid to or for members (Part IX, column (A), line 4)		
15	Salaries, other compensation, employee benefits (Part IX, column (A), lines 5–10)		
16a	Professional fundraising fees (Part IX, column (A), line 11e)		
b	Total fundraising expenses (Part IX, column (D), line 25) ▶		
17	Other expenses (Part IX, column (A), lines 11a–11d, 11f–24e)		
18	Total expenses. Add lines 13–17 (must equal Part IX, column (A), line 25)		
19	Revenue less expenses. Subtract line 18 from line 12		

Net Assets or Fund Balances

		Beginning of Current Year	End of Year
20	Total assets (Part X, line 16)		
21	Total liabilities (Part X, line 26)		
22	Net assets or fund balances. Subtract line 21 from line 20		

Part II Signature Block

Under penalties of perjury, I declare that I have examined this return, including accompanying schedules and statements, and to the best of my knowledge and belief, it is true, correct, and complete. Declaration of preparer (other than officer) is based on all information of which preparer has any knowledge.

Sign Here	▶ Signature of officer		Date
	▶ Type or print name and title		

Paid Preparer Use Only	Print/Type preparer's name	Preparer's signature	Date	Check ☐ if self-employed	PTIN
	Firm's name ▶			Firm's EIN ▶	
	Firm's address ▶			Phone no.	

May the IRS discuss this return with the preparer shown above? (see instructions) . . . . ☐ Yes ☐ No

For Paperwork Reduction Act Notice, see the separate instructions.   Cat. No. 11282Y   Form **990** (2016)

The Form 990-EZ

As noted earlier, the Form 990-EZ, the *Short Form Return of Organizations Exempt from Income Tax*, can be filed when a nonprofit's gross receipts are less than

$200,000 and total assets are less than $500,000 at the end of the tax year. This filing is highly recommended, since it is one-third the size of the full Form 990. The main elements of the form are contained within its first two pages, which are reproduced in the following two exhibits. Though these pages still require a significant amount of work, they represent a major compression of the reporting requirements of the Form 990. The main emphasis of the 990-EZ is on reporting the financial results and position of the nonprofit, its service accomplishments, and the compensation of its officers, directors, and contractors.

The Form 990-N

As noted earlier, the Form 990-N, the *e-Postcard*, can be filed when a nonprofit's gross receipts are $50,000 or less. A nonprofit should always opt in favor of using the 990-N when it is allowable to do so, since the filing requirements are so minimal. Only the following information must be submitted:

- Legal name of the entity
- Any other (doing business as) names used by the entity
- Mailing address
- Website address
- Employer identification number
- Name and address of a principal officer of the organization, which is usually the president, a vice president, or the secretary or treasurer
- The entity's tax year
- Whether gross receipts are still $50,000 or less
- Whether the entity has gone out of business

The amount of reporting is clearly far less than for the other variations on the Form 990, essentially just identifying the organization and establishing whether it still exists. The form is filed through an on-line web page. The IRS provides a link to the form on its website; the form is maintained by a third party organization.

Form 990-EZ, Page 1

Form **990-EZ**	**Short Form** **Return of Organization Exempt From Income Tax** Under section 501(c), 527, or 4947(a)(1) of the Internal Revenue Code (except private foundations)	OMB No. 1545-1150 **2016**
Department of the Treasury Internal Revenue Service	▶ Do not enter social security numbers on this form as it may be made public. ▶ Information about Form 990-EZ and its instructions is at *www.irs.gov/form990*.	**Open to Public Inspection**

A For the 2016 calendar year, or tax year beginning _____, 2016, and ending _____, 20____

B Check if applicable:	**C** Name of organization 🔲	**D** Employer identification number 🔲
☐ Address change		
☐ Name change	Number and street (or P.O. box, if mail is not delivered to street address) 🔲 Room/suite	**E** Telephone number
☐ Initial return		
☐ Final return/terminated	City or town, state or province, country, and ZIP or foreign postal code	**F** Group Exemption
☐ Amended return		Number ▶ 🔲
☐ Application pending		

G Accounting Method: ☐ Cash ☐ Accrual Other (specify) ▶ _____

I Website: ▶ _____

H Check ▶ ☐ if the organization is **not** required to attach Schedule B 🔲 (Form 990, 990-EZ, or 990-PF).

J Tax-exempt status (check only one) — ☐ 501(c)(3) ☐ 501(c)( ) ◀ (insert no.) ☐ 4947(a)(1) or ☐ 527

K Form of organization: ☐ Corporation ☐ Trust ☐ Association ☐ Other

L Add lines 5b, 6c, and 7b to line 9 to determine gross receipts. If gross receipts are $200,000 or more, or if total assets (Part II, column (B) below) are $500,000 or more, file Form 990 instead of Form 990-EZ . . . . ▶ $ _____

Part I	**Revenue, Expenses, and Changes in Net Assets or Fund Balances** (see the instructions for Part I) 🔲

Check if the organization used Schedule O to respond to any question in this Part I . . . . ☐

Revenue	**1** Contributions, gifts, grants, and similar amounts received		**1**
	2 Program service revenue including government fees and contracts		**2**
	3 Membership dues and assessments		**3**
	4 Investment income		**4**
	5a Gross amount from sale of assets other than inventory	**5a**	
	b Less: cost or other basis and sales expenses	**5b**	
	c Gain or (loss) from sale of assets other than inventory (Subtract line 5b from line 5a) . . .		**5c**
	6 Gaming and fundraising events		
	a Gross income from gaming (attach Schedule G if greater than $15,000)	**6a**	
	b Gross income from fundraising events (not including $ _____ of contributions from fundraising events reported on line 1) (attach Schedule G if the sum of such gross income and contributions exceeds $15,000) . .	**6b**	
	c Less: direct expenses from gaming and fundraising events . .	**6c**	
	d Net income or (loss) from gaming and fundraising events (add lines 6a and 6b and subtract line 6c)		**6d**
	7a Gross sales of inventory, less returns and allowances	**7a**	
	b Less: cost of goods sold	**7b**	
	c Gross profit or (loss) from sales of inventory (Subtract line 7b from line 7a)		**7c**
	8 Other revenue (describe in Schedule O)		**8**
	9 **Total revenue.** Add lines 1, 2, 3, 4, 5c, 6d, 7c, and 8 . . . . ▶		**9**
Expenses	**10** Grants and similar amounts paid (list in Schedule O)		**10**
	11 Benefits paid to or for members		**11**
	12 Salaries, other compensation, and employee benefits 🔲		**12**
	13 Professional fees and other payments to independent contractors 🔲 . . .		**13**
	14 Occupancy, rent, utilities, and maintenance		**14**
	15 Printing, publications, postage, and shipping		**15**
	16 Other expenses (describe in Schedule O) 🔲		**16**
	17 **Total expenses.** Add lines 10 through 16 . . . . ▶		**17**
Net Assets	**18** Excess or (deficit) for the year (Subtract line 17 from line 9)		**18**
	19 Net assets or fund balances at beginning of year (from line 27, column (A)) (must agree with end-of-year figure reported on prior year's return)		**19**
	20 Other changes in net assets or fund balances (explain in Schedule O)		**20**
	21 Net assets or fund balances at end of year. Combine lines 18 through 20 . . . ▶		**21**

For Paperwork Reduction Act Notice, see the separate instructions.　　Cat. No. 10642I　　Form **990-EZ** (2016)

Form 990-EZ, Page 2

Form 990-EZ (2016)				Page **2**

Part II   **Balance Sheets** (see the instructions for Part II)

Check if the organization used Schedule O to respond to any question in this Part II . . . . ☐

		(A) Beginning of year	(B) End of year
22	Cash, savings, and investments	**22**	
23	Land and buildings	**23**	
24	Other assets (describe in Schedule O)	**24**	
25	**Total assets**	**25**	
26	**Total liabilities** (describe in Schedule O)	**26**	
27	**Net assets or fund balances** (line 27 of column (B) **must** agree with line 21) . .	**27**	

Part III   **Statement of Program Service Accomplishments** (see the instructions for Part III)

Check if the organization used Schedule O to respond to any question in this Part III . . ☐

What is the organization's primary exempt purpose? _____

Describe the organization's program service accomplishments for each of its three largest program services, as measured by expenses. In a clear and concise manner, describe the services provided, the number of persons benefited, and other relevant information for each program title.

Expenses
(Required for section 501(c)(3) and 501(c)(4) organizations; optional for others.)

28 ....

....

....

  (Grants $ _____) If this amount includes foreign grants, check here . . . . ▶ ☐   **28a**

29 ....

....

....

  (Grants $ _____) If this amount includes foreign grants, check here . . . . ▶ ☐   **29a**

30 ....

....

....

  (Grants $ _____) If this amount includes foreign grants, check here . . . . ▶ ☐   **30a**

31 Other program services (describe in Schedule O) . . . .

  (Grants $ _____) If this amount includes foreign grants, check here . . . . ▶ ☐   **31a**

32 **Total program service expenses** (add lines 28a through 31a) . . . . ▶   **32**

Part IV   **List of Officers, Directors, Trustees, and Key Employees** (list each one even if not compensated—see the instructions for Part IV)

Check if the organization used Schedule O to respond to any question in this Part IV . . . . ☐

(a) Name and title	(b) Average hours per week devoted to position	(c) Reportable compensation (Forms W-2/1099-MISC) (if not paid, enter -0-)	(d) Health benefits, contributions to employee benefit plans, and deferred compensation	(e) Estimated amount of other compensation

Form **990-EZ** (2016)

The Form 990-T

The Form 990-T must be filed by any nonprofit that has gross income of $1,000 or more from a regularly conducted, unrelated trade or business. Unrelated income is considered to be any income derived from activities not substantially related to the tax-exempt purpose of a nonprofit. As just noted, the income is reportable if it is regularly conducted; this implies that the activity is conducted on an ongoing basis.

EXAMPLE

Archimedes Education runs a café on its premises, which is mostly intended to handle the lunch needs of its employees. Given the high quality of its meals, the café charges prices that are well above the cost of the meals, resulting in substantial profits. Since this is an ongoing business that is unrelated to the educational nature of the organization, any income from the café should be reported on a Form 990-T.

EXAMPLE

Archimedes Education needs a new computer for its graphics department, so the staff conducts a one-time bake sale to raise money for it. Since this is a one-time, nonrecurring event, the proceeds from the bake sale are not considered to be reportable on a Form 990-T.

EXAMPLE

Archimedes Education routinely sells its mailing list of donors to for-profit businesses. Doing so does not contribute to the non-profit purpose of the entity, and so is considered unrelated taxable income that should be reported on a Form 990-T.

The intent of this form is to ferret out taxable income, and requires that a nonprofit pay taxes on this income. Since a nonprofit of any size may generate this type of income, it is entirely possible that even a small nonprofit filing a Form 990-N may also have to file a Form 990-T. The form contains the following primary sections:

- *Part I, Unrelated Trade or Business Income.* State all sources of revenue from unrelated activities.
- *Part II. Deductions Not Taken Elsewhere.* State all expenses associated with the unrelated activities.
- *Part III, Tax Computation.* Calculate the amount of income tax due.
- *Part IV, Tax and Payments.* Derive the amount of the tax payable to the government.

It may also be necessary to file a number of additional schedules that provide additional information about rent income, unrelated debt-financed income, investment income, advertising income, and similar items.

The Form 1099

A nonprofit must file a Form 1099-MISC, Miscellaneous Income, to report payments of $600 or more to individuals who are not classified as employees (usually independent contractors) in exchange for services performed. This form must also be filed for each individual for whom a nonprofit has withheld any federal income tax under backup withholding rules (irrespective of the amount). A sample Form 1099-MISC is shown below.

Sample Form 1099-MISC

Send the form to recipients no later than January 31 for payments made during the preceding calendar year. Also, send a copy of the form to the IRS no later than February 28, along with a Form 1096, Annual Summary and Transmittal of U.S. Information Returns, which aggregates the information on the individual Forms 1099.

> **Note:** The Form 1099-MISC does not have to be issued to corporations, except for fish purchases for cash, attorney's fees, medical services, and substitute payments in lieu of dividends or tax-exempt interest.

Explanations of the key fields on the Form 1099-MISC are:

- *Box 1, Rents.* Enter amounts of $600 or more for all types of rent payments, such as for real estate rentals and equipment rentals.

- *Box 2, Royalties.* Enter amounts of $10 or more for such items as oil and gas or mineral property royalties, as well as for patents, copyrights, and trade names.

- *Box 3, Other income.* Enter amounts in this box that do not clearly fall into one of the other categories, such as prizes and awards paid to individuals who are not employees, and punitive damages received.

- *Box 4, Federal income tax withheld.* Enter any amount of federal income tax withheld for persons who did not furnish the organization with a taxpayer identification number.

- *Box 5, Fishing boat proceeds.* Enter the recipient's share of the proceeds from a catch, as well as cash payments up to $100 per trip that are contingent upon a minimum catch, and which are paid solely for extra duties (such as being the cook) for which such payments are traditional in the industry.

- *Box 6, Medical services.* Enter amounts of $600 or more made to each physician or supplier of medical services. If the payments are to a corporation, report the payments in this form.

- *Box 7, Nonemployee compensation.* Most of the reporting on the form is in this field. Consider this box to be the default location in which to report payments. Examples of such payments are professional service fees, referral fees, payments by attorneys to witnesses or experts in legal adjudication, commissions paid to non-employees, and directors' fees.

- *Box 8, Substitute payments.* Enter the total amount received by a broker for a customer in lieu of dividends or tax-exempt interest resulting from the loan of a customer's securities, if the amount is $10 or more.

- *Box 9, Consumer products.* Check this box if $5,000 or more of consumer products have been sold to a person on a buy-sell or commission basis for resale. Do not enter a monetary amount in this box.

- *Box 10, Crop insurance proceeds.* Enter crop insurance proceeds of at least $600 paid to farmers.

- *Box 13, Golden parachute payments.* Enter any amount of excess golden parachute payments. The amount is considered excess if it exceeds three times the average annual compensation for services included in an individual's gross income over the most recent five tax years.

- *Box 14, Attorney payments.* Enter amounts of $600 or more to an attorney in connection with legal services provided.

- *Box 15a, Section 409A deferrals.* Enter amounts of $600 or more deferred during the year under a nonqualified plan.

- *Box 15b, Section 409A income.* Enter all amounts deferred that are includible in income under section 409A because a nonqualified compensation plan does not satisfy the requirements of section 409A. Do not include amounts that are considered to be subject to a substantial risk of forfeiture.

- *Boxes 16-18, State and local withholdings.* It is not necessary to enter information in these fields, since they are only for internal use, and are not required by the IRS. There is room in these boxes to report payments for up to two states.

The Form 1099-MISC is comprised of several copies, which are used as follows:

- *Copy A*. To be filed by the nonprofit with the summary-level Form 1096 with the IRS. A sample of the Form 1096 is shown next.
- *Copy 1*. To be filed by the nonprofit with the state tax department.
- *Copy B*. To be sent to the individual ("recipient") who provided services to the nonprofit.
- *Copy 2*. To be filed by the recipient with the recipient's state income tax return.
- *Copy C*. To be retained by the nonprofit.

If a nonprofit generates at least 250 Forms 1099, they must be filed electronically.

The Form 1096, Annual Summary and Transmittal of U.S. Information Returns, is a summary-level document that aggregates the information on a batch of Forms 1099. List on this form the number of accompanying Forms 1099, check off the type of Forms 1099 (there are several varieties), and enter the total amount of federal income tax withheld on the forms. A sample form is shown below.

Sample Form 1096

The Form W-2

Following the end of every calendar year, and no later than January 31, an employer must issue the multi-part Form W-2, on which it itemizes the wages it paid to each employee during the year, as well as the taxes that it withheld from employee pay. It issues this form to anyone who was paid wages by the organization at any time during the year, even if they no longer work for the business. This information forms the basis for the personal income tax returns completed by all employees for the federal government and the state government in which they reside. An example of the Form W-2 is shown below.

Sample Form W-2

22222	Void ☐	a Employee's social security number	For Official Use Only ▶ OMB No. 1545-0008		
b Employer identification number (EIN)			1 Wages, tips, other compensation	2 Federal income tax withheld	
c Employer's name, address, and ZIP code			3 Social security wages	4 Social security tax withheld	
			5 Medicare wages and tips	6 Medicare tax withheld	
			7 Social security tips	8 Allocated tips	
d Control number			9 Verification code	10 Dependent care benefits	
e Employee's first name and initial	Last name	Suff.	11 Nonqualified plans	12a See instructions for box 12	
			13 Statutory employee / Retirement plan / Third-party sick pay	12b	
			14 Other	12c	
				12d	
f Employee's address and ZIP code					
15 State Employer's state ID number	16 State wages, tips, etc.	17 State income tax	18 Local wages, tips, etc.	19 Local income tax	20 Locality name

Form **W-2** Wage and Tax Statement   **2017**   Department of the Treasury—Internal Revenue Service

Copy A For Social Security Administration — Send this entire page with Form W-3 to the Social Security Administration; photocopies are not acceptable.

For Privacy Act and Paperwork Reduction Act Notice, see the separate instructions.

Cat. No. 10134D

The Form W-2 contains a large number of fields, but many of them are not needed to report the compensation and tax information for a typical employee; many of the fields are only required to report unusual compensation arrangements. The payroll system prints these forms automatically after the end of the calendar year. If payroll has been outsourced, the supplier will issue them on the organization's behalf. Thus, the Form W-2 is usually not an especially difficult document to produce.

The Form W-2 is comprised of several copies, which are used as follows:

- *Copy A.* Send this copy to the Social Security Administration.
- *Copy 1.* Send this copy to the state, city, or local tax department.
- *Copy B.* The recipient sends this copy to the IRS as part of his or her federal tax return.
- *Copy C.* This copy is intended for the employee's records.
- *Copy 2.* The recipient attaches this copy to his or her state, city, or local income tax return.
- *Copy D.* This copy is intended for the employer's records.

Tip: More than one Form W-2 can be issued to an employee. For example, if more items must be reported than will fit in one box on the form, do so on an additional form. If so, fill in the same identifying information in boxes "a" through "f" that were completed for the first Form W-2 for the employee.

Explanations of the key fields on the Form W-2 are:

- *Box a, Social security number.* Enter the employee's social security number. This should be the number shown on the employee's social security card.
- *Box b, Employer identification number (EIN).* Enter the EIN assigned to the employer by the IRS.
- *Box c, Employer address.* Enter the employer's mailing address.
- *Box d, Control number.* Use this box to identify an individual Form W-2. The IRS does not use the information in this box.
- *Box e, Employee name.* Enter the name of the employee that is shown on his or her social security card. If the name is too long, print the full last name, and enter initials for the first and middle names. Do not include titles in the name.
- *Box f, Employee address.* Enter the mailing address of the employee. A post office box number is acceptable.
- *Box 1, Wages, tips, other compensation.* Enter the total amount of taxable compensation paid to the employee during the calendar year.
- *Box 2, Federal income tax withheld.* Enter the total amount withheld from the employee's pay for federal income taxes during the calendar year. Include the 20% excise tax on excess parachute payments (if any).
- *Box 3, Social security wages.* Enter the amount of total wages paid during the calendar year that are subject to the social security tax.
- *Box 4, Social security tax withheld.* Enter the total amount of social security taxes withheld from the employee's pay during the calendar year. Do not include the matching amount of social security tax paid by the employer.
- *Box 5, Medicare wages and tips.* Enter the amount of total wages paid during the calendar year that are subject to the Medicare tax.
- *Box 6, Medicare tax withheld.* Enter the total amount of Medicare taxes withheld from the employee's pay during the calendar year. Do not include the matching amount of Medicare tax paid by the employer.
- *Box 7, Social security tips.* Enter the amount of tips reported by the employee to the employer, even if there were not sufficient employee funds to collect the social security tax related to the tips.
- *Box 8, Allocated tips.* If the employer is a food or beverage establishment, enter the amount of tips allocated to the employee.
- *Box 9.* Do not use this box.
- *Box 10, Dependent care benefits.* Enter the total dependent care benefits paid to the employee under a dependent care assistance program, or incurred on the employee's behalf by the employer.

- *Box 11, Nonqualified plans.* Enter any distributions to the employee from a nonqualified plan. Also report the amount of these distributions within the total in Box 1.
- *Box 12, Coded items.* Use the IRS codes in the following table to record the dollar amount of the indicated items. There is space within Box 12 for four coded items.
- *Box 13, Checkboxes.* Check the "Statutory employee" box if an employee is a statutory employee whose earnings are not subject to federal income tax withholding, but which are subject to social security and Medicare taxes. Check the "Retirement plan" box if the employee was an active participant in a variety of types of pension plans. Check the "Third-party sick pay" box if the filer is a third-party sick pay payer who is filing a Form W-2 for an insured party's employee, or an employer reporting sick pay payments made to an employee by a third party.
- *Box 14, Other.* If 100% of a vehicle's annual lease value was included in an employee's income, enter it here. Other information may be entered in that box for payments made to an employee, such as union dues, uniform payments, and educational assistance payments.
- *Boxes 15–20, State and local income tax information.* Report state and local income tax information in these boxes. This includes the two-letter abbreviation of the name of the state, and the employer's state ID number. There is room to report wages and taxes for two states and two localities.

Form W-3

Once an employer creates Forms W-2 for its employees, it takes Copy A of these forms and aggregates selected information on them into a Form W-3, *Transmittal of Wage and Tax Statements*. It then submits all of the Copy A versions of the Forms W-2, as well as the Form W-3, to the government no later than February 28. An example of the Form W-3 is shown below. Explanations of the key fields on the Form W-3 are:

- *Box a, Control number.* Use this box to identify a Form W-3. The IRS does not use the information in this box.
- *Box b, Kind of payer.* Check the box that applies to the employer. Check only one box. The most common box to check is the "941" box, which indicates that the organization files the Form 941, Employer's Quarterly Federal Tax Return.
- *Box b, Kind of employer.* Check the box that applies to the employer. Check only one box. The most common box to check is the "None apply" box.
- *Box b, Third-party sick pay.* Check this box if the entity is a third-party sick pay payer, or is reporting sick pay payments made by a third party.
- *Box c, Total number of Forms W-2.* Enter the number of Forms W-2 that accompany this Form W-3.

- *Box d, Establishment number.* Use this box to identify different establishments within the business. It is allowable to file a separate Form W-3 for each establishment, along with accompanying Forms W-2, even if all of the establishments use the same employer identification number.
- *Box e, Employer identification number.* Enter the EIN assigned to the employer by the IRS. If an EIN has not yet been received when the Form W-3 is filed, enter "Applied for" in this box.
- *Box f, Employer's name.* Enter the name of the employer, which should be the same one used on the Form 941.
- *Box g, Employer's address.* Enter the employer's mailing address.
- *Box h, Other EIN used this year.* Enter any other employer identification number used during the year on the Form 941 that is different from the EIN stated on this form.
- *Boxes 1-8.* Enter the wages, tax withholdings, and tip allocations in these boxes that are the totals from the corresponding Forms W-2 being submitted along with this form.
- *Box 10, Dependent care benefits.* Enter the total of the dependent care benefits reported in box 10 of the accompanying Forms W-2.

Sample Form W-3

- *Box 11, Nonqualified plans.* Enter the total amount in box 11 of the accompanying Forms W-2.
- *Box 12a, Deferred compensation.* Enter the total for the following IRS codes in box 12 on the accompanying Forms W-2: codes D through H, S, Y, AA, BB, and EE. Do not enter the codes themselves.
- *Box 13, For third-party sick pay use only.* If the entity is a third-party payer of sick pay, enter the aggregate amount of third-party sick pay recap.
- *Box 14, Income tax withheld by payer of third-party sick pay.* Enter the total income tax withheld by third-party payers on sick pay payments to employees.
- *Box 15, State | Employer's state ID number.* Enter the two-letter abbreviation of the state being reported on the accompanying Forms W-2, as well as the ID number assigned to the employer by the state. If more than one state is being reported, enter an "X" here, and do not enter a state ID number.
- *Boxes 16-19.* Enter the total amount of state/local wages and income taxes in the accompanying Forms W-2. If the Forms W-2 contain amounts for more than one state or locality, combine them into one reported amount.
- *Contact information.* Enter the name of the person most familiar with the payroll information on the report. An appropriate choice might be the payroll manager.

As was the case for the Form W-2, the organization's payroll software should generate the Form W-3 automatically. If not, be sure to verify that the information on the accompanying Forms W-2 add up to the totals printed on the Form W-3. Also, verify that the totals on the Form W-3 match the aggregate of the amounts listed on all Forms 941 filed during the year.

Payroll Taxes

A nonprofit is liable for the same payroll taxes that are incurred by a for-profit entity. This means that a nonprofit must calculate social security and Medicare taxes for each employee, as well as matching amounts to be provided by the nonprofit, and forward these funds to the government in a timely manner. In this section, we describe the most common types of payroll taxes, how these taxes are to be deposited with the government, and how payroll tax information is to be subsequently reported to the government.

Social Security Tax

The social security tax began with the passage of the Social Security Act in 1935, which established Old Age and Survivor's Insurance. The insurance was to be funded by compulsory deductions from the pay of wage earners. Initially, these deductions were set at 1% of gross wages, and were to be paid by both the employer and the employee, and would continue until retirement age, which was set at 65. By 1948, the amount of these deductions had increased to 3%. Employers have been

212

and continue to be responsible for withholding the social security tax from employee pay.

The tax rate for social security is now governed by the Federal Insurance Contributions Act (FICA). Because of this association, social security taxes are now closely associated with the acronym "FICA".

This tax has increased in size over time, along with the maximum wage cap (also known as the *wage base limit*) to which it applies. The social security tax rate is only applied to a person's wages up to the amount of the wage base cap. Do not apply the tax to any wages earned above the wage cap. For example, on earnings of $150,000 in 2017, the amount of employer tax paid would be $7,886.40, which is calculated as follows:

$$6.2\% \text{ Tax rate} \times \$127,200 \text{ Wage cap} = \$7,886.40$$

The following table shows the recent history of the social security tax for the past few years. Note the drop in the employee portion of the tax in 2011 and 2012.

Tax Year	FICA Tax Rate	Wage Cap
2017	6.2%	$127,200
2016	6.2%	118,500
2015	6.2%	118,500
2014	6.2%	117,000
2013	6.2%	113,700
2012	4.2% Employee / 6.2% Employer	110,100
2011	4.2% Employee / 6.2% Employer	106,800
2010	6.2%	106,800
2009	6.2%	106,800
2008	6.2%	102,000

Note that social security is matched by the employee, so the total tax amount paid to the government by the employer is 12.4% (with the exceptions of 2011 and 2012, as noted in the preceding table). A self-employed person is responsible for paying the full amount of the 12.4%.

EXAMPLE

Benjamin Mayhew earned $200,000 in 2017. Based on the $127,200 wage cap in place that year, his employer must deduct $7,886.40 from his gross pay and match it with another $7,886.40 for a total payment of $15,772.80.

The age at which full social security retirement benefits are payable depends on the year of birth of the individual. The following table states the full retirement age for different years of birth.

Age at Which Full Social Security Benefits Are Available

Year of Birth	Full Retirement Age
1943-1954	66
1955	66 and 2 months
1956	66 and 4 months
1957	66 and 6 months
1958	66 and 8 months
1959	66 and 10 months
1960+	67

An individual can retire as early as age 62, but will be paid roughly 25% less than the amount that would have been paid if the person had chosen to wait until his or her full retirement age.

Conversely, a person can choose to continue working beyond the full retirement age. If so, the individual is adding extra years of work to his or her social security record, which may result in higher benefits upon retirement. Further, one can choose to delay retirement until age 70 in exchange for an automatic increase by a certain percentage (usually about 8% per year) from the full retirement age until age 70.

Widows and widowers can begin receiving social security benefits at age 60, or at age 50 if they are disabled.

Medicare Tax

Medicare is a health insurance program that is administered by the United States government, and which is primarily available to those 65 years old or older, as well as to those with certain disabilities. It is funded through the Medicare tax, though participants must also pay a portion of all health insurance costs incurred. The program has been in existence since 1965.

Since 1986, the Medicare tax rate that is paid by an employee has been 1.45% (plus matching of the same amount by the employer), and 2.9% for self-employed workers. There is no cap on the Medicare tax for employed and self-employed people; thus, everyone must pay it, irrespective of the amount of money that they earn.

EXAMPLE

Archimedes Education employs Mr. Smith, who earns $5,000 of gross pay in the most recent pay period. Archimedes withholds $72.50 ($5,000 × .0145) from the pay of Mr. Smith, matches the $72.50 from its own funds, and forwards $145.00 to the government.

As of 2014, an additional Medicare tax of 0.9% was imposed, which applies to all wages earned in excess of $250,000 for married filers, and in excess of $200,000 for single and head of household filers.

Types of Tax Deposit Schedules

There are two deposit schedules, known as the *monthly deposit schedule* and the *semiweekly deposit schedule*, which state when to deposit payroll taxes. The accountant must determine which of these deposit schedules will be followed before the beginning of each calendar year. The selection of a deposit schedule is based entirely on the tax liability reported during a *lookback period*.

The deposit schedule is based on the total taxes (i.e., federal income taxes withheld, social security taxes, and Medicare taxes) reported in line 8 of the Forms 941 in a four-quarter lookback period. The lookback period begins on July 1 and ends on June 30. The decision tree for selecting a deposit period is:

- If the organization reported $50,000 or less of taxes during the lookback period, use the monthly deposit schedule.
- If the organization reported more than $50,000 of taxes during the lookback period, use the semiweekly deposit schedule.

EXAMPLE

Norrona Software, a provider of free desktop software to poverty-stricken countries, had used the monthly deposit schedule in previous years, but its payroll expanded considerably in the past year, which may place it in the semiweekly deposit schedule. Norrona's payroll manager calculates the amount of taxes paid during its lookback period to see if the semiweekly deposit schedule now applies. The calculation is:

Lookback Period	Taxes Paid
July 1 – September 30, 2016	$8,250
October 1 – December 31, 2016	14,750
January 1 – March 31, 2017	17,500
April 1 – June 30, 2017	19,000
Total	$59,500

Since the total amount of taxes that Norrona paid during the lookback period exceeded $50,000, the organization must use the semiweekly deposit schedule during the next calendar year.

Tip: A new employer has no lookback period, and so is automatically considered a monthly schedule depositor for its first calendar year of business.

If a business qualifies to use the monthly deposit schedule, deposit employment taxes on payments made during a month by the 15th day of the following month.

EXAMPLE

Archimedes Education is a monthly schedule depositor that pays its staff on the 15th and last business day of each month. Under the monthly deposit schedule, Archimedes must deposit the combined tax liabilities for all of its payrolls in a month by the 15th day of the following month. The same deposit schedule would apply if Archimedes had instead paid its employees every day, every other week, twice a month, once a month, or on any other payroll schedule.

The total payroll taxes withheld for each of Archimedes' payrolls in September are noted in the following table, along with the amount of its tax liability that will be due for remittance to the government on October 15:

	Federal Income Tax Withheld	Social Security Tax Withheld	Medicare Tax Withheld
Sept. 15 payroll	$1,500.00	$620.00	$145.00
Sept. 30 payroll	1,250.00	558.00	130.50
Sept. total withheld	$2,750.00	$1,178.00	$275.50
Employer tax matching	--	1,178.00	275.50
Tax deposit due Oct. 15	$2,750.00	$2,356.00	$551.00

Archimedes' tax liability to be remitted on October 15 is $5,657.00, which is calculated as the total of all withholdings and employer matches for federal income taxes, social security taxes, and Medicare taxes ($2,750.00 + $2,356.00 + $551.00).

If a nonprofit qualifies to use the semiweekly deposit schedule, remit payroll taxes using the following table:

Payment Date	Corresponding Deposit Date
Wednesday, Thursday, or Friday	Following Wednesday
Saturday, Sunday, Monday, Tuesday	Following Friday

If a nonprofit has more than one pay date during a semiweekly period and the pay dates fall in different calendar quarters, make separate deposits for the liabilities associated with each pay date.

EXAMPLE

Norrona Software has a pay date on Wednesday, June 29 (second quarter) and another pay date on Friday, July 1 (third quarter). Norrona must make a separate deposit for the taxes associated with each pay date, even though both dates fall within the same semiweekly period. Norrona should pay both deposits on the following Wednesday, July 6.

Note that the semiweekly deposit method does not mean that a nonprofit is required to make two tax deposits per week – it is simply the name of the method. Thus, if an organization has one payroll every other week, it would remit taxes only every other week.

The differentiating factor between the monthly and semiweekly deposit schedules is that a nonprofit must remit taxes much more quickly under the semiweekly method. The monthly method uses a simpler and more delayed tax deposit schedule, which is ideal for smaller organizations.

The Form 941

Following each calendar quarter, any employer that pays wages subject to income tax withholding, or social security and Medicare taxes, must file a Form 941, the *Employer's Quarterly Federal Tax Return*. File the Form 941 by the last day of the month following the calendar quarter to which it applies. Thus, the filing dates for the Form 941 are:

Quarter Ending	Form 941 Due Date
March 31	April 30
June 30	July 31
September 30	October 31
December 31	January 31

The following exhibit contains a sample of the Form 941, as completed by a semiweekly filer that has no unusual exceptions from the normal tax reporting. In the form, the employer and the reporting period are identified in the header block, the amount of taxes to be deposited and the amount already deposited are noted in Part 1, and the organization's deposit schedule appears in Part 2. These are the key components of the form.

The form shown in the exhibit is sufficient for all employers on a monthly filing schedule. An employer on the semiweekly filing schedule must also add Schedule B to the form, which itemizes the dates on which all payroll tax liabilities were incurred during the calendar quarter. Schedule B is shown in a following exhibit. In some situations, a nonprofit may need to make a payment alongside the Form 941. If so, complete Form 941-V, Payment Voucher, to document the amount of the payment. In the exhibit, we have not entered a payment amount in Form 941-V, since all deposits related to the calendar quarter were already made and listed in Schedule B.

Form 941, Employer's Quarterly Federal Tax Return (Page 1)

Form **941 for 2016:** Employer's QUARTERLY Federal Tax Return	950114

(Rev. January 2016) Department of the Treasury — Internal Revenue Service

OMB No. 1545-0029

Employer identification number (EIN) 8 4 – 0 1 2 3 4 5 6

Name (not your trade name) Norrona Software

Trade name (if any)

Address 123 Main Street
Number Street Suite or room number

Anywhere CO 80111
City State ZIP code

Foreign country name Foreign province/county Foreign postal code

Report for this Quarter of 2016
(Check one.)

[X] 1: January, February, March

[ ] 2: April, May, June

[ ] 3: July, August, September

[ ] 4: October, November, December

Instructions and prior year forms are available at www.irs.gov/form941.

Read the separate instructions before you complete Form 941. Type or print within the boxes.

Part 1: Answer these questions for this quarter.

1 Number of employees who received wages, tips, or other compensation for the pay period including: Mar. 12 (Quarter 1), June 12 (Quarter 2), Sept. 12 (Quarter 3), or Dec. 12 (Quarter 4) ... 1 | 28

2 Wages, tips, and other compensation . . . . 2 | 284000 . 00

3 Federal income tax withheld from wages, tips, and other compensation . . . . . 3 | 28400 . 00

4 If no wages, tips, and other compensation are subject to social security or Medicare tax [ ] Check and go to line 6.

		Column 1		Column 2	
5a	Taxable social security wages . .	284000 . 00	× .124 =	29536 . 00	
5b	Taxable social security tips . . .	.	× .124 =	.	
5c	Taxable Medicare wages & tips.	284000 . 00	× .029 =	8236 . 00	
5d	Taxable wages & tips subject to Additional Medicare Tax withholding	.	× .009 =	.	

5e Add Column 2 from lines 5a, 5b, 5c, and 5d . . . . 5e | 37772 . 00

5f Section 3121(q) Notice and Demand—Tax due on unreported tips (see instructions) . . 5f | .

6 Total taxes before adjustments. Add lines 3, 5e, and 5f . . . . 6 | 66172 . 00

7 Current quarter's adjustment for fractions of cents . . . . 7 | .

8 Current quarter's adjustment for sick pay . . . . 8 | .

9 Current quarter's adjustments for tips and group-term life insurance . . . 9 | .

10 Total taxes after adjustments. Combine lines 6 through 9 . . . . . . 10 | 66172 . 00

11 Total deposits for this quarter, including overpayment applied from a prior quarter and overpayments applied from Form 941-X, 941-X (PR), 944-X, or 944-X (SP) filed in the current quarter . . . . 11 | 66172 . 00

12 Balance due. If line 10 is more than line 11, enter the difference and see instructions . . . 12 | .

13 Overpayment. If line 11 is more than line 10, enter the difference | . | Check one: [ ] Apply to next return. [ ] Send a refund.

▶ You MUST complete both pages of Form 941 and SIGN it.

Next ▶

Form 941, Employer's Quarterly Federal Tax Return (Page 2)

Name (not your trade name)	Employer identification number (EIN)
Norrona Software	84-0123456

Part 2: Tell us about your deposit schedule and tax liability for this quarter.

If you are unsure about whether you are a monthly schedule depositor or a semiweekly schedule depositor, see section 11 of Pub. 15.

14 Check one:
☐ Line 10 on this return is less than $2,500 or line 10 on the return for the prior quarter was less than $2,500, and you did not incur a $100,000 next-day deposit obligation during the current quarter. If line 10 for the prior quarter was less than $2,500 but line 10 on this return is $100,000 or more, you must provide a record of your federal tax liability. If you are a monthly schedule depositor, complete the deposit schedule below; if you are a semiweekly schedule depositor, attach Schedule B (Form 941). Go to Part 3.

☐ **You were a monthly schedule depositor for the entire quarter.** Enter your tax liability for each month and total liability for the quarter, then go to Part 3.

Tax liability:	Month 1	.
	Month 2	.
	Month 3	.
Total liability for quarter		.	Total must equal line 10.

☐ **You were a semiweekly schedule depositor for any part of this quarter.** Complete Schedule B (Form 941), Report of Tax Liability for Semiweekly Schedule Depositors, and attach it to Form 941.

Part 3: Tell us about your business. If a question does NOT apply to your business, leave it blank.

15 If your business has closed or you stopped paying wages . . . . ☐ Check here, and

enter the final date you paid wages [/ /] .

16 If you are a seasonal employer and you do not have to file a return for every quarter of the year . . ☐ Check here.

Part 4: May we speak with your third-party designee?

Do you want to allow an employee, a paid tax preparer, or another person to discuss this return with the IRS? See the instructions for details.

☒ Yes. Designee's name and phone number [John Smith] [303-238-1234]

Select a 5-digit Personal Identification Number (PIN) to use when talking to the IRS. ☐ ☐ ☐ ☐ ☐

☐ No.

Part 5: Sign here. You MUST complete both pages of Form 941 and SIGN it.

Under penalties of perjury, I declare that I have examined this return, including accompanying schedules and statements, and to the best of my knowledge and belief, it is true, correct, and complete. Declaration of preparer (other than taxpayer) is based on all information of which preparer has any knowledge.

X Sign your name here [ ]

| Print your name here | Arlo Jones |
| Print your title here | Controller |

Date [/ /]

Best daytime phone [303-238-1234]

Paid Preparer Use Only

Check if you are self-employed . . . ☐

Preparer's name		PTIN	
Preparer's signature		Date	/ /
Firm's name (or yours if self-employed)		EIN	
Address		Phone	
City		State		ZIP code	

Form **941** (Rev. 1-2016)

Form 941, Schedule B

Schedule B (Form 941):

Report of Tax Liability for Semiweekly Schedule Depositors

960311

(Rev. January 2014)   Department of the Treasury — Internal Revenue Service

OMB No. 1545-0029

Employer identification number (EIN): 8 4 – 0 1 2 3 4 5 6

Name (not your trade name): Norrona Software

Calendar year: 2 0 1 6   (Also check quarter)

Report for this Quarter...
(Check one.)

- [X] 1: January, February, March
- [ ] 2: April, May, June
- [ ] 3: July, August, September
- [ ] 4: October, November, December

Use this schedule to show your TAX LIABILITY for the quarter; DO NOT use it to show your deposits. When you file this form with Form 941 or Form 941-SS, DO NOT change your tax liability by adjustments reported on any Forms 941-X or 944-X. You must fill out this form and attach it to Form 941 or Form 941-SS if you are a semiweekly schedule depositor or became one because your accumulated tax liability on any day was $100,000 or more. Write your daily tax liability on the numbered space that corresponds to the date wages were paid. See Section 11 in Pub. 15 (Circular E), Employer's Tax Guide, for details.

Month 1

1		9		17		25	
2		10		18		26	
3		11		19		27	
4		12		20		28	
5		13		21		29	
6		14		22		30	
7		15	9625 . 00	23		31	9625 . 00
8		16		24			

Tax liability for Month 1: 19250 . 00

Month 2

1		9		17		25	
2		10		18		26	
3		11		19		27	
4		12		20		28	10025 . 00
5		13		21		29	
6		14		22		30	
7		15	10025 . 00	23		31	
8		16		24			

Tax liability for Month 2: 20050 . 00

Month 3

1		9		17		25	
2		10		18		26	
3		11		19		27	
4		12		20		28	
5		13		21		29	
6		14		22		30	
7		15	13436 . 00	23		31	13436 . 00
8		16		24			

Tax liability for Month 3: 26872 . 00

Fill in your total liability for the quarter (Month 1 + Month 2 + Month 3) ▶
Total must equal line 10 on Form 941 or Form 941-SS.

Total liability for the quarter: 66172 . 00

For Paperwork Reduction Act Notice, see separate instructions.   IRS.gov/form941   Cat. No. 11967Q   Schedule B (Form 941) (Rev. 1-2014)

Form 941-V, Payment Voucher

Form **941-V** Department of the Treasury Internal Revenue Service	**Payment Voucher** ▶ Don't staple this voucher or your payment to Form 941.	OMB No. 1545-0029 2016

1 Enter your employer identification number (EIN). 84-0123456	2 **Enter the amount of your payment.** ▶ Make your check or money order payable to "United States Treasury"	Dollars	Cents

3 Tax Period		4 Enter your business name (individual name if sole proprietor). Norrona Software
◉ 1st Quarter	○ 3rd Quarter	Enter your address. 123 Main Street
○ 2nd Quarter	○ 4th Quarter	Enter your city, state, and ZIP code or your city, foreign country name, foreign province/county, and foreign postal code. Anywhere, CO 80111

If a nonprofit goes out of business, file a final Form 941 return for the last quarter in which wages were paid.

If a nonprofit does not file a Form 941 in a timely manner (not including filing extensions), the IRS imposes a failure-to-file penalty of 5% of the unpaid tax due with that return, up to a maximum penalty of 25% of the tax due. In addition, for each whole month or part of a month that an organization pays late, there is an additional failure-to-pay penalty of ½% of the amount of the tax, up to a maximum of 25% of the tax due. If both penalties apply in a month, the failure-to-file penalty is reduced by the amount of the failure-to-pay penalty. The IRS may waive these penalties if one can present a reasonable cause for failing to file the Form 941 or pay the tax due.

Summary

The Form 990 is considered a key document for any nonprofit, since the information contained within it is also made available to the public, and so could play a role in the decisions of donors to contribute funds. Accordingly, be sure to allocate a significant amount of time to its completion, and review it several times to ensure that the form is properly representative of the operations of the organization. Also, post the completed form to an archives section on the nonprofit's website, and refer any inquiring parties to the archive. Doing so reduces the work associated with supplying this information to outsiders, since they can download the reports themselves.

In this chapter, we also noted the substantial amount of tax reporting associated with compensation payments to contractors and employees. For more information about the methods used to accumulate work hours, derive gross pay, and calculate income tax withholdings, refer to the latest annual edition of the author's *Payroll Management* book.

Chapter 19
Closing the Books

Introduction

The concept of closing the books refers to summarizing the information in the accounting records into the financial statements at the end of a reporting period. Many steps are required to do so. In this chapter, we give an overview of closing journal entries and the most prevalent closing activities that a nonprofit is likely to need.

The closing process does not begin *after* a reporting period has been completed. Instead, the accounting staff should be preparing for it well in advance. By doing so, the department can complete a number of activities in a leisurely manner before the end of the month, leaving fewer items for the busier period immediately following the end of the period. Accordingly, we have grouped closing steps into the following categories:

1. *Prior closing steps*. These are the steps needed to complete the processing of the financial statements, and which can usually be completed before the end of the reporting period.
2. *Core closing steps*. These are the steps required for the creation of financial statements, and which cannot be completed prior to the end of the reporting period.
3. *Delayed closing steps*. These are the activities that can be safely delayed until after the issuance of the financial statements, but which are still part of the closing process.

The sections in this chapter do not necessarily represent the exact sequence of activities that a nonprofit should follow when closing the books; one can alter the sequence based on the unique processes of an organization, and the availability of employees to work on them.

> **Related Podcast Episodes:** Episodes 16 through 25 and 160 of the Accounting Best Practices Podcast discuss closing the books. The episodes are available at: **accountingtools.com/podcasts** or **iTunes**

Journal Entries

An important part of the closing process is the use of journal entries to refine the reported financial results. In this section, we discuss various aspects of journal entries – the accruals concept, adjusting entries, reversing entries, and closing entries.

The Accruals Concept

An *accrual* allows one to record expenses and revenues for which a nonprofit expects to expend cash or receive cash, respectively, in a future reporting period. The offset to an accrued expense is an accrued liability account, which appears in the statement of financial position. The offset to accrued revenue is an accrued asset account (such as unbilled fees), which also appears in the statement of financial position. Examples of accruals are:

- *Revenue accrual.* A nonprofit's employees work billable hours on a project that it will eventually invoice for $5,000. It can record an accrual in the current period so that its current statement of activities shows $5,000 of revenue, even though it has not yet billed the recipient.
- *Expense accrual – interest.* An organization has a loan with the local bank for $1 million, and pays interest on the loan at a variable rate of interest. The invoice from the bank for $3,000 in interest expense does not arrive until the following month, so the nonprofit accrues the expense in order to show the amount on its statement of activities in the proper month.
- *Expense accrual – wages.* A nonprofit pays its employees at the end of each month for their hours worked through the 25th day of the month. To fully record the wage expense for the entire month, it also accrues $32,000 in additional wages, which represents the cost of wages for the remaining days of the month.

Most accruals are initially created as reversing entries, so that the accounting software automatically cancels them in the following month. This happens when revenue is expected to be billed, or supplier invoices to actually arrive, in the next month. The concept is addressed later in the Reversing Entries sub-section.

Adjusting Entries

Adjusting entries are journal entries that are used at the end of an accounting period to adjust the balances in various general ledger accounts to more closely align the reported results and financial position of a business to meet the requirements of an accounting framework, such as GAAP or International Financial Reporting Standards (IFRS).

An adjusting entry can be used for any type of accounting transaction; here are some of the more common ones:

- To record depreciation and amortization for the period
- To record an allowance for doubtful accounts
- To record accrued revenue
- To record accrued expenses
- To record previously paid but unused expenditures as prepaid expenses
- To adjust cash balances for any reconciling items noted in the bank reconciliation

Adjusting entries are most commonly of three types, which are:

- *Accruals*. To record a revenue or expense that has not yet been recorded through a standard accounting transaction.
- *Deferrals*. To defer a revenue or expense that has occurred, but which has not yet been earned or used.
- *Estimates*. To estimate the amount of a reserve, such as the allowance for doubtful accounts.

When a journal entry is recorded for an accrual, deferral, or estimate, it usually impacts an asset or liability account. For example, if an expense is accrued, this also increases a liability account. Or, if revenue recognition is deferred to a later period, this also increases a liability account. Thus, adjusting entries impact the statement of financial position, not just the statement of activities.

Reversing Entries

When a journal entry is created, it may be to record revenue or an expense other than through a more traditional method, such as issuing an invoice to a donor or recording an invoice from a supplier. In these situations, the journal entry is only meant to be a stopgap measure, with the traditional recordation method still being used at a later date. This means that the accounting department has to eventually create a journal entry that is the *opposite* of the original entry, thereby cancelling out the original entry. The concept is best explained with an example.

EXAMPLE

The controller of Archimedes Education has not yet received an invoice from a key supplier of training materials by the time he closes the books for the month of May. He expects that the invoice will be for $20,000, so he records the following accrual entry for the invoice:

	Debit	Credit
Training materials (expense)	20,000	
Accrued expenses (liability)		20,000

This entry creates an additional expense of $20,000 for the month of May.

The controller knows that the invoice will arrive in June and will be recorded upon receipt. Therefore, he creates a reversing entry for the original accrual in early June that cancels out the original entry. The entry is:

	Debit	Credit
Accrued expenses (liability)	20,000	
Training materials (expense)		20,000

The invoice then arrives, and is recorded in the normal manner through the accounts payable module in Archimedes' accounting software. This creates an expense during the month of June of $20,000. Thus, the net effect in June is:

June reversing entry	-$20,000
Supplier invoice	+20,000
Net effect in June	$0

Thus, the accrual entry shifts recognition of the expense from June to May.

Any accounting software package contains an option for automatically creating a reversing journal entry when a journal entry is initially set up. Always use this feature when a reversing entry will be needed. By doing so, one can avoid the risk of forgetting to manually create the reversing entry, and also avoid the risk of creating an incorrect entry.

Tip: There will be situations where there is not an expectation to reverse a journal entry for a few months. If so, consider using an automated reversing entry in the *next* month, and creating a replacement journal entry in each successive month. While this approach may appear time-consuming, it ensures that the original entry is *always* flushed from the books, thereby avoiding the risk of carrying a journal entry past the date when it should have been eliminated.

Common Adjusting Entries

This section contains a discussion of the journal entries that a nonprofit is most likely to need to close the books, along with an example of the accounts most likely to be used in the entries.

Depreciation

This entry is used to gradually charge the investment in fixed assets to expense over the useful lives of those assets. The amount of depreciation is calculated from a spreadsheet or fixed asset software, and is based on a systematic method for spreading recognition of the expense over multiple periods. If the election is made to charge the entire depreciation expense in a lump sum to a single account, the entry is:

	Debit	Credit
Depreciation expense	xxx	
Accumulated depreciation		xxx

In this entry, the accumulated depreciation account is a contra asset account, which means that it carries a negative balance that offsets a related asset account (in this case, the fixed assets account on the statement of financial position).

A more common approach is to charge the depreciation expense to individual departments or programs, based on their usage of fixed assets. This entry increases the number of depreciation line items, though there is no need to make a similar allocation of accumulated depreciation among different accounts. An example of this format is:

	Debit	Credit
Depreciation – Management and administration	xxx	
Depreciation – Fundraising	xxx	
Depreciation – Program A	xxx	
Depreciation – Program B	xxx	
Accumulated depreciation		xxx

If a nonprofit also has intangible assets recorded in the accounting records, charge them to expense over their useful lives. The entry is identical to the depreciation entry, except that we substitute the word "amortization" for "depreciation." A sample entry is:

	Debit	Credit
Amortization expense	xxx	
Accumulated amortization		xxx

It is less necessary to charge amortization expense to individual departments or programs, since it is not always easy to trace the usage of a specific intangible asset. Instead, it is more commonly charged to the management and administration function.

Allowance for Doubtful Accounts

If a nonprofit sells services on credit or accepts commitments for future donations, there is a strong likelihood that a portion of the resulting accounts receivable will eventually become bad debts. If so, update the allowance for doubtful accounts each month. This account is a contra asset account that offsets the balance in the accounts receivable account. Set the balance in this allowance to match the best estimate of how much of the month-end accounts receivable will eventually be written off as bad debts. A sample entry is:

	Debit	Credit
Bad debts expense	xxx	
Allowance for doubt accounts		xxx

Accrued Revenue

If an organization has engaged in work for a client but has not yet billed the client, it may be possible to recognize some or all of the revenue associated with the work performed to date. The offset to the revenue is a debit to an accrued accounts receivable account. Do not record this accrual in the standard trade accounts receivable account, since that account should be reserved for actual billings to clients. A sample of the accrued revenue entry is:

	Debit	Credit
Accounts receivable – accrued	xxx	
Sales		xxx

It is also possible for the reverse situation to arise, where a customer is invoiced in advance of completing work on the billed items. In this case, *reduce* recorded sales by the amount of unearned revenue by crediting an unearned sales (liability) account. A sample entry is:

	Debit	Credit
Sales	xxx	
Unearned sales (liability)		xxx

Accrued Expenses

If there are supplier invoices expected but which have not yet been received, estimate the amount of the expense and accrue it with a journal entry. There are any number of expense accounts to which such transactions might be charged; in the following sample entry, we assume that the expense relates to a supplier invoice for utilities that has not yet arrived.

	Debit	Credit
Utilities expense	xxx	
Accrued expenses (liability)		xxx

This is likely to be the most frequent of the adjusting entries, as there may be a number of supplier invoices that do not arrive by the time an organization officially closes its books.

Prepaid Assets

Occasionally, an organization will make a significant payment in advance to a third party. This advance may be for something that will be charged to expense in a later period, or it may be a deposit that will be returned at a later date. These payments should initially be recorded as assets, usually in the prepaid assets account. Situations where one may record a prepaid asset include:

- Rent paid before the month to which it applies
- Medical insurance paid before the month to which it applies
- Rent deposit, to be returned at the conclusion of a lease
- Utilities deposit, to be retained until the organization cancels service

Most of these transactions have the same journal entry, which is:

	Debit	Credit
Prepaid expenses	xxx	
Cash		xxx

The name of the debited account can vary. We use "Prepaid expenses" in the sample entry, but "Prepaid assets" is also used.

Closing Entries

Closing entries are journal entries used to flush out all temporary accounts at the end of an accounting period and transfer their balances into permanent accounts. Doing so resets the temporary accounts to begin accumulating new transactions in the next accounting period. A *temporary account* is an account used to hold balances during an accounting period for revenue, expense, gain, and loss transactions. These accounts are flushed into the net assets account at the end of an accounting period, leaving them with zero balances at the beginning of the next reporting year.

The basic sequence of closing entries is:

1. Debit all revenue accounts and credit the income summary account, thereby clearing out the revenue accounts.
2. Credit all expense accounts and debit the income summary account, thereby clearing out all expense accounts.
3. Close the income summary account to the net assets account. If there was a profit in the period, this entry is a debit to the income summary account and a credit to the net assets account. If there was a loss in the period, this entry is a credit to the income summary account and a debit to the net assets account.

The result of these activities is to move the net profit or loss for the period into the net assets account, which appears in the statement of financial position.

Since the income summary account is only a transitional account, it is also acceptable to close directly to the net assets account and bypass the income summary account entirely.

EXAMPLE

Archimedes Education is closing its books for the most recent accounting period. Archimedes had $50,000 of revenues and $45,000 of expenses during the period. For simplicity, we assume that all of the expenses were recorded in a single account; in a normal environment, there might be dozens of expense accounts to clear out. The sequence of entries is:

1. Empty the revenue account by debiting it for $50,000, and transfer the balance to the income summary account with a credit. The entry is:

	Debit	Credit
Revenue	50,000	
Income summary		50,000

2. Empty the expense account by crediting it for $45,000, and transfer the balance to the income summary account with a debit. The entry is:

	Debit	Credit
Income summary	45,000	
Expenses		45,000

3. Empty the income summary account by debiting it for $5,000, and transfer the balance to the net assets account with a credit. The entry is:

	Debit	Credit
Income summary	5,000	
Net assets		5,000

These entries have emptied the revenue, expense, and income summary accounts, and shifted the net profit for the period to the net assets account.

We should point out that a practicing accountant rarely uses any of these closing entries, since they are handled automatically by any accounting software package. Instead, the basic closing step is to access an option in the software to close the accounting period. Doing so automatically populates the net assets account and prevents any further transactions from being recorded in the system for the period that has been closed.

Prior Closing Steps: Update Reserves

If a nonprofit is using the accrual basis of accounting, create a reserve in the expectation that expenses will be incurred in the future that are related to revenues generated now. This concept is called the matching principle. Under the matching principle, record the cause and effect of a business transaction at the same time. Thus, when revenue is recorded, also record within the same accounting period any expenses directly related to that revenue. An example of this type of expense is the allowance for doubtful accounts; this allowance is used to charge to expense the amount of bad debts expected from a certain amount of sales or pledges, before there is precise knowledge of which items will not be paid.

There is no need to create a reserve if the balance in the account is going to be immaterial. Instead, many nonprofits can generate perfectly adequate financial statements that only have a few reserves, while charging all other expenditures to expense as incurred.

Core Closing Steps: Issue Customer and Donor Invoices

Part of the closing process may include the issuance of month-end invoices to customers. This may relate to program services, or perhaps to acknowledgements of pledges. Irrespective of the number of invoices to be issued, invoices are always an important part of the closing process, because they are the primary method for recognizing revenue. Consequently, a significant part of the closing process is normally spent verifying that all possible invoices have, in fact, been created.

If some revenues are considered to not yet be billable, but to have been fully earned by the organization, accrue the revenue with a journal entry.

The accounting software should have an accounts receivable module that is used to enter customer invoices. This module automatically populates the accounts receivable account in the general ledger when invoices are created. Thus, at month-end, one can print the open accounts receivable report and have the grand total on it match the ending balance in the accounts receivable general ledger account. This means that there are no reconciling items between the open accounts receivable report and the general ledger account.

If there is a difference between the two numbers, it is almost certainly caused by the use of a journal entry that debited or credited the accounts receivable account. Such a journal entry should *never* be created, because there is so much detail in the accounts receivable account that it is very time-consuming to wade through it to ascertain the source of the variance.

The primary transaction that the accounting staff will be tempted to record in the accounts receivable account is accrued revenue. Instead, create a current asset account called "Accrued Revenue Receivable" and enter the accruals in that account. By doing so, normal accounts receivable transactions are segregated from special month-end accrual transactions. Accrual transactions require special monitoring, since they may linger for several months, so keeping them in a separate account makes it easier to reconcile accounts receivable.

Core Closing Steps: Reconcile the Bank Statement

Closing cash is all about the bank reconciliation, because it matches the amount of cash recorded by the organization to what its bank has recorded. Once a bank reconciliation has been constructed, the accountant can be reasonably confident that the amount of cash appearing on the statement of financial position is correct.

A bank reconciliation is the process of matching the balances in an entity's accounting records for a cash account to the corresponding information on a bank statement, with the goal of ascertaining the differences between the two and booking changes to the accounting records as appropriate. The information on the bank statement is the bank's record of all transactions impacting the entity's bank account during the past month.

At a minimum, conduct a bank reconciliation shortly after the end of each month, when the bank sends the nonprofit a bank statement containing the bank's beginning cash balance, transactions during the month, and its ending cash balance. It is even better to conduct a bank reconciliation every day based on the bank's month-to-date information, which should be accessible on the bank's web site. By completing a daily bank reconciliation, problems can be spotted and corrected immediately.

The following bank reconciliation procedure assumes that a bank reconciliation is being constructed in an accounting software package, which makes the reconciliation process easier:

1. Enter the bank reconciliation software module. A listing of uncleared checks and uncleared deposits will appear.
2. Check off in the bank reconciliation module all checks that are listed on the bank statement as having cleared the bank.
3. Check off in the bank reconciliation module all deposits that are listed on the bank statement as having cleared the bank.
4. Enter as expenses all bank charges appearing on the bank statement, and which have not already been recorded in the nonprofit's records.
5. Enter the ending balance on the bank statement. If the book and bank balances match, post all changes recorded in the bank reconciliation, and close the module. If the balances do not match, continue reviewing the bank reconciliation for additional reconciling items. Look for the following issues:

   - Checks recorded in the bank records at a different amount from what is recorded in the nonprofit's records.
   - Deposits recorded in the bank records at a different amount from what is recorded in the nonprofit's records.
   - Checks recorded in the bank records that are not recorded at all in the nonprofit's records.
   - Deposits recorded in the bank records that are not recorded at all in the nonprofit's records.

- Inbound wire transfers from which a lifting fee has been extracted. A lifting fee is the transaction fee charged to the recipient of a wire transfer, which the recipient's bank imposes for handling the transaction. The term also applies to foreign bank processing fees, which may be applied to a variety of other financial transactions besides a wire transfer.

EXAMPLE

Archimedes Education is closing its books for the month ended April 30. Archimedes' controller must prepare a bank reconciliation based on the following issues:

1. The bank statement contains an ending bank balance of $320,000.
2. The bank statement contains a $200 check printing charge for new checks that the organization ordered.
3. The bank statement contains a $150 service charge for operating the bank account.
4. The bank rejects a deposit of $500, due to not sufficient funds, and charges Archimedes a $10 fee associated with the rejection.
5. The bank statement contains interest income of $30.
6. Archimedes issued $80,000 of checks that have not yet cleared the bank.
7. Archimedes deposited $25,000 of checks at month-end that were not deposited in time to appear on the bank statement.

Based on this information, the controller creates the following reconciliation:

	$	Item No.	Adjustment to Books
Bank balance	$320,000	1	
- Check printing charge	-200	2	Debit expense, credit cash
- Service charge	-150	3	Debit expense, credit cash
- NSF fee	-10	4	Debit expense, credit cash
- NSF deposit rejected	-500	4	Debit receivable, credit cash
+ Interest income	+30	5	Debit cash, credit interest income
- Uncleared checks	-80,000	6	None
+ Deposits in transit	+25,000	7	None
Book balance	$264,170		

There are several problems that continually arise as part of the bank reconciliation to be aware of. They are:

- *Uncleared checks that continue to not be presented.* There will be a residual number of checks that either are not presented to the bank for payment for a long time, or which are never presented for payment. In the short term, treat them in the same manner as any other uncleared checks – just keep them in the uncleared checks listing in the accounting software, so they will be an ongoing reconciling item. In the long term, contact the payee to see if they ever received the check; the accounting department will likely need to void the old check and issue them a new one.

- *Checks clear the bank after having been voided.* As just noted, if a check remains uncleared for a long time, the accountant will probably void the old check and issue a replacement check. But what if the payee then cashes the original check? If it was voided with the bank, the bank should reject the check when it is presented. If the check was not voided with the bank, record the check with a credit to the cash account and a debit to indicate the reason for the payment. If the payee has not yet cashed the replacement check, void it with the bank at once to avoid a double payment. Otherwise, it will be necessary to pursue repayment of the second check with the payee.
- *Deposited checks are returned.* There are cases where the bank will refuse to deposit a check, usually because it is drawn on a bank account located in another country. In this case, the original entry related to that deposit must be reversed, which will be a credit to the cash account to reduce the cash balance, with a corresponding debit (increase) in the accounts receivable account.

The three items noted here are relatively common; the accountant will likely have to deal with each one at least once a year.

Core Closing Steps: Calculate Depreciation

Once all fixed assets have been recorded in the accounting records for the month, calculate the amount of depreciation (for tangible assets) and amortization (for intangible assets). This is a significant issue for nonprofits with a large investment in fixed assets, but may be so insignificant in other situations that it is sufficient to only record depreciation at the end of the year.

If fixed assets are being constructed (as would be the case for a facility or nonprofit headquarters) and the organization has incurred debt to do so, it may be necessary to capitalize some interest expense into the cost of the fixed assets.

Core Closing Steps: Accounts Payable

Accounts payable can be a significant bottleneck in the closing process. The reason is that some suppliers only issue invoices at the end of each month when they are closing *their* books, so the organization will not receive their invoices until several days into the next month. This circumstance usually arises either when a supplier ships something near the end of the month or when it is providing a continuing service. There are several choices for dealing with these items:

1. *Do nothing.* If management is willing to wait a few days, the invoices will arrive in the mail, so the accountant can record the invoices and close the books. The advantage of this approach is a high degree of precision and perfect supporting evidence for all expenses. It is probably the best approach

at year-end, if the financial statements will be audited. The downside is that it can significantly delay the issuance of financial statements.

2. *Accrue continuing service items.* As just noted, suppliers providing continuing services are more likely to issue invoices at month-end. When services are being provided on a continuing basis, it is usually easy to estimate what the expense should be, based on prior invoices. Thus, it is not difficult to create reversing journal entries for these items at the end of the month. It is likely that these accruals will vary somewhat from the amounts on the actual invoices, but the differences should be immaterial.

3. *Accrue based on purchase orders.* As just noted, suppliers issue invoices at month-end when they ship goods near that date. If the nonprofit is using purchase orders to order these items, the supplier is supposed to issue an invoice containing the same price stated on the purchase order. Therefore, if an item is received at the receiving dock but there is no accompanying invoice, use the purchase order to create a reversing journal entry that accrues the expense associated with the received item.

In short, we strongly recommend using accruals to record expenses for supplier invoices that have not yet arrived. The sole exception is the end of the fiscal year, when the outside auditors may expect a greater degree of precision and supporting evidence, and will expect the accounting department to wait for actual invoices to arrive before closing the books.

The accounting software should have an accounts payable module that is used to enter supplier invoices. This module automatically populates the accounts payable account in the general ledger with transactions. Thus, at the end of the month, one can print the open accounts payable report and have the grand total on that report match the ending balance in the accounts payable general ledger account; there are no reconciling items between the open accounts payable report and the general ledger.

If there is a difference between the two numbers, it is almost certainly caused by the use of a journal entry that debited or credited the accounts payable account. Such a journal entry should *never* be created, because there is so much detail in the accounts payable account that it is very time-consuming to wade through it to ascertain the source of the variance.

The one transaction that the accounting staff will be tempted to record in the accounts payable account is the accrued expense. Instead, create a current liability account in the general ledger called "Accrued Expenses" and enter the accruals in that account. By doing so, normal accounts payable transactions are being properly segregated from special month-end accrual transactions.

This differentiation is not a minor one. Accrual transactions require more maintenance than standard accounts payable transactions, because they may linger through multiple accounting periods, and so should be monitored to know when to eliminate them from the general ledger. This problem can be addressed with reversing journal entries, but some accruals may not be designated as reversing entries, which calls for long-term tracking. If accrued expenses were to be lumped into the accounts payable account, it would be very difficult to continually monitor the outstanding accruals.

In summary, restrict the accounts payable account to standard payables transactions, which makes it extremely easy to reconcile at month-end. Any transactions related to accounts payable but which are entered via journal entries should be recorded in a separate account.

Core Closing Steps: Review Journal Entries

It is entirely possible that some journal entries were made incorrectly, in duplicate, or not at all. Print the list of standard journal entries and compare it to the actual entries made in the general ledger, just to ensure that they were entered in the general ledger correctly. Another test is to have someone review the detailed calculations supporting each journal entry, and trace them through to the actual entries in the general ledger. This second approach takes more time, but is useful for ensuring that all necessary journal entries have been made correctly.

If there is an interest in closing the books quickly, the latter approach could interfere with the speed of the close; if so, authorize this detailed review at a later date, when someone can conduct the review under less time pressure. However, any errors found can only be corrected in the *following* accounting period, since the financial statements will already have been issued.

Core Closing Steps: Reconcile Accounts

It is important to examine the contents of the statement of financial position accounts to verify that the recorded assets and liabilities are supposed to be there. It is quite possible that some items are still listed in an account that should have been flushed out of the statement a long time ago, which can be quite embarrassing if they are still on record when the auditors review the nonprofit's books at the end of the year. Here are several situations that a proper account reconciliation would have caught:

- *Prepaid assets.* A nonprofit pays $10,000 to an insurance company as an advance on its regular monthly medical insurance, and records the payment as a prepaid asset. The asset lingers on the books until year-end, when the auditors inquire about it, and the organization then charges the full amount to expense.
- *Accrued revenue.* An entity accrues revenue of $50,000 for a program services contract, but forgets to reverse the entry in the following month, when it invoices the full $50,000 to the client. This results in the double recordation of revenue, which is not spotted until year-end. The controller then reverses the accrual, thereby unexpectedly reducing revenues for the full year by $50,000.
- *Depreciation.* A nonprofit calculates the depreciation on several hundred assets with an electronic spreadsheet, which unfortunately does not track

when to stop depreciating assets. A year-end review finds that the organization charged $40,000 of excess depreciation to expense.

- *Accumulated depreciation.* A nonprofit has been disposing of its assets for years, but has never bothered to eliminate the associated accumulated depreciation from its statement of financial position. Doing so reduces both the fixed asset and accumulated depreciation accounts by 50%.
- *Accounts payable.* An entity does not compare its accounts payable detail report to the general ledger account balance, which is $8,000 lower than the detail. The auditors spot the error and require a correcting entry at year-end, so that the account balance matches the detail report.

These issues and many more are common problems encountered at year-end. To prevent the extensive embarrassment and error corrections caused by these problems, conduct account reconciliations every month for the larger accounts, and occasionally review the detail for the smaller accounts, too. The following are some of the account reconciliations to conduct, as well as the specific issues to look for:

Sample Account Reconciliation List

Account	Reconciliation Discussion
Cash	There can be a number of unrecorded checks, deposits, and bank fees that will only be spotted with a bank reconciliation. It is permissible to do a partial bank reconciliation a day or two before the close, but completely ignoring it is not a good idea.
Accounts receivable, trade	The accounts receivable detail report should match the account balance. If not, a journal entry was probably created that should be eliminated from this account.
Accounts receivable, other	This account usually includes a large proportion of accounts receivable from employees, which are probably being deducted from their paychecks over time. This is a prime source of errors, since payroll deductions may not have been properly reflected in this account.
Accrued revenue	It is good practice to reverse all accrued revenue out of this account at the beginning of every period, thereby forcing the creation of new accruals every month. Thus, if there is a residual balance in the account, it probably should not be there.
Prepaid assets	This account may contain a variety of assets that will be charged to expense in the short term, so it may require frequent reviews to ensure that items have been flushed out in a timely manner.
Fixed assets	It is quite likely that fixed assets will initially be recorded in the wrong fixed asset account, or that they are disposed of incorrectly. Reconcile the account to the fixed asset detail report at least once a quarter to spot and correct these issues.

Account	Reconciliation Discussion
Accumulated depreciation	The balance in this account may not match the fixed asset detail if accumulated depreciation was not removed from the account upon the sale or disposal of an asset. This is not a critical issue, but still warrants occasional review.
Accounts payable, trade	The accounts payable detail report should match the account balance. If not, a journal entry was probably included in the account, and the entry should be reversed.
Accrued expenses	This account can include a large number of accruals for such expenses as wages, vacations, and benefits. It is good practice to reverse all of these expenses in the month following recordation. Thus, if there is a residual balance, there may be an excess accrual still on the books.
Notes payable	The balance in this account should exactly match the account balance of the lender, barring any exceptions for in-transit payments to the lender.

The number of accounts that can be reconciled makes it clear that this is one of the larger steps involved in closing the books. Selected reconciliations can be skipped from time to time, but doing so presents the risk of an error creeping into the financial statements and not being spotted for quite a few months. Consequently, there is a significant risk of issuing inaccurate financial statements if some reconciliations are continually avoided.

Core Closing Steps: Close Subsidiary Ledgers

Depending on the type of accounting software used, it may be necessary to resolve any open issues in subsidiary ledgers, create a transaction to shift the totals in these balances to the general ledger (called *posting*), and then close the accounting periods within the subsidiary ledgers and open the next accounting period. This may involve ledgers for inventory, accounts receivable, and accounts payable.

Other accounting software systems (typically those developed more recently) do not have subsidiary ledgers, or at least use ones that do not require posting, and so are essentially invisible from the perspective of closing the books. Posting is the process of copying either summary-level or detailed entries in an accounting journal into the general ledger. Posting is needed in order to have a complete record of all accounting transactions in the general ledger. Posting may be done at any time, in batches, or at the end of an accounting period.

Core Closing Steps: Create Financial Statements

When all of the preceding steps have been completed, print the financial statements, which include the following items:

- Statement of activities
- Statement of financial position

- Statement of cash flows
- Reporting of expenses by nature and function

If the financial statements are only to be distributed internally, it may be acceptable to only issue the statement of activities and statement of financial position, and dispense with the other items just noted. Reporting to people outside of the nonprofit generally calls for issuance of the complete set of financial statements, including disclosures.

Core Closing Steps: Review Financial Statements

Once all of the preceding steps have been completed, review the financial statements for errors. There are several ways to do so, including:

- *Horizontal analysis*. Print reports that show the statement of activities, statement of financial position, and statement of cash flows for the past twelve months on a rolling basis. Track across each line item to see if there are any unusual declines or spikes in comparison to the results of prior periods, and investigate those items. This is the best review technique.
- *Budget versus actual*. Print a statement of activities or a report on expenses by nature and function that shows budgeted versus actual results, and investigate any larger variances. This is a less effective review technique, because it assumes that the budget is realistic, and also because a budget is not usually available for the statement of financial position or statement of cash flows.

There will almost always be problems with the first iteration of the financial statements. Expect to investigate and correct several items before issuing a satisfactory set of financials. To reduce the amount of time needed to review financial statement errors during the core closing period, consider doing so a few days prior to month-end; this may uncover a few errors, leaving a smaller number to investigate later on.

Core Closing Steps: Accrue Tax Liabilities

Once the financial statements have been created, there may be a need to accrue an income tax liability based on the amount of net profit or loss for those activities outside of the core mission of the organization. There are several issues to consider when creating this accrual:

- *Income tax rate*. In most countries that impose an income tax, the tax rate begins at a low level and then gradually moves up to a higher tax rate that corresponds to higher levels of income. When accruing income taxes, use the average income tax rate expected for the full year. Otherwise, the first quarter of the year will have a lower tax rate than later months, which is caused by the tax rate schedule, rather than any change in a nonprofit's operational results.

- *Losses.* If the entity has earned a taxable profit in a prior period of the year, and has now generated a loss, accrue for a tax rebate, which will offset the tax expense that was recorded earlier. Doing so creates the correct amount of tax liability when looking at year-to-date results. If there was no prior profit and no reasonable prospect of one, do not accrue for a tax rebate, since it is more likely than not that the entity will not receive the rebate.

Once the income tax liability has been accrued, print the complete set of financial statements.

Core Closing Steps: Close the Month

Once all accounting transactions have been entered in the accounting system, close the month in the accounting software. This means prohibiting any further transactions in the general ledger in the old accounting period, as well as allowing the next accounting period to accept transactions. These steps are important, so that transactions are not inadvertently entered into the wrong accounting periods.

> **Tip:** There is a risk that an accounting person might access the accounting software to re-open an accounting period to fraudulently adjust the results from a prior period. To avoid this, password-protect the relevant data entry screens in the software.

Core Closing Steps: Add Disclosures

If the nonprofit is issuing financial statements to readers other than the management team, consider adding disclosures to the basic set of financial statements. There are many disclosures required under GAAP. It is especially important to include a complete set of disclosures if the financial statements are being audited. If so, the auditors will offer advice regarding which disclosures to include. Allocate a large amount of time to the proper construction and error-checking of disclosures, for they contain a number of references to the financial statements and subsets of financial information extracted from the statements, and this information could be wrong. Thus, every time a new iteration of the financial statements is created, the disclosures must be updated.

If financial statements are being issued solely for the management team, do not include any disclosures. By avoiding them, the accounting staff can cut a significant amount of time from the closing process. Further, the management team is already well aware of how the business is run, and so presumably does not need the disclosures. If there are disclosure items that are unusual (such as violating the covenants on a loan), attach just those items to the financial statements, or note them in the cover letter that accompanies the financial statements.

Core Steps: Issue Financial Statements

The final core step in closing the books is to issue the financial statements. There are several ways to do this. If there is an interest in reducing the total time required for someone to receive the financial statements, convert the entire package to PDF documents and e-mail them to the recipients. Doing so eliminates the mail float that would otherwise be required. If a number of reports are being incorporated into the financial statement package, this may require the purchase of a document scanner.

When issuing financial statements, always print a copy for the accounting department and store it in a binder. This gives ready access to the report during the next few days, when managers from around the organization are most likely to contact the department with questions about it.

Delayed Closing Steps: Issue Invoices

From the perspective of closing the books, it is more important to formulate all customer invoices than it is to issue those invoices to customers.

Taking this delaying step can delay a nonprofit's cash flow. The problem is that a customer is supposed to pay an invoice based on pre-arranged terms that may also be stated on the invoice, so a delayed receipt of the invoice delays the corresponding payment. However, this is not necessarily the case. The terms set with customers should state that they must pay the organization following a certain number of days from the invoice date, not the date when they receive the invoices. Thus, if invoices are printed that are dated as of the last day of the month being closed and then mailed a few days later, the entity should still be paid on the usual date.

From a practical perspective, this can still be a problem, because the accounting staff of the customer typically uses the current date as the default date when it enters supplier invoices into its accounting system. If they do so, the organization will likely be paid late. Follow up with any customers that appear to be paying late for this reason, but this will likely be a continuing problem.

Delayed Closing Steps: Closing Metrics

If there is an interest in closing the books more quickly, consider tracking a small set of metrics related to the close. The objective of having these metrics is not necessarily to attain a world-class closing speed, but rather to spot the bottleneck areas of the close that are preventing a more rapid issuance of the financial statements. Thus, it is useful to have a set of metrics that delve sufficiently far into the workings of the closing process to spot the bottlenecks. An example of such metrics follows. Note that the total time required to close the books and issue financial statements is six days, but that the closing time for most of the steps needed to close the books is substantially shorter. Only the bank reconciliation metric reveals a long closing interval. Thus, this type of metric measurement and presentation allows one to quickly spot where there are opportunities to compress the closing process.

Sample Metrics Report for Closing the Books

	Day 1	Day 2	Day 3	Day 4	Day 5	Day 6
Issue financials	xxx	xxx	xxx	xxx	xxx	**Done**
Supplier invoices	xxx	**Done**				
Customer invoices	xxx	xxx	**Done**			
Accrued expenses	xxx	xxx	**Done**			
Bank reconciliation	xxx	xxx	xxx	**Done**		
Fixed assets	xxx	**Done**				
Payroll	**Done**					

Delayed Closing Steps: Document Future Closing Changes

After reviewing the closing metrics in the preceding step, the accountant will likely want to make some improvements to the closing process. It is possible to incorporate these changes into a schedule of activities for the next close, and review any resulting changes in responsibility with the accounting staff. Do this as soon after the close as possible, since this is the time when any problems with the close will be obvious, and there will be more interest in fixing them during the next close.

Even if there is a general level of satisfaction with the timing of closing activities, it is possible that one or more employees in the accounting department will be on vacation during the next close, so incorporate their absence into the plan. Further, if there are inexperienced people in the department, consider including them in peripheral closing activities, and then gradually shifting them into positions of greater responsibility within the process. Thus, from the perspective of improvements, employee absences, and training, it is important to document any changes to the next closing process.

Delayed Closing Steps: Update Closing Procedures

When first implementing a rigorous set of closing procedures, it is likely that they will not yield the expected results. Some steps may be concluded too late to feed into another step, or some activities may be assigned to the wrong employee. As these issues are gradually sorted through, the closing procedures and schedule of events can be updated. This process will require a number of iterations, after which the closing procedures will yield more satisfactory results. Further, every time the nonprofit changes its operations, the procedures should be updated again. Examples of situations that may require a change in the closing procedures are:

Situation	Impact on Closing Procedure
New accounting software	Every accounting package has a different built-in methodology for closing the books, which must be incorporated into the closing procedures.
New business transaction procedures	If other parts of the business alter their approaches to processing purchasing, program activities, and so forth, it will be necessary to adjust the closing procedures for them.
Acquisition or sale of a subsidiary	Add procedures to encompass new lines of business, while shutting down closing activities for those segments that have been disposed of.
Change in bank accounts	Different banks have different systems for providing on-line access to bank account information, which may alter the bank reconciliation procedure.

The preceding list is by no means all-encompassing. It merely illustrates the fact that the accountant should consider the impact of almost *any* change in the organization on the closing procedures. It is quite likely that at least minor tweaking will be needed every few months for even the most finely-tuned closing procedures. In particular, be wary of closing steps that are no longer needed, or whose impact on the financial statements have become so minor that their impact is immaterial; such steps clutter up the closing process and can significantly delay the issuance of financial statements.

Summary

This chapter has outlined a large number of steps that are needed to close the books. It may appear that the level of organization required to close the books in this manner is overkill. However, consider that the primary work product of the accounting department is the financial statements. If the department can establish a reputation for consistently issuing high-quality financial statements within a reasonable period of time, this will likely be the basis for the organization's view of the entire department.

There are a number of techniques available that allow a nonprofit to close its books and issue financial statements within just a few days. For a comprehensive discussion of these techniques, see the author's *Closing the Books* book.

Chapter 20
Nonprofit Budgeting

Introduction

A budget is a financial model of expected revenues and expenses. It is used as a basis of comparison, to see if actual results are tracking along with expectations. If not, management can take action to bring actual results back into line with expectations. A budget is a necessary financial control for a nonprofit, which typically operates with little room for financial shortfalls. In this chapter, we describe the basic modeling approach for revenue and expense budgets, and also other issues related to grant budgets, the frequency of budget recasting, cash forecasting, and similar topics.

> **Related Podcast Episodes:** Episodes 71, 130, and 131 of the Accounting Best Practices Podcast discuss budget model improvements, the problems with budgeting, and operating without a budget, respectively. These episodes are available at: **accountingtools.com/podcasts** or **iTunes**

The Revenue Budget

The amount of revenue that a nonprofit expects to receive during the next year drives the amount of expenditures that it can undertake during that period. This means that a reasonable method for predicting revenue is critical to a nonprofit. There are several ways to quantify predicted revenue. If an organization relies upon specific grants to generate most of its revenue, one budgeting method is to itemize expected receipts by grant, as noted in the following exhibit.

Budgeting can be especially difficult for a nonprofit when it is uncertain of the sources of support that it will need in the upcoming budget period. If so, one option is to create a Resource Development line item, which is used to budget for sources of support that are not yet apparent. This subcategory is shown in the following exhibit, where resource development comprises the bulk of all budgeted revenue.

Sample Revenue Budget by Grant

Contract	Quarter 1	Quarter 2	Quarter 3	Quarter 4
Existing Grants:				
HHS #01327	$175,000	$175,000	$25,000	$--
HHS #AC124	460,000	460,000	460,000	25,000
HHS #BG0047	260,000	280,000	280,000	260,000
Subtotal	$895,000	$915,000	$765,000	$285,000
Resource Development:				
DOA Farm Analysis	$--	$--	$150,000	$300,000
BLM Lease Analysis	--	210,000	600,000	550,000
NGS Survey Review	10,000	80,000	80,000	100,000
Subtotal	$10,000	$290,000	$830,000	$950,000
Totals	$905,000	$1,205,000	$1,595,000	$1,235,000

If a nonprofit runs one or more programs, an alternative is to itemize expected revenues by program, with additional detail located in a supporting schedule. An example for several programs follows.

Sample Program Revenue Budget

	Quarter 1	Quarter 2	Quarter 3	Quarter 4
Program A revenue	$905,000	$1,205,000	$1,595,000	$1,235,000
Program B revenue	880,000	920,000	1,115,000	970,000
Totals	$1,785,000	$2,125,000	$2,710,000	$2,205,000

Or, if a large amount of revenue comes from individual donors, it can make sense to itemize expected receipts from the largest donors, and then cluster all smaller expected donations into a single line item. Doing so focuses attention on contacting the largest existing donors to maintain high levels of contact, thereby improving the odds of receiving a continuing stream of donations from them. The following sample exhibit illustrates the layout of this format. Note that the individual donors listing is in order by size of expected donations, so the most attention is paid to those at the top of the list.

Sample Donor Revenue Budget

	Quarter 1	Quarter 2	Quarter 3	Quarter 4
Smith, Donald	$55,000	$-	$10,000	$45,000
Arbuckle, Mary	38,000	25,000	15,000	5,000
Davis, Eduardo	50,000	-	-	-
Emery, Francis	-	24,000	-	24,000
Bingo, Marco	-	-	40,000	-
McKenzie, Elwood	7,000	7,000	7,000	7,000
Druthers, Kinsey	-	25,000	-	-
All other donors	70,000	35,000	60,000	85,000
Totals	$220,000	$116,000	$132,000	$166,000

If a nonprofit earns revenues from several or all of the sources just described, it can make sense to derive a master revenue budget that aggregates all of the various revenue sources, with each source summarized in a single line item. For example, the following exhibit aggregates all of the revenue totals from the preceding sample exhibits.

Sample Master Revenue Budget

	Quarter 1	Quarter 2	Quarter 3	Quarter 4
Contract revenue	$905,000	$1,205,000	$1,595,000	$1,235,000
Program revenue	1,785,000	2,125,000	2,710,000	2,205,000
Donor revenue	220,000	116,000	132,000	166,000
Totals	$2,910,000	$3,446,000	$4,437,000	$3,606,000

There can be a large amount of uncertainty in the projected revenue figures. If so, consider conducting a periodic recasting of the budget to see if the projections have changed, and altering expenditures to be in proper alignment with expected revenues.

The Management and Administration Budget

The management and administration budget contains those expenses attributable to a variety of support functions, including accounting, treasury, human resources, and general management. It also includes expenses that are not easily allocated elsewhere, such as the cost of directors and officers insurance. When creating this budget, consider the following issues:

- *Compensation*. The largest item in this budget is usually employee compensation, so pay particular attention to the formulation of this amount and test it for reasonableness. See the Compensation Budget section for more information.

- *Historical basis.* The amounts in this budget are frequently carried forward from actual results in the preceding year. This may be reasonable, but some costs may disappear due to changes in the structure of the organization, or increase due to contractually scheduled price increases. Be sure to verify these items.
- *Step costs.* Determine when any step costs may be incurred, such as additional staff to support reporting requirements for new grants, and incorporate them into the budget.
- *Zero-base analysis.* It may be useful to occasionally re-create this budget from the ground up, justifying the need for each expense. This is a time-consuming process, but may uncover a few expense items that can be eliminated.

The following example illustrates the basic layout of a management and administration budget.

EXAMPLE

Newton Education compiles the following management and administration budget, which is organized by expense line item:

	Quarter 1	Quarter 2	Quarter 3	Quarter 4
Audit fees	$35,000	$0	$0	$0
Bank fees	500	500	500	500
Insurance	5,000	5,500	6,000	6,000
Payroll taxes	10,000	10,500	10,500	11,000
Property taxes	0	25,000	0	0
Rent	11,000	11,000	11,000	14,000
Salaries	140,000	142,000	144,000	146,000
Supplies	2,000	2,000	2,000	2,000
Travel and entertainment	4,500	8,000	4,000	4,000
Utilities	2,500	3,000	3,000	4,000
Other expenses	1,500	1,500	1,500	2,000
Total expenses	$212,000	$209,000	$182,500	$189,500

The preceding example reveals a common characteristic of most line items in the management and administration budget, which is that most costs are fixed over the short term, and so only vary slightly from period to period. The exceptions are pay increases and scheduled events, such as audits. Otherwise, the main reason for a sudden change in an expense is a step cost, such as increasing the headcount.

If these costs are simply carried forward into the budget from the previous year, it will be difficult to tell if the organization is being efficient in its expenditures. To find out, consider separating the management and administration costs into their constituent parts, such as the cost of the accounting, treasury, and human resources departments, and calculate each of these costs as a percentage of total revenues. Then compare these percentages to the industry average or a best-in-class benchmark. The comparison may reveal that some parts of this budget are operating at excessively high cost levels.

The Fundraising Budget

The fundraising budget contains somewhat different expense line items than are usually found in the management and administration budget. There is a greater emphasis on compensation, advertising, and travel expenditures. An example of this budget format follows.

Fundraising Budget by Expense Type

Expense Type	Quarter 1	Quarter 2	Quarter 3	Quarter 4
Salaries and wages	$270,000	$275,000	$320,000	$380,000
Payroll taxes	22,000	27,000	35,000	41,000
Promotions	0	50,000	85,000	42,000
Advertising	20,000	22,000	22,000	28,000
Grant research	0	0	35,000	0
Travel and entertainment	40,000	20,000	80,000	70,000
Office expenses	15,000	15,000	21,000	21,000
Other	5,000	5,000	5,000	5,000
Totals	$382,000	$484,000	$723,000	$727,000

When reviewing the fundraising budget, there are several areas that call for detailed analysis. The first is the relationship between the expenditures *for* the fundraising staff and corresponding revenues generated *by* that staff. Consider the following factors when deciding whether this expenditure is reasonable:

- *Historical trend.* If the fundraising staff has historically been able to generate a certain amount of contributions per person, it should be quite difficult for them to exceed this productivity level in the new budget year, so be wary of large presumed productivity increases.
- *Diminishing returns.* It is increasingly difficult to extract more donations from existing target groups, so question such revenue increases where the related expenses do not increase to an even greater extent.

The second area to investigate is the justification for promotional expenditures. The fundraising staff should provide an analysis of the estimated number of target contributors reached, and the conversion rate for those contributors. This is a difficult analysis area, since projections are difficult to verify.

Program and Grant Budgets

A program generates its own revenue and incurs its own expenses, so the budget for it looks just like the statement of activities; there are one or more revenue line items, which are offset by a set of expected expenses. We do not provide a sample budget for a program, since the types of revenues and expenses incurred will vary substantially by program. However, the general budget format already shown for the management and administration budget will serve for a program, with the addition of revenues.

When a government issues a grant to a nonprofit, there is usually an expectation that the nonprofit will formulate a budget for the funds to be spent. This budget is then loaded into the grants tracking module of the accounting software, and is used as a monitoring tool for funds expended against specific grants.

It is especially difficult to allocate expenses to grants, since some (such as staff time) may involve several different grants or other activities. If there is not a consistent or logical basis of allocation for these expenditures, it is quite likely that, over time, the amounts charged against grant budgets will not be supportable. This can be a significant problem when grant expenditures are audited. Consequently, the accounting staff needs to spend an especially large amount of time examining budget-versus-actual reports for grants, to ensure that allocations were correctly assigned to each grant.

The Compensation Budget

A key component of any budget is the derivation of the compensation to be paid to employees. It is not usually itemized as a separate budget. Instead, it is integrated into the various departmental and program budgets, so that managers can more easily see the compensation information pertaining to their areas of responsibility. We have segregated it in this section in order to delve into the various technical aspects of its construction.

The Compensation Budget

The key goals of a compensation budget are to itemize the pay rates of all employees, the dates on which their pay is expected to be altered, and all associated payroll taxes. Bonus payments and their associated payroll taxes are generally handled separately, or may not be included in the budget at all if it is unlikely that employees will earn them.

The compensation budget in the following example separates the calculation of compensation, social security taxes, Medicare taxes, and unemployment taxes. The separate calculation of these items is the only way to achieve a reasonable level of accuracy in the calculation of payroll taxes, since there are different tax rates and wage caps associated with each of the taxes. A wage cap is the maximum amount of annual compensation subject to a tax. The pertinent information related to each of the indicated payroll taxes is:

Tax Type	Tax Rate	2017 Wage Cap
Social security	6.20%	$127,200
Medicare	1.45%	No cap
Unemployment	Varies by state	Varies by state

In a lower-wage environment, there may be few employees whose pay exceeds the social security wage cap, which makes the social security tax budget quite simple to calculate. However, in situations where compensation levels are quite high, expect to meet social security wage caps within the first two or three quarters of the year. Given the size of the social security match paid by employers, it is especially important to budget for the correct amount of tax; otherwise, the compensation budget could be inaccurate by a significant amount.

The simplest of the tax calculations is for the Medicare tax, since there is no wage cap for it. We have presented its calculation in the following example as a table in which we calculate it for each individual employee. However, given the lack of a wage cap, a budget for it can be more easily created with a single line item that multiplies total compensation in every budget period by the Medicare tax rate.

A 501(c)(3) nonprofit does not have to pay the federal unemployment tax, which is quite a small amount. However, these nonprofits must pay either the state unemployment tax or directly reimburse the state for any unemployment claims made – which can be a substantial amount. Given the risk that an employee layoff can trigger a large amount of unemployment reimbursement, we strongly recommend that these nonprofits elect to pay the unemployment rate assigned to them by the state, thereby making it easier to plan for the expense.

These concepts are noted in the following example, where we present separate budgets for base pay, social security, Medicare, and state unemployment taxes, and then aggregate them into a master compensation budget.

EXAMPLE

Newton Education is starting up a small group that will create advanced physics classes for high school students. The board of directors decides to create a separate compensation budget for the group, which includes five employees. Pay levels are high, given the advanced nature of the subject matter. The compensation budget is as follows, with quarters in which pay raises are scheduled being highlighted. Note that the annual salary is stated in each calendar quarter.

Base Pay Budget

	Quarter 1	Quarter 2	Quarter 3	Quarter 4
Erskin, Donald	$75,000	$75,000	$79,500	$79,500
Fells, Arnold	45,000	46,250	46,250	46,250
Gainsborough, Amy	88,000	88,000	88,000	91,500
Harmon, Debra	68,500	68,500	70,000	70,000
Illescu, Adriana	125,000	125,000	125,000	125,000
Annual compensation	$401,500	$402,750	$408,750	$412,250
Quarterly compensation	$100,375	$100,688	$102,188	$103,063

Social Security Budget (6.2% tax, $127,200 wage cap as of 2017)

	Quarter 1	Quarter 2	Quarter 3	Quarter 4
Erskin, Donald	$1,163	$1,163	$1,232	$1,232
Fells, Arnold	698	717	717	717
Gaisborough, Amy	1,364	1,364	1,364	1,418
Harmon, Debra	1,062	1,062	1,085	1,085
Illescu, Adriana	1,938	1,938	1,938	1,938
Totals	$6,225	$6,244	$6,336	$6,390

Medicare Budget (1.45% tax, no wage cap)

	Quarter 1	Quarter 2	Quarter 3	Quarter 4
Erskin, Donald	$272	$272	$288	$288
Fells, Arnold	163	168	168	168
Gaisborough, Amy	319	319	319	332
Harmon, Debra	248	248	254	254
Illescu, Adriana	453	453	453	453
Totals	$1,455	$1,460	$1,482	$1,495

State Unemployment Tax Budget (3.5% tax, $10,000 wage cap)

	Quarter 1	Quarter 2	Quarter 3	Quarter 4
Erskin, Donald	$350	$0	$0	$0
Fells, Arnold	350	0	0	0
Gaisborough, Amy	350	0	0	0
Harmon, Debra	350	0	0	0
Illescu, Adriana	350	0	0	0
Totals	$1,750	$0	$0	$0

Newton then shifts the summary totals from each of the preceding tables into a master compensation budget, as follows:

Master Compensation Budget

	Quarter 1	Quarter 2	Quarter 3	Quarter 4
Total base pay	$100,375	$100,688	$102,188	$103,063
Total social security	6,225	6,244	6,336	6,390
Total Medicare	1,455	1,460	1,482	1,495
Total unemployment	1,750	0	0	0
Grand totals	$109,805	$108,392	$110,006	$110,948

In the preceding example, compensation is shown in each quarter on an annualized basis, since it is easier to review the budget for errors when the information is presented in this manner. The information is then stepped down to a quarterly basis, which is used to calculate taxes in the tax budgets.

In the model, any change in pay is assumed to occur as of the first day of an accounting period. If this is not the case, listing the full amount of the revised compensation level will result in an excessively high budgeted compensation in that period. This may be a minor issue if the amount of compensation changes is small. Alternatively, enter a reduced amount of pay change in that period and the full amount of the change in compensation in the next period.

Treatment of Hourly Pay and Overtime

In the preceding example, we assumed that all employees were paid salaries. In environments where employees are paid an hourly wage, the format of the budget can be altered to instead list the hourly pay rate for each employee and then multiply it by the standard number of working hours in the year to arrive at annual compensation. This is useful when hourly rate information should be verified against payroll records. However, we recommend itemizing pay based on an annual rate of pay, rather than an hourly rate of pay, because employees may be expected to work more or fewer hours than the standard number of hours in a year. Doing so also creates more consistency within the budget model, so that the compensation of both salaried and hourly employees is presented in terms of their annual compensation.

Overtime is difficult to predict at the level of an individual employee, but can be estimated at a more aggregated level. It is easiest to use the historical proportion of overtime hours, adjusted for expectations in the budget period. This means that an overtime percentage can be multiplied by the aggregate amount of employee compensation to derive the amount of budgeted overtime pay. The following example illustrates the concept.

EXAMPLE

Newton Education operates a production line for physics training manuals that is only operated for part of the year. Newton prefers to deactivate the production line for the first half of the calendar year and then run it with substantial employee overtime during the third quarter and a portion of the fourth quarter of the year. This results in the following overtime budget, which also assumes that a production crew is still working during the first half of the year – they just happen to be working on other publications.

	Quarter 1	Quarter 2	Quarter 3	Quarter 4
Total wage expense	$250,000	$255,000	$270,000	$240,000
Overtime percentage	0%	2%	28%	12%
Overtime pay	$0	$5,100	$75,600	$28,800
Social security for overtime pay	$0	$316	$4,687	$1,786
Medicare for overtime pay	0	$74	$1,096	$418
Total overtime compensation	$0	$390	$5,783	$2,204

The trouble with the overtime calculation format just presented is that it does not account for the social security wage cap, which is calculated at the level of the individual employee. It is easiest to simply assume that the wage cap is never reached, which may result in some excess amount of social security tax being budgeted. Realistically, few employees who are paid on an hourly basis will exceed the wage cap, so this should be a minor issue for most nonprofits.

The Benefits Budget

A key part of employee compensation is the benefits paid to each employee, since benefits can comprise a large part of total compensation. Budgeting for benefits can be a problem under the following combination of circumstances:

- The organization-paid portion is significant; and
- The amount of the expense varies based on the number of dependents covered by the benefits; and
- Employees may opt into or out of the coverage.

If a nonprofit is faced with this much variability, it may be necessary to create the benefits budget with line items for each employee. However, if there are many benefits, this can result in an inordinately large budget that is difficult to update.

An alternative approach is to avoid compiling the benefits budget at the level of the individual employee. Instead, create a moderate level of detail for those few benefits that cost the most (usually medical insurance), and aggregate the cost of all other benefits in a few line items. This approach is easy to maintain and provides a reasonably accurate picture of benefit expenses. The following example illustrates the concept.

EXAMPLE

The controller of Newton Education is compiling the budgeted amount of benefits for the management and administration staff. This budget provides additional detail for medical insurance, since it is the key benefit provided by the organization, and the amount of the expense varies markedly, depending on the number of dependents. The cost of dental and life insurance is much lower, so these expenses are only shown in aggregate, and based on total headcount. The calculation of the total amount of 403(b) pension matching is based on the following factors:

- 85% of the staff will enroll in the pension plan
- Newton will match employee pension deductions up to a maximum of $3,000 per year
- Newton's payment of the pension match will be distributed over the four quarters in proportions of 35%, 25% 20%, and 20%. This distribution is based on some employees having more than $3,000 deducted from their pay, so that the pension match is completed earlier in the year for those employees.

	Quarter 1	Quarter 2	Quarter 3	Quarter 4
Total management and administration compensation	$705,000	$726,000	$767,000	$767,000
Medical insurance headcount:				
Single coverage	12	12	14	14
Married coverage	17	16	16	16
Family coverage	5	7	7	7
No coverage	10	10	10	10
Total headcount	44	45	47	47
Medical insurance employer cost				
Single coverage ($1,050/qtr each)	$12,600	$12,600	$14,700	$14,700
Married coverage ($1,575/qtr each)	26,775	25,200	25,200	25,200
Family coverage ($2,500/qtr each)	12,500	17,500	17,500	17,500
Total medical employer cost	$51,875	$55,300	$57,400	$57,400
Total employer dental expense	$9,250	$9,500	$10,000	$10,000
Total employer life insurance expense	2,380	2,450	2,590	2,590

	Quarter 1	Quarter 2	Quarter 3	Quarter 4
403(b) pension assumptions:				
Proportion enrolled in pension plan	85%	85%	85%	85%
Matching cap	$3,000	$3,000	$3,000	$3,000
Matching distribution	35%	25%	20%	20%
403(b) pension matching*	$39,270	$28,688	$23,970	$23,970
Total benefits expense	$102,775	$95,938	$93,960	$93,960

* Calculated as the quarterly total headcount × proportion enrolled in the pension plan × matching cap × matching distribution percentage

Budget Recasting

Nonprofits typically have reduced financial resources, and so must be extremely careful in spending cash. This means that a nonprofit manager may need to continually recast the budget, perhaps on a monthly basis, to ensure that planned expenditures are closely adhering to the most recent forecast of cash inflows. If a manager were to instead allow expenses to follow the budget for several months in a row without paying attention to contributions and other sources of cash, it is quite possible that a nonprofit could find itself out of business in short order.

This recasting issue is particularly common in the area of government grants. A nonprofit typically creates a budget for each government grant, so that it knows exactly how much it can spend in relation to the grant amounts that it expects to receive. However, governments have issues with their own funding, so the amounts that a nonprofit is paid may vary considerably from initial expectations. Alternatively, the government may mandate that the uses to which funds are to be put will be altered. For both of these reasons, it is relatively common for grant-related budgets to be adjusted throughout the year.

Budget Linkages

A budget is only useful to a nonprofit if it is matched against actual expenditures in the financial statements. This means that the statement of activities and/or a report on expenses by nature and function should contain an additional column that shows the available year-to-date budget next to actual expenditures, as well as a variance column. Management uses these reports to verify how well actual expenditures are tracking against the plan.

For a greater level of control, consider having the purchasing staff review the amount of available budgeted funding before issuing any purchase orders. Doing so is a more effective way to manage expenditures than a budget-versus-actual financial statement, since the purchasing staff can prevent expenditures from occurring in the first place. For this approach to work, the purchasing staff must have access to a report that subtracts actual expenditures to-date from the budget, thereby revealing the amount of budgeted funds that are still available for use.

Cash Forecasting

The executive director needs to know the amount of cash that will probably be on hand in the near future, in order to make fundraising and expense reduction decisions. This is accomplished with a cash forecast, which should be sufficiently detailed to inform management of projected cash shortfalls and excess funds on at least a weekly basis. This section covers the details of how to create and fine-tune a cash forecast.

Related Podcast Episode: Episode 187 of the Accounting Best Practices Podcast discusses cash forecasting accuracy. The episode is available at: **accounting-tools.com/podcasts** or **iTunes**

The cash forecast can be divided into two parts: near-term cash flows that are highly predictable (typically covering a one-month period) and medium-term cash flows that are largely based on revenues that have not yet occurred and supplier invoices that have not yet arrived. The first part of the forecast can be quite accurate, while the second part yields increasingly tenuous results after not much more than a month has passed. It is also possible to create a long-term cash forecast that is essentially a modified version of the entity's budget, though its utility is relatively low. The following exhibit shows the severity of the decline in accuracy for short-term and medium-term forecasts. In particular, there is an immediate decline in accuracy as soon as the medium-term forecast replaces the short-term forecast, since less reliable information is used in the medium-term forecast.

Variability of Actual from Forecasted Cash Flow Information

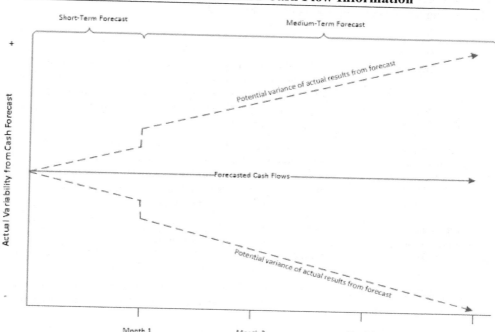

Through the remainder of this section, we will deal separately with how to construct the short-term and medium-term portions of the cash forecast.

The Short-Term Cash Forecast

The short-term cash forecast is based on a detailed accumulation of information from a variety of sources within the organization. The bulk of this information comes from the accounts receivable, accounts payable, and payroll records. Since this forecast is based on detailed itemizations of cash inflows and outflows, it is sometimes called the *receipts and disbursements method*.

The forecast needs to be sufficiently detailed to create an accurate cash forecast, but not so detailed that it requires an inordinate amount of labor to update. Consequently, include a detailed analysis of only the *largest* receipts and expenditures, and aggregate all other items. The detailed analysis involves the manual prediction of selected cash receipts and expenditures, while the aggregated results are scheduled based on average dates of receipt and payment.

Tip: Use detailed analysis of cash items in the cash forecast for the 20% of items that comprise 80% of the cash flows, and aggregate the remaining 80% of items that comprise 20% of the cash flows.

256

The following table notes the treatment of the key line items in a cash forecast, including the level of detailed forecasting required.

+/-	Line Item	Discussion
+	Beginning cash	This is the current cash balance as of the creation date of the cash forecast, or, for subsequent weeks, it is the ending cash balance from the preceding week. Do not include restricted cash in this number, since this cash may not be available to pay for expenditures.
+	Accounts receivable and pledges	Do not attempt to duplicate the detail of the aged accounts receivable report in this section of the forecast. However, the largest receivables should be itemized, stating the period in which cash receipt is most likely to occur. All other receivables can be listed in aggregate.
-	Employee compensation	This is possibly the largest expense item, so be especially careful in estimating the amount. It is easiest to base the compensation expense on the amount paid in the preceding period, adjusted for any expected changes.
-	Payroll taxes	List this expense separately, since it is common to forget to include it when aggregated into the employee compensation line item.
-	Contractor compensation	If there are large payments to subcontractors, list them in one or more line items.
-	Key supplier payments	If there are large payments due to specific suppliers, itemize them separately. It may be necessary to change the dates of these payments in the forecast in response to estimated cash positions.
-	Large recurring payments	These are usually large ongoing payments, such as rent and medical insurance, which can be itemized on separate lines of the forecast.
-	Debt payments	If there are significant principal or interest payments coming due, itemize them in the report.
-	Expense reports	If there are a large number of expense reports in each month, they are probably clustered near month-end. It is usually possible to estimate the amount likely to be submitted.
=	Net cash position	This is the total of all the preceding line items.
+/-	Financing activities	Add any new debt, which increases cash flow, or the reduction of debt, which decreases cash flow. Also add any investments that mature during the period.
	Ending cash	This is the sum of the net cash position line item and the financing activities line item.

The following example illustrates a cash forecast, using the line items described in the preceding table.

EXAMPLE

The controller of Suture Indigent Medical Care constructs the following cash forecast for each week in the month of September.

+/-	Line Item	Sept. 1-7	Sept. 8-14	Sept. 15-22	Sept. 23-30
+	Beginning cash	$50,000	$30,000	$2,000	$0
+	Accounts receivable				
+	Alpha Pharmaceuticals	120,000		60,000	
+	St. Joseph's Burn Center		85,000		52,000
+	Third Degree Burn Center	29,000		109,000	
+	Other receivables	160,000	25,000	48,000	60,000
+	Other receivables	10,000		5,000	
-	Employee compensation	140,000		145,000	
-	Payroll taxes	10,000		11,000	
-	Contractor compensation				
-	Bryce Contractors	8,000		8,000	
-	Johnson Contractors	14,000		12,000	
-	Key supplier payments				
-	Chico Biomedical	100,000		35,000	
-	Stanford Research	20,000	80,000	29,000	14,000
-	Other suppliers	35,000	40,000	30,000	48,000
-	Large recurring payments				
-	Medical insurance				43,000
-	Rent				49,000
-	Debt payments		18,000	20,000	
-	Expense reports	12,000	0	0	21,000
=	Net cash position	$30,000	$2,000	-$66,000	-$63,000
+/-	Financing activities			66,000	63,000
=	Ending cash	$30,000	$2,000	$0	$0

The forecast reveals a cash shortfall beginning in the third week, which will require a cumulative total of $129,000 of additional financing if the organization wants to meet its scheduled payment obligations.

The format is designed with the goal of giving sufficient visibility into cash flows to reveal the causes of unusual cash shortfalls or overages, without burying the reader in an excessive amount of detail. To meet this goal, note the use of the "Other receivables" and "Other suppliers" line items in the exhibit. They are used to aggregate smaller projected transactions that do not have a major impact on the forecast, but which would otherwise overwhelm the document with an excessive amount of detail if they were listed individually.

A possible addition to the cash forecast is the use of a *target balance*. This is essentially a "safety stock" of cash that is kept on hand to guard against unexpected cash requirements that were not planned for in the cash forecast. All excess cash above the target balance can be invested, while any shortfalls below the target balance should be funded (perhaps with debt or a special call for donations). If a target balance had been incorporated into the preceding cash forecast example in the amount of $10,000, the amount would have been listed for the week of September 1-7 as a deduction from the ending cash position, leaving $20,000 of cash available for investment purposes.

The model we have outlined in this section requires a weekly update. It only covers a one-month period, so its contents become outdated very quickly. Ideally, block out time in the department work schedule to complete the forecast at the same time, every week. Unless the organization is operating in an extremely tight cash flow environment, we do not recommend daily updates of cash forecasts – the time required to create these forecasts is excessive in comparison to the additional precision gained from the more frequent updates.

> **Tip:** Do not schedule an update of the cash forecast on a Monday or Friday, since too many of these days involve holidays. Instead, schedule the forecast update on any other business day, thereby increasing the odds of completing a new forecast every week.

The very short-term portion of the cash forecast may be subject to some tweaking, usually to delay a few supplier payments to adjust for liquidity problems expected to arise over the next few days. To incorporate these changes into the forecast, use a preliminary draft of the forecast to coordinate changes in the timing of payments with the controller, and then record the delays in the forecast before finalizing it.

The Medium-Term Cash Forecast

The medium-term cash forecast extends from the end of the short-term forecast through whatever time period is needed to develop investment and funding strategies. Typically, this means that the medium-term forecast begins one month into the future.

The components of the medium-term forecast are largely comprised of formulas, rather than the specific data inputs used for a short-term forecast. For example, if the fundraising manager were to contribute estimated revenue figures for each forecasting period, a standard time lag between the billing date and payment date can be incorporated into the estimation of when cash will be received from donors, governments, and program clients.

The concept of a formula-filled cash forecast that automatically generates cash balance information breaks down in some parts of the forecast. In the following areas, the accounting staff will need to make manual updates to the forecast:

- *Fixed costs.* Some costs are entirely fixed, such as rent, and so will not vary with revenue volume. The accounting staff should be aware of any contractually-mandated changes in these costs, and incorporate them into the forecast.
- *Step costs.* If revenues change significantly, the fixed costs just described may have to be altered by substantial amounts. For example, a certain revenue level may mandate hiring another accounting person. Be aware of the activity levels at which these step costs will occur.
- *Seasonal / infrequent costs.* There may be expenditures that only arise at long intervals, such as for the organization's Christmas party. These amounts are manually added to the forecast.
- *Contractual items.* Both cash inflows and outflows may be linked to contract payments, as can be the case with service contracts. If so, the exact amount and timing of each periodic payment can be transferred from the contract directly into the cash forecast.

The methods used to construct a medium-term cash forecast are inherently less accurate than the much more precise information used to derive a short-term forecast. The problem is that much of the information is derived from the estimated revenue figure, which rapidly declines in accuracy just a few months into the future. Because of this inherent level of inaccuracy, do not extend the forecast over too long a period of time. Instead, settle upon a time range that provides useful information for planning purposes. Any additional forecasting beyond that time period will waste staff time to create, and may yield misleading information.

Summary

It is critical for a nonprofit to maintain and monitor a budget, since nonprofits rarely have sufficient cash reserves to soften the impact of excessively low revenues or high expenses. This means that the management team should build a review of the budget versus actual report into its monthly (if not weekly) management meetings. If this analysis indicates that there will be a funding shortfall, the team must take action at once to remedy the situation.

The budget-versus-actual report should be supplemented by a cash forecast that is regularly updated. Cash forecasts can be inaccurate, so be sure to examine the forecast regularly to see how well its results compare to actual cash balances. If there are ongoing differences, it may be necessary to revise the cash forecast model or the manner in which it is updated.

Chapter 21
Accounting Controls

Introduction

Accounting controls are the means by which we gain a reasonable assurance that a nonprofit will operate as planned, that its financial results are fairly reported, and that it complies with laws and regulations. They are usually constructed to be an additional set of activities that overlay or are directly integrated into the basic operations of an organization.

In this chapter, we explore the extent to which controls should be installed, give an overview of control principles, and note how to install a set of controls. We also delve more deeply into controls for four areas that are of particular concern to most nonprofits – cash receipts, fixed assets, payables, and payroll.

> **Related Podcast Episode:** Episode 135 of the Accounting Best Practices Podcast discusses fine tuning the control system. The episode is available at: **accounting-tools.com/podcasts** or **iTunes**

The Proper Balance of Control Systems

A person who has been trained in control systems will likely want to install every possible control, and will then feel satisfied that he or she has saved the organization from an impending failure. Those on the receiving end of these controls have a different opinion of the situation, which is that controls slow down transactions, require more staff, and have the same general effect on a nonprofit as pouring sand into the gas tank of a car.

Because of these radically differing views of the utility of control systems, it is useful to adopt a set of controls that are based on the following points:

- *Risk – monetary*. If a control can prevent a large loss, such as one that could bankrupt a nonprofit, then it makes sense to install it, as long as the probability of the event is reasonably high. For example, having two people involved in every wire transfer transaction is a reasonable precaution, given the amount of funds that could be transferred out in a single wire transfer. Conversely, if a control can never save more than a few dollars (such as locking the office supply cabinet) it is entirely likely that the sheer annoyance caused by the control outweighs any possible savings to be achieved from it.
- *Risk – financial statements*. A nonprofit must understand its performance, and it can only do so with reliable financial statements. Consequently, controls over recordkeeping should be among the most comprehensive in an

organization. However, this does not necessarily call for an oppressive amount of controls in those areas where the amounts involved are essentially immaterial to the financial statements.

- *Repetitiveness.* Only install comprehensive controls for those transactions that a nonprofit will engage in on a recurring basis. For example, if an organization sells excess assets to a foreign customer once a year and wants to hedge the outstanding receivable, a once-a-year transaction does not require an elaborate control system (unless the receivable is for a large amount – see the preceding point about risk). Thus, it behooves a nonprofit to concentrate on a finely-tuned set of controls for the 20% of its processes that make up 80% of its business (the Pareto Principle). Of the remaining 80% of the nonprofit's processes, those items involving the most inherent risk should be the prime candidates for strong controls.

- *Offsetting controls.* It may be acceptable to have weak controls in one part of an operation, as long as there are offsetting controls elsewhere. For example, it may not be necessary to have someone sign checks, as long as all purchases are initiated with an authorizing purchase order. This concept can be used to great effect if there is a good business reason to keep one process running as smoothly as possible (i.e., without controls), with offsetting controls in a less noticeable part of the organization.

- *Cost.* The cost of controls must be balanced against the expected reduction in risk. This is not a simple calculation to make, for it can be quite difficult to estimate the reduction of risk that will be achieved by implementing a control. One approach to quantifying risk is to multiply the risk percentage by the exposure to the business, which is known as the *expected loss*. See the following example.

  Conversely, it is easy enough to measure the labor cost and other factors required to implement and maintain a control, so there is a tendency for nonprofits to focus on the up-front cost of a control and downplay the savings that may or may not arise from having the control. The result tends to be a control level that is lower than it should be.

EXAMPLE

Archimedes Education operates a payroll system that pays employees on a semi-monthly basis. When there are a significant number of data errors in the payroll, Archimedes' payroll manager requires that the payroll be run again, at a cost of $5,000.

The payroll manager is considering the installation of an automated data validation software package that is expected to reduce the payroll data error rate from 8% to 1%, at a software rental cost of $250 per payroll. The cost–benefit analysis is:

- *No data validation.* There is an 8% chance of incurring a $5,000 payroll reprocessing cost, which is an expected loss of $400 ($5,000 exposure × 8% risk) per payroll.

- *Data validation.* There is a 1% chance of incurring a $5,000 payroll reprocessing cost, which is an expected loss of $50 ($5,000 exposure × 1% risk) per payroll. There is also a charge of $250 per payroll for the software rental cost.

Thus, there is a reduction of $350 in the expected loss if the control is implemented, against which there is a control cost of $250. This results in a net gain of $100 per payroll by using the control. Changes in the estimated probabilities can have a significant impact on the outcome of this analysis.

The resulting system should be one where some failures will still occur, but either in such small amounts that they do not place the organization at risk, or where the probability of occurrence is very low. It is difficult to maintain this balance between controls and operational effectiveness over time, seeing that a growing nonprofit is constantly in a state of flux, expanding some programs, curtailing others, and installing any number of new systems. It is the job of the controller to watch the interaction of these processes with existing control systems, and know when it is an acceptable risk to pare back some controls, while introducing new ones elsewhere.

It is quite common to see a control system that lags behind the current state of its processes, usually due to inattention by the controller. This means that some controls are so antiquated as to be essentially meaningless (while still annoying the staff), while new systems are devoid of controls, and will only see new ones when a system failure occurs.

In summary, there is a balance between the system of controls and the efficient operation of a nonprofit that is difficult to manage. A good controller will understand the needs of employees to keep operations efficient, and so should be willing to subsist in some areas on control systems that may appear rather skimpy, as long as the tradeoff is between a notable improvement in efficiency and the risk of only modest losses that would have been prevented by controls.

Control Principles

There are a number of principles to keep in mind when constructing a system of controls for a nonprofit. These principles are frequently the difference between a robust control system and one that appears adequate on paper, but which never seems to work in practice. The principles are:

- *Separation of duties.* The separation of duties involves assigning different parts of a process to different people, so that collusion would be required for someone to commit fraud. For example, one person opens the mail and records a list of the checks received, while a different person records them in the accounting system and a third person deposits the checks. By separating these tasks, it is much more difficult for someone to (for example) remove a check from the incoming mail, record a receivables credit in the accounting system to cover his tracks, and cash the check into his own account. Unfortunately, there is a major downside to the separation of duties, which is that shifting tasks among multiple people interferes with the efficiency of a process. Consequently, only use this control principle at the minimum level needed to establish the desired level of control – too much of it is not cost-effective.

- *Process integration.* Controls should be so thoroughly intertwined with business transactions that it is impossible for employees *not* to perform them as part of their daily activities. This level of integration substantially reduces the incidence of errors and the risk of fraud. An example of minimal process integration that will likely result in frequent control problems is requiring employees to record this information by hand on a paper form.

- *Management support.* The management team must make it abundantly clear to employees that it thoroughly supports the system of controls. This does not mean that a general statement of ethics is included in the employee manual. Instead, it means that management takes the time to explain controls to employees, is highly visible in investigating control breaches, and takes sufficient remedial action to make it clear to the entire staff that controls are to be taken seriously. Management also does not override its own controls, nor does it set performance standards that are so difficult to attain that employees would be forced to circumvent controls in order to meet the standards.

- *Responsibility.* No control system will work unless people are made responsible for them. This means that someone should be assigned responsibility for every control, and that they receive regular updates on the status of those controls. It would also be useful if the status of their controls are noted in their compensation reviews, and have a direct impact on changes in their pay.

- *Conscientious application.* Employees cannot simply treat controls in a perfunctory manner. Instead, there should be a culture that encourages the close examination of control breaches to determine what went wrong, and how the system can be adjusted to reduce the risk that the same issue will occur again. This level of conscientious behavior must be encouraged by the management team through constant reinforcement of the message that the system of controls is important. It also requires the availability of communication channels through which employees can anonymously report suspected improprieties.

- *Systems knowledge.* It is impossible to expect employees to conscientiously inspect controls unless they already know how systems operate. This calls for the ongoing training of employees to ensure that they thoroughly understand all aspects of the systems with which they are involved. This requires not only an initial training session for new employees, but also reminder sessions that are timed to coincide with any changes in processes and related controls, as well as thorough documentation of the systems. A good level of systems knowledge may call for the use of procedures, training materials, and a core group of trainers.

- *Error reporting.* It is impossible to know if a control is functioning properly unless there is a system in place for reporting control breaches. This may be a report generated by a computer system, but it may also call for open communication channels with employees, donors, and suppliers to solicit any errors that have been found. In this latter case, error reporting is strongly supported by a management group that is clearly interested in spotting errors and correcting them in a way that does not cast blame on those reporting the information. In addition, errors should be communicated all the way up through the organization to the audit committee and board of directors, who can enforce the establishment of enhanced controls.

- *Staffing.* There must be an adequate number of employees on hand to operate controls. Otherwise, there will be great pressure to avoid manual controls, since they take too much time to complete. This is actually a profitability issue, since a nonprofit experiencing losses is more likely to cut back on staffing, which in turn impacts the control system.

- *Outlier analysis.* Most businesses create control systems to deal with problems they have seen in the past, or which have been experienced elsewhere in the industry. They rarely create controls designed to mitigate outlier issues – that is, problems that occur very infrequently. The sign of a great control system is one in which employees take the time to examine the control system from a high level, and in light of the current and future business environment, to see if there are any outlier events that present a risk of loss in sufficiently large amounts to warrant the addition of controls. This outlier analysis requires excellent knowledge of the industry and a perceptive view of the direction in which it is headed.

Of the principles just noted, management support is the most crucial. Without it, a system of controls is like a building with no supporting framework – the entire structure crashes to the ground if there is any pressure placed upon it at all. For example, the control system may appear to have proper separation of duties, but this makes no difference if the management team ignores these separations for transactions that it has an interest in ramming through the system.

Constructing a System of Controls

The preceding discussion has revolved around the general concept of controls and the principles that should underlie them. But how is a system of controls created? What are the nuts and bolts of building a system? The primary steps are:

1. *Understand the new system.* Work with the systems analysts who have designed the new system to understand what it is designed to do, and each step in the process flow. This may call for the use of flowcharts and walkthroughs of test transactions. The result may be a formal report describing the system, probably including a preliminary set of procedures.

2. *Explore possible control breaches.* Work with the internal and external auditors, department managers, and systems analysts to estimate where control breaches are most likely to arise in the prospective system.
3. *Quantify possible control breaches.* Estimate the number of occurrences of each type of control breach, the maximum and most likely amounts that a control breach would cost, and their impact on key performance metrics.
4. *Design controls.* Based on the quantification of control breaches, design controls that will cost-effectively mitigate risks and be so thoroughly integrated into the underlying process that they will be as robust as possible.
5. *Implement the controls.* Install the controls, along with all necessary documentation, forms, systems, and training, and oversee the initial rollout to ensure that it is operating as planned.
6. *Test the system.* A system of controls does not necessarily operate as planned, perhaps due to a misperception of how the underlying system operates, a bad control design, technology issues, poor employee training, and so on. To detect these issues, test the system of controls by feeding incorrect transactions into it, and see if the controls detect the transactions. If not, adjust the controls and repeat the exercise as many times as necessary.
7. *Conduct a post-implementation review.* All systems change over time, so expect control redundancy and gaps to appear as systems change. Review systems at least once a year, and more frequently if there have been major changes, to see if the existing system of controls should be adjusted.

In a larger organization, it may be cost-effective to hire a controls analyst who deals with these matters on a full-time basis. In a smaller nonprofit, it is more likely that this work will be handled by the controller, who might consider outsourcing it to a consultant.

Cash Controls

Cash receipts is an area in which a poorly-controlled nonprofit can lose a large amount of money, since cash is one of the more easily negotiable assets, and so is a continual target for theft. In addition, it is a high-volume application, so some data entry errors will arise occasionally that will require time-consuming investigation and correction.

Related Podcast Episode: Episode 12 of the Accounting Best Practices Podcast discusses cash receipt controls. The episode is available at: **accounting-tools.com/podcasts** or **iTunes**

In this section, we cover the controls that can be imposed on the core cash receipts activities. The list appears long, because different controls apply only to certain types of cash receipt, such as checks, cash, or credit cards.

1. Accept Cash

This section includes controls for three very different types of payment – checks sent to the organization, checks sent to a lockbox, and cash. After perusing these controls, it will be clear that the area most inundated with controls is the receipt of cash, which are needed to prevent theft. The controls are:

- *Open the mail and record cash receipts.* Someone not otherwise involved in the handling or recordation of cash receipts opens the mail, records all cash and checks received, and then forwards the cash receipts to the cashier. To strengthen this control, have two people jointly open the mail.

> **Tip:** If there is only one person in the mailroom, call in a clerk from another part of the nonprofit just to participate in the recordation of cash receipts.

- *Endorse for deposit only.* The person opening the mail should also immediately endorse all checks received with a "For Deposit Only" stamp, preferably one that also lists the entity's bank account number. This makes it much more difficult for someone to extract a check and deposit it into some other account.
- *Direct payments to lockbox.* An excellent control is to set up a lockbox at a bank, and direct customers and donors to send their payments directly to the bank. This eliminates all risk of cash or checks being stolen from within the nonprofit, and may also accelerate the recognition of cash in the nonprofit's bank account by a day or so.
- *Record cash in cash register.* The primary purpose of a cash register is as its name indicates – it registers the amount of cash received. Therefore, when there is any reasonable expectation for a large number of cash receipts, always have a cash register available for recording the transactions.
- *Record cash on pre-numbered receipts.* In situations where relatively small quantities of cash are anticipated, it may not be cost-effective to operate a cash register. If so, record cash received on pre-numbered receipts, and be sure to use the receipts consecutively. By doing so, the numbers on the receipts can be scanned to see if any receipts are missing. A missing receipt indicates that cash has not been recorded.
- *Give receipt to customer or donor.* If a customer or donor is paying with cash, have cashiers give them a copy of the receipt. If the cash is recorded in a cash register, the amount printed on the receipt will match the amount punched into the register. If the cash is recorded on pre-numbered receipts, the form should be a two-part form, so that the amount written on it by the clerk is identical for the versions kept by the customer and the nonprofit. Handing over a receipt is a reasonable control, since it means that the recipient might examine the receipt to see if the amount recorded matches what they paid.

- *Document fundraisers.* When a fund raising event is held, validate the amount of the winning bid with the person who placed the bid, to ensure that the amount of cash recorded matches the amount paid by the person. Also, have a second person reconcile the bid documentation and the deposit slip to ensure that all funds were received and that they were deposited correctly.
- *Document table sponsors.* When a table is sponsored at a fund raiser, payments for a table may be made at the event. If so, provide a sealable envelope at each table, in which sponsors can place their cash payments. Then have two people collect, open, and document the contents of the envelopes. Also, send a confirmation letter to each donor, so that donors will have a chance to complain if the amount is incorrect.

2. Record Cash

The recordation of cash within the accounting system is essentially the same for all types of payment, with the main difference being that the cashier should record the type of payment received when recording each payment. Thus, there should be a "cash," "check," or "credit card" flag in the software. This makes it easier to later track down the types of cash payments made. The controls for recording cash are:

- *Apply cash at once.* There are several reasons why the cashier should apply cash to programs or customer accounts as soon as the cash is received. First, it removes overdue accounts receivable from the aged receivables report, and therefore keeps the collection staff from wasting time on collection calls. Also, immediate cash application means that the cash will then be shifted off the premises and deposited, leaving little time for anyone to steal it.

Tip: Encourage donors to include the name of the program to which they are donating on their check payments, so that these checks can be applied more easily.

- *Apply cash based on check copies.* This control can be applied in two situations. If a nonprofit is using a bank lockbox, the bank will either mail copies of all checks and remittance advices received to the organization, or it will make them available on a website as scanned images; in either case, the cashier uses these documents as the basis for cash applications. In the second situation, the cashier photocopies all checks, thereby allowing for the immediate deposit of the checks and a somewhat more leisurely application of the payments to outstanding receivables.
- *Record undocumented receipts in a clearing account.* One of the best ways to destroy accounts receivable record accuracy is to apply cash receipts to receivables even when there is no indication of the invoice numbers to which they should be applied. Instead, these receipts should always be recorded into a clearing account for further review.

- *Match documents.* The cashier should match the initial list of checks generated by the person opening the mail to the related cash receipts journal. This highlights cash that the cashier may not have applied to receivables, and will also spot any cash that was removed between the mailroom and the cashier's office.

3. Deposit Cash

The depositing of cash and checks is essentially the same, since they are routinely recorded under a single deposit slip and transported to the bank together. This means that their deposit-related controls are identical. However, if a nonprofit uses remote deposit capture to scan checks on-site and send an electronic file to the bank, there are different controls for those checks. The controls are noted below:

- *Deposit daily.* If checks or cash are left on-site overnight, there is an increased chance that they may be stolen. To mitigate this risk, always deposit cash and checks at the end of every business day.
- *Lock up cash during transport.* Store all cash in a locked container while transporting it to the bank for deposit. This is not a good control, since someone could steal the entire container. A better approach for transporting large amounts of cash is to hire an armored car company to transport the cash on behalf of the entity.
- *Match cash receipts journal to bank receipt.* When funds are deposited at the bank, the bank clerk hands over a receipt for the amount deposited. The person transporting the cash to the bank gives this receipt to the cashier, who compares it to the cash receipts journal. If the numbers do not match, it may mean that the person transporting the cash removed some cash prior to the deposit, though it may also mean that either the cashier or the bank incorrectly recorded the amount of cash.

Credit card payments do not involve the handling of cash, so their controls are quite different from the ones used for cash. Possible controls include:

- *Use a form to take down information.* If a nonprofit manually enters credit card information into an on-line site, there is a significant chance that the information it enters will be incorrect in some respect, and so will be rejected. To reduce this risk, use a standard form to take down the name, billing address, and credit card information associated with the card being used to pay an invoice, as well as the name and address to which a receipt should be sent, and the number of the invoice being paid. The form should also require a phone number for the person paying the invoice, in case someone needs to call them back to verify the information or ask for a different credit card number.
- *Reconcile credit card receipts to pledges and accounts receivable.* When cash appears on the bank statement from a credit card transaction, have a procedure to trace it back to cash applied to specific accounts receivable or

pledges. Otherwise, there is a chance that the accountant will process a credit card but forget to also process the matching cash receipt against the related invoice or pledge.

> **Tip:** When entering credit card payments in the cash receipts system, always designate them as credit card payments. A report can then be created that shows only the credit card payments assigned to pledges receivable during the month. Compare the amounts on this report to the receipts appearing on the bank statement to ensure that all credit card payments were applied against open receivables.

Fixed Asset Controls

In this section, we cover the controls that can be imposed on the various stages of the fixed asset life cycle. This life cycle encompasses the initial acquisition of assets, as well as their depreciation and disposal.

> **Related Podcast Episode:** Episode 15 of the Accounting Best Practices Podcast discusses fixed asset controls. The episode is available at: **accountingtools.com/podcasts** or **iTunes**

1. Fixed Asset Acquisition

The key focus of controls for the acquisition of key assets is to ensure that the entity needs the assets. This means that controls are designed to require an evaluation of how a proposed acquisition will fit into operations, and what kind of return on investment it will generate. A secondary set of controls is also needed to ensure that all acquisition transactions are forced to follow this review process. With these goals in mind, consider using the following controls:

- *Require an approval form.* There should be an approval form that requires an applicant to describe the asset, how it is to be used, and the return on investment that will be generated (if any). This standardizes the information about each fixed asset, and also provides a handy signature form for various approvals.
- *Require independent analysis of the approval form.* Someone who is skilled in asset analysis should review each submitted approval form. This analysis includes a verification that all supporting documents are attached to the form, that all assumptions are reasonable, and that the conclusions reached appear to be valid. The person conducting this analysis does not necessarily render an opinion on whether to acquire the asset, but should point out any flaws in the proposal. This person should *not* report to the person who submitted the proposal, since that would be a conflict of interest.
- *Require multi-level approvals for more expensive assets.* If an asset request is *really* expensive, impose a requirement for a number of approvals by people in positions of increasing levels of authority. Though clearly time-consuming, the intent is to make a number of people aware of the request, so

that the organization as a whole will be absolutely sure of its position before allowing a purchase to proceed.

- *Focus more attention on rush requests.* Someone may try to avoid the usual review steps in order to obtain an asset right now on a rush basis. These are precisely the sorts of situations where it may make sense to impose a tighter review, since the rush nature of the purchase may be keeping people from due deliberation of the alternatives available. The exact nature of this control will vary under the circumstances, but the key point is to not eliminate *all* reviews and approvals just because someone says that an asset must be bought at once.

- *Impose a mandatory waiting period.* Though controversial, it may make sense to impose a waiting period before any asset is purchased, on the grounds that due deliberation may reveal that some assets are simply not needed, and so should not be bought. Taken to extremes, such a control can result in an excessively plodding organization, so use it with care.

- *Do not issue a purchase order without a signed approval form.* Train the purchasing staff to not order fixed assets unless the requestor has a signed approval form. Better yet, route all such purchase orders to a senior executive, such as the executive director, for approval.

- *Conduct milestone reviews.* For longer-term asset installations, there should be a series of milestone events at which the management team responsible for the project examines expenditures to date, progress on the project, and any issues relating to the remaining tasks to be completed. Though rare, the team may occasionally use the information obtained in this review to cancel the project entirely. A more common response is a variety of adjustments to improve the odds of successful completion within the cost budget.

The controls noted here will absolutely slow down the fixed asset acquisition process, and with good reason – part of their intent is to encourage more deliberation of why an asset is being acquired. Nonetheless, these controls will appear onerous to those people trying to obtain assets that are relatively inexpensive, so it is certainly acceptable to adopt a reduced set of controls for such assets, perhaps simply treating them as accounts payable that require a single approval signature on a purchase order.

Similarly, a more streamlined set of controls can be considered for assets that must be acquired at once. However, keep in mind that some managers intent on subverting the system of controls can characterize *everything* as a rush requirement, just to avoid the usual reviews and approvals. Consequently, if a reduced set of controls is adopted for such purchases, at least conduct an after-the-fact review of the circumstances of these purchases, to see if the reduced controls were actually justified.

2. Fixed Asset Depreciation

Depreciation calculation errors are extremely common, since there are opportunities to incorrectly enter the asset amount, useful life, salvage value, and depreciation method in whatever calculation spreadsheet or software is being used. Here are several controls that can mitigate this problem:

- *Conduct separate review of master file additions.* Have a second person review any records added to the fixed asset master file. This review should involve a comparison of the amounts paid to the amount listed in the master file, to ensure that the amount being depreciated is correct. Also, verify that the asset classification in which each asset is placed is the correct one, since this usually drives the depreciation method used and the useful life over which it will be depreciated. Further, verify that any salvage value used has been properly substantiated. Finally, verify that the recorded asset location is correct, so that anyone attempting to locate the asset in the future will be able to find it.
- *Audit depreciation calculations.* Periodically review a selection of the depreciation calculations, to see if an asset is being depreciated over the correct useful life, with the correct depreciation method, and with a verifiable salvage value. Errors will be more common if this information is being maintained on an electronic spreadsheet, given the greater risk of manual errors in this format.

3. Fixed Asset Disposal

There tends to be some amount of fixed asset "leakage" out of any organization, especially for smaller and more mobile assets, such as computers. In many cases, the resale value of these items near the end of their useful lives is so small that a nonprofit may very well be justified in giving them away to employees or simply dropping them into the scrap bin. However, there may be some residual value remaining in these assets, so consider using the following controls to recapture that value:

- *Conduct asset disposition reviews.* The goals of this review are to decide whether a nonprofit continues to need a fixed asset, and if not, how to obtain the highest price for it. If this control is not used, assets tend to remain on the premises long after they are no longer needed, and lose value during that time.
- *Require signed approval of asset dispositions.* Create a form that describes the asset to be disposed of, the method of disposition, and the cash to be received (if any). The person whose authorization is required could be a specialist in asset disposition, or perhaps the purchasing manager, who might have some knowledge of asset values. The point of this control is to require a last look by someone who might know of a better way to gain more value from a disposal.

- *Monitor cash receipts from asset sales.* Most fixed assets are sold for cash, and sometimes for large amounts of cash. Given the amount of funds involved, it can be quite a temptation for employees to find ways to either not record asset sales or falsify sale documents to record smaller sales, and then pocket the undocumented cash. This situation can be monitored by requiring that a bill of sale from the purchasing entity accompany the documentation for each asset sale. It is also useful to periodically audit asset sale transactions, if only to show the staff that these transactions are being monitored.
- *Send copy of disposal form to accounting.* If there is an asset disposal form that must be filled out prior to the disposal of a fixed asset, route a copy of it to the accounting department, so that the accounting staff can write off the asset and stop recording a periodic depreciation charge for it.

Payables Controls

Accounts payable is an area in which a poorly-controlled department can lose a large amount of money, as well as annoy those suppliers who are being paid late. In this section, we describe the control systems needed to remediate these issues.

> **Related Podcast Episode:** Episode 13 of the Accounting Best Practices Podcast discusses accounts payable controls. The episode is available at: **accounting-tools.com/podcasts** or **iTunes**

1. Verify Obligation to Pay

The verification of obligation to pay can be accomplished through one of several possible controls. They are:

- *Invoice approval.* The person in a position to authorize payment signifies his or her approval of a supplier invoice. However, this is actually a relatively weak control if the approver only sees the supplier invoice, since there is no way to tell if the goods or services were received, or if the prices being charged were what the nonprofit originally agreed to. The approver may also want to know which general ledger account will be charged. Consequently, it is better to have the payables staff first assemble the supplier invoice, authorizing purchase order, and receiving documentation into a packet, then stamp the invoice with a signature block that includes the account number to be charged, and *then* have the approver review it. This approach gives reviewers a *very* complete set of information to work with.

> **Tip:** Approvers are busy, and so have a bad habit of only giving supplier invoices a perfunctory review before approving them. To prevent this, the accounts payable manager can set up appointments with each approver, bring the invoices to them, and discuss the invoices with them. This approach also ensures that every invoice will be returned promptly.

> **Tip:** If invoices are sent out for approvals prior to being entered in the payable system, maintain a log of the invoices that are out for approval, and cross them off when they are eventually returned. This makes it easier to determine which invoices have *not* been returned.

- *Purchase order approval.* The purchasing department issues a purchase order for every purchase made. By doing so, the purchasing staff is, in essence, approving all expenditures before they have been made, which may prevent some expenditures from ever occurring. Since this control entails a certain amount of work by the purchasing staff, they will likely ask employees to request items on a formal purchase requisition form.

> **Tip:** In practice, it will be inordinately expensive to enforce the use of purchase orders for everything. Instead, this control is more enforceable for larger purchases, with an automatic exemption for all purchases below a minimum dollar amount.

- *Complete a three-way match.* The payables staff matches the supplier invoice to the related purchase order and proof of receipt before authorizing payment. This approach supersedes the need for individual invoice approval, since approval is based on the purchase order instead. It is also better than approving only based on the purchase order, since it also verifies receipt of the goods. However, this control is also painfully slow and can break down if there is missing paperwork.

> **Tip:** Always allow the payables staff some margin for which invoices can be approved under the three-way match. For example, the price on an invoice might be acceptable if it is within 0.5% of the amount on the purchase order, while the received quantity is acceptable if it is within a similar margin. Without these margins, very few invoices would ever be paid. Also, there should be exemptions from three-way matching, such as tax payments, royalty payments, insurance, and benefit payments, where the required paperwork may not be available.
>
> **Tip:** It seems to be easiest for receiving reports to go astray, so consider having them prenumbered, which helps to determine which reports are missing.

- *Manual duplicate payment search.* A computerized payables system conducts an automatic search for duplicate invoice numbers. This is a much more difficult endeavor in an entirely manual accounting system. In this case, the payables clerk can search through the vendor file and unpaid invoices file to see if an invoice just received from a supplier has already been paid. In many situations, the volume of incoming supplier invoices makes this so difficult that the payables staff abandons any attempt to identify duplicate invoices, and simply accepts that it will occasionally pay for such items.

2. Data Entry

There are several ways to ensure that all supplier invoices have been entered in the accounts payable system, though these controls have varying degrees of success. The controls are:

- *Record after approval.* This control forces the accounts payable staff to verify the approval of every invoice before entering it into the system.

> **Tip:** This control can be an expensive one, since some invoices will inevitably not be approved in time to be paid by their due dates. To avoid late penalties, use automatic approvals of smaller and recurring invoices, and have several alternate approvers available if the primary approvers are not available.

- *Record prior to approval.* This control places greater priority on paying suppliers than it does on obtaining authorizations to pay, since every invoice received is recorded in the payables system at once. This control works best where purchase orders have already been used to authorize a purchase.

> **Tip:** When recording supplier invoices in advance, consider using *negative approvals*. This means that approvers receive a copy of each invoice, but only contact the payables staff if they *do not* approve an invoice. This largely eliminates the amount of feedback that the payables staff can expect from authorizers.

- *Adopt an invoice numbering guideline.* Perhaps the largest problem in the area of payables data entry is duplicate payments. This would not appear to be a problem, since most companies use accounting software that automatically detects duplicate invoices and prevents duplicate payments. However, there can be inconsistency in how invoice numbers are recorded. For example, should invoice number 0000078234 be recorded with the leading zeros or without them? If the same invoice is presented to the payables staff twice, and it is recorded as 0000078234 one time and 78234 the next time, the system will not flag them as being duplicate invoices. The same problem arises with dashes in an invoice number; an invoice number of 1234-999 could be recorded as 1234-999 or as 1234999.

  A simple control over the duplicate invoice problem is a one-page description of how invoice numbers are to be recorded, which is to be posted prominently next to the computer of every accounts payable data entry person for easy reference. A sample statement follows.

Invoice Number Policy

Leading zeros: Always delete all leading zeros from an invoice number.

    <u>For example</u>: Record 0000078234 as 78234

Dashes: Always delete all dashes from an invoice number.

    <u>For example</u>: Record 1234-999 as 1234999

No invoice number: Enter the invoice date as a six-digit number.

    <u>For example</u>: Enter an invoice dated July 9, 2014 as 070914

<u>3. Payment</u>

The bulk of the controls noted below pertain to payment by check, since that is still the predominant form of payment. Several controls near the bottom of the list are targeted at electronic payments. The controls are:

- *Split check printing and signing.* One person should prepare checks, and a different person should sign them. By doing so, there is a cross-check on the issuance of cash.
- *Store all checks in a locked location.* Unused check stock should *always* be stored in a locked location. Otherwise, checks can be stolen and fraudulently filled out and cashed. This means that any signature plates or stamps should also be stored in a locked location.

> **Tip:** If there is a signature stamp or plate, store it in a different locked location from the check stock, and keep the keys to the two locations in different spots. Ideally, different people should be responsible for the check stock and the signature plate. This makes it more difficult for someone to obtain both and generate valid-looking check payments.

- *Secure check-printing equipment.* Some printers are only used for check printing. If so, keep them in a locked location so that no one can print checks and have the integrated signature plate automatically sign the checks.
- *Track the sequence of check numbers used.* Maintain a log in which are listed the range of check numbers used during a check run. This is useful for determining if any checks in storage might be missing. This log should not be kept with the stored checks, since someone could steal the log at the same time they steal checks.
- *Issue checks in numerical order.* This is not actually a control, but rather a means of ensuring that there are few gaps in the sequence of check numbers that need to be investigated. From a practical perspective, checks are nearly always used in batches, so they will always be issued in numerical order.

- *Require manual check signing.* A nonprofit can require that all checks be signed. This is actually a relatively weak control, since few check signers delve into why checks are being issued, and rarely question the amounts paid. If an organization chooses to use a signature plate or stamp instead, it is much more important to have a strong purchase order system; the purchasing staff becomes the de facto approvers of invoices by issuing purchase orders earlier in the payables process flow.

Tip: If a nonprofit requires manual check signing, do everything possible to strengthen the control. This means assembling a voucher package for each check that the check signer can review, and having a payables person sit with the check signer to answer questions during signing sessions.

- *Require an additional check signer.* If the amount of a check exceeds a certain amount, require a second check signer. This control supposedly gives multiple senior-level people the chance to stop making a payment. In reality, it is more likely to only introduce another step into the payment process without really strengthening the control environment.
- *Stamp invoices "paid".* In a purely manual payables environment, there is a risk of paying an invoice more than once, so a reasonable control is to stamp each paid invoice, or even perforate it with a "paid" stamp. This control is less necessary (if at all) in a computerized system, which automatically tracks which invoices have been paid.

Tip: If the choice is made to not use a "paid" stamp in a computerized environment, be sure to install a consistent procedure for assigning an invoice number to those invoices that are not numbered. Otherwise, the copies of the same invoice could be assigned different invoice numbers and then paid.

- *Lock up undistributed checks.* If a nonprofit does not distribute checks at once, they should be stored in a locked location. Otherwise, there is a risk of theft, with the person stealing the checks modifying them sufficiently to cash them.
- *Use positive pay.* Positive pay is a program under which a nonprofit sends a file containing its check payment information to its bank; if a check is presented for payment and it is not on the list of checks issued by the organization, the bank rejects it. This can eliminate check fraud, though there is some question of whether it is more beneficial to the bank (which could be liable for accepting fraudulent checks) or the nonprofit.

> **Tip:** It is easy to forget to notify the bank of check payments, especially manual checks that are created outside of the normal check printing process. Therefore, have an iron-clad bank notification system in place before enacting positive pay. It may help to run positive pay on a test basis for a few months to see how many check notifications were not made, and what caused them.

- *Initiate banking transactions from a dedicated computer.* It is possible for someone to use keystroke logging software to detect the user identification and password information that a business uses to authorize direct deposit and wire transfer information. To reduce the risk, set up a separate computer that is only used to initiate transactions with the bank. This reduces the risk that keystroke logging software might be inadvertently downloaded onto the machine from an e-mail or other transaction.
- *Pay from a separate account.* There is a risk that someone could use an ACH debit transaction to move funds out of a nonprofit's bank account. To reduce this risk, only shift sufficient funds into a checking account to cover the amount of outstanding checks, ACH payments, and wire transfers that have not yet cleared the bank. Also, arrange with the bank to block all ACH debit transactions.
- *Password-protect the direct deposit file.* Some nonprofits accumulate bank account information for their supplier payments in a computer file, while others may access it online in their bank's systems. In either case, the file should be password protected to prevent tampering with the accounts. Also, the password should be changed regularly, and certainly after anyone with access to the file has left the organization.
- *Different person verifies or approves wire transfers.* When a nonprofit authorizes a wire transfer, one person issues the instructions to the bank, and a different person verifies or approves the transaction.

> **Tip:** If a different person is to verify or approve each wire transfer, set up the e-mail address of the verifying person in the confirmation contact list in the bank's records, so that notifications are automatically sent to that person.

> **Tip:** Direct deposit and wire transfer payments are frequently made outside of the accounts payable system, which means that someone has to manually record these payments in the payables system. If they forget to do so, there is a risk that these items will be paid again, or paid by check. Consequently, be sure to set up a default payment type for each supplier in the vendor master file, and stick to that payment type. Treat any request for a different type of payment as a policy violation, which requires extra approvals.

Payroll Controls

Payroll requires the assembly and marshaling of a great deal of timekeeping information, which presents the risk of many errors when it is converted into the payroll database. It is also an area in which fraud can be rife. Both circumstances require the creation of a robust system of controls, which are described in this section.

> **Related Podcast Episode:** Episode 14 of the Accounting Best Practices Podcast discusses payroll controls. The episode is available at: **accounting-tools.com/podcasts** or **iTunes**

1. Collect Time Information

Controls are needed over time collection to ensure that all timesheets have been collected, and that the amounts reported are valid. These controls are:

- *Install automated timekeeping.* Install computerized time clocks. These clocks have a number of built-in controls, such as only allowing employees to clock in or out for their designated shifts, not allowing overtime without a supervisory override, and (for biometric clocks) eliminating the risk of buddy punching. Buddy punching occurs when a third party clocks an employee in and out of a timekeeping system, even though the employee is not working. Also, any exception reports generated by these clocks should be sent to supervisors for review.
- *Match timesheets to employee list.* There is a risk that an employee will not turn in a timesheet in a timely manner, and so will not be paid. To avoid this problem, print a list of active employees at the beginning of payroll processing, and check off the names on the list when their timesheets are received.

> **Tip:** Be sure to use the most recent employee list from the human resources department. In particular, the list must flag which employees are new, because they may not know that they need to submit a timesheet.

- *Verify hours worked.* Have supervisors approve hours worked by their employees, to prevent the employees from charging more time than they actually worked.

> **Tip:** The payroll staff is usually operating under an extremely tight deadline for payroll processing, so make sure that all supervisors have designated alternates available to review timesheets, in case they are not available.

- *Verify overtime worked.* Even if supervisors are not required to approve the hours worked by employees, at least have supervisors approve overtime hours worked. There is a pay premium associated with these hours, so the cost to the nonprofit is higher, and is a temptation for employees to claim them.

Tip: An additional control to consider is to track overtime hours by employee on a trend line. This may highlight those employees who persistently record very small amounts of overtime on a continuing basis, on the theory that a supervisor will approve these small amounts without much investigation.

- *Confirm self-service changes.* When employees enter their own updates to the payroll system, it should send them a confirming e-mail, describing the changes made.

2. Data Entry

It is quite easy to make mistakes when manually entering timekeeping information into a payroll system, and when setting up electronic payment information. Also, ensure that changes to employee deductions and pay rates have been authorized. The related controls are:

- *Verify aggregation calculations.* If payroll is being manually calculated, have a second person verify the aggregation of hours worked. A second person is more likely to conduct a careful examination than the person who originated the calculations.
- *Match entered totals to timesheets.* If there has been a history of errors in entering timekeeping information into the payroll software, consider adding a control to match the entered totals to the aggregated totals listed on employee timesheets. If automated timekeeping systems are in use, this information will be entered automatically, and no control is needed.
- *Require change authorizations.* Only allow a change to an employee's marital status, withholding allowances, or deductions if the employee has submitted a written and signed request for the nonprofit to do so. Otherwise, there is no proof that the employee wanted a change to be made. The same control applies for any pay rate changes requested by a manager.
- *Require pre-noting.* Pre-noting is used to conduct a trial test of a direct deposit transaction. Though this feature delays the start of direct deposits by one payroll, it is quite useful for spotting incorrect bank numbers and account codes. It is especially important when employees are allowed to alter their direct deposit information with a self-service system, since they are more likely than the payroll staff to input incorrect information. In particular, they may use information from their bank account deposit slips, rather than their checks; deposit slips do not necessarily contain the correct bank and account number information.

3. Calculate Gross and Net Pay

If payroll is being calculated manually, there is a risk that taxes will be incorrectly calculated, and that taxes and deductions may be incorrectly applied to gross pay. There are fewer concerns if payroll software is used, though the following payroll register controls should still be employed. The controls are:

- *Review calculations.* If payroll calculations are being conducted manually, have a second person verify the payroll calculations, tracing back to the summary totals to be paid to each employee, and checking taxes, deductions, and net pay calculations.
- *Review preliminary payroll register.* In a computerized system, the first evidence that the payroll clerk may have made a mistake will appear on the preliminary payroll register. A major control is to engage in as many iterations of this report as necessary, printing the register, looking for mistakes, correcting the mistakes, printing a replacement register, and so on.
- *Manager approves final payroll register.* Once all time information has been entered in the payroll system and wages and related deductions have been calculated, print a final payroll register that summarizes this information, and have a manager review and approve it.

Tip: Auditors consider a reviewed and signed payroll register as evidence of a strong payroll control, so retain copies of the final, signed registers for all payrolls.

---

4. Payment

The bulk of the controls noted below pertain to payment by check, since that is still a predominant form of payment. Several controls near the bottom of the list are targeted at cash payments. Many payment controls are necessary for checks, because there are risks of fraud and errors in multiple places during their storage, printing, and distribution. The controls are:

- *Use a separate bank account.* Pay employees from a separate checking account, and fund it only in the amount of the checks paid out. Doing so prevents someone from fraudulently increasing the amount on an existing paycheck or creating an entirely new one, since the funds in the account will not be sufficient to pay for the altered check.
- *Split check printing and signing.* One person should prepare checks, and a different person should sign them. By doing so, there is a cross-check on the issuance of cash.
- *Store all checks in a locked location.* Unused check stock should *always* be stored in a locked location. Otherwise, checks can be stolen and fraudulently filled out and cashed. This means that any signature plates or stamps should also be stored in a locked location.

Tip: If there is a signature stamp or plate, store it in a different locked location from the check stock, and keep the keys to the two locations in different spots. Ideally, different people should be responsible for the check stock and the signature plate. This makes it more difficult for someone to obtain both and generate valid-looking check payments.

- *Secure check-printing equipment.* Some printers are only used for check printing. If so, keep them in a locked location so that no one can print checks and have the integrated signature plate automatically sign the checks.
- *Track the sequence of check numbers used.* Maintain a log in which are listed the range of check numbers used during a check run. This is useful for determining if any checks in storage might be missing. This log should not be kept with the stored checks, since someone could steal the log at the same time they steal checks.
- *Issue checks in numerical order.* This is not actually a control, but rather a means of ensuring that there are few gaps in the sequence of check numbers that need to be investigated. From a practical perspective, checks are nearly always used in batches, so they will always be issued in numerical order.
- *Match check total to calculations.* If paychecks are being manually created, have a second person compare the amount on the checks to the net pay amounts indicated in the payroll register. The person who writes the checks is less likely to be thorough in matching these amounts.

Tip: A common mistake is to cut a manual check for the gross pay amount, rather than the net pay amount listed on the payroll register. To keep this from happening, use a highlighter to mark the net pay amounts on the register prior to writing checks.

- *Sign checks.* In a smaller nonprofit where there are few employees, it may make sense to avoid a signature plate or stamp, in favor of manual check signing. Doing so increases the odds that the check signer may spot an issue. A further control here is to require two check signers for really large payments, just to introduce an additional reviewer.

Tip: When there are multiple forms of payment, having someone sign checks may no longer be adequate. An alternative is to have someone periodically compare the amounts actually paid to the approved payroll register to ensure that they match.

- *Hand checks to employees.* Where possible, hand checks directly to employees. Doing so prevents a type of fraud where a payroll clerk creates a check for a ghost employee and pockets the check. A ghost employee is a fake employee record to which payments are fraudulently made. It could be an entirely fabricated person, or else a former employee whose record still indicates that he or she is an active employee. If this is too inefficient a control, consider distributing checks manually on an occasional basis.

- *Lock up undistributed checks.* If a nonprofit does not distribute checks at once, they should be stored in a locked location. Otherwise, there is a risk of theft, with the person stealing the checks modifying them sufficiently to cash them.
- *Use ink on pay envelope.* When there are cash payments to employees, use ink to note the pay amount on the outside of each pay envelope, which makes it more difficult for someone to alter the amount to be paid.
- *Match payroll register to pay envelope.* When there are cash payments to employees, have a second person match the amount of cash in each pay envelope to the amount specified on the payroll register. This makes it more difficult for a payroll clerk to collude with an employee to pay him or her more cash. The second person should then initial each verified envelope, seal it, and transport all verified envelopes to the employees for distribution.
- *Obtain a receipt.* When there are cash payments to employees, have them sign a receipt in exchange that states the amount paid and the date of payment. Doing so gives the organization proof of payment, in case an employee later complains of being shortchanged or not paid at all. To make this control even more effective, insist on having each employee count the money in his or her pay envelope, rather than just signing off on the receipt without looking.

5. Remit Taxes

A nonprofit is liable for remitting the correct amount of withheld, matching, and other payroll taxes to various government entities, so be sure to use the following control to avoid late payment penalties:

- *Verify tax remittances.* The penalties associated with a late or missing tax remittance are severe, so have someone independently verify the amount of tax to remit, verify that the funds were actually sent to the government, and that the organization received a receipt in exchange.

Tip: Outsourcing payroll processing eliminates the tax remittance problem, since the supplier is now responsible for it.

Summary

It is especially important to install and maintain a strong system of controls in a nonprofit, because of the generally lower pay levels. When employees are paid less than their peers in for-profit entities, there is a risk that they will rationalize that they deserve a higher level of compensation, which can lead to fraud.

A key point to take away from this chapter is that there is no boilerplate system of controls that can be inserted into a nonprofit. Instead, the control system must be fashioned to meet the risk profile of an organization, while accepting minor losses in areas where it is more important to pare back on controls in favor of having more efficient business processes. Consequently, it takes a deep knowledge of a nonprofit's processes to set up and continually tweak a system of controls that yields the proper blend of risk aversion and operational performance.

Even if a correct set of controls is installed and they are designed to match the risk profile of a nonprofit, this does not mean that they will work properly; excellent control implementation demands a culture of conscientious examination of controls and control breaches by the entire organization. Only through a continuing and entity-wide focus on the importance of controls is it possible to have a robust set of controls. Thus, a top-notch control system involves both the controls themselves and the commitment of the organization behind them.

Chapter 22
Nonprofit Policies

Introduction

It is useful for a nonprofit to have a small number of policies in place that provide boundaries for the actions that the board of directors expects the staff to take. Doing so keeps "out of bounds" transactions from occurring, and provides a solid foundation for a system of procedures. In this chapter, we describe the reasons for a number of sample policies that can be used in the basic operations of a nonprofit's accounting department, as well as in related nonprofit operations.

General Accounting Policies

In this section, we note why policies are needed to govern the handling of cash, fixed assets, payables, and payroll, and provide sample policies.

Cash

A potentially significant control problem arises when a nonprofit retains cash and checks on its premises for any period of time. When this happens, there is an increased risk that employees, visitors, and volunteers will have an opportunity to abscond with the funds. This risk can be mitigated by forcing cash to be sent to the bank as soon as possible, as described by the following procedure:

> All cash and checks shall be deposited on the same day as the date of receipt.

Fixed Assets

Donors sometimes put a stipulation on how donated fixed assets are to be used. But what if there is no such restriction? A nonprofit could theoretically sell off such assets at once, but doing so might annoy donors. Accordingly, it may be useful to adopt a policy that mandates a certain usage period, such as the following:

> Donated assets shall be held and used for a period of at least one-half of their estimated remaining useful lives, unless there is no practical use for the assets.

An entire collection may be donated to a nonprofit. If so, there should be a policy in place for how to account for it. The choices are to not recognize it, recognize it, or to capitalize prospectively (that is, only additions to the collection). A sample policy is:

> All collections with an appraised fair value exceeding $___ shall be capitalized.

The basis of valuation for a purchased fixed asset is its cost, while the basis of valuation for a contributed fixed asset is its fair value. This can be noted in a formal policy, such as:

> All fixed assets purchased by the organization shall be recorded at cost, including any costs to bring these assets to their intended location and condition. All donated fixed assets shall be recorded at their fair value, as determined by an independent appraiser.

The typical nonprofit runs on a tight budget, and so cannot afford to squander cash on unneeded assets. Accordingly, it makes sense to impose especially stringent controls over the purchase of fixed assets. The following policy requires extra documentation prior to a purchase, which inherently incorporates an approval process:

> Employees must submit a capital budgeting request for any asset purchase exceeding $___.

A capitalization limit should be placed on the recordation of fixed assets, so that smaller expenditures are charged to expense. Doing so reduces the paperwork burden on the accounting staff. A typical capitalization policy is:

> All expenditures for fixed assets of less than $___ shall be charged to expense in the period incurred.

Fixed assets should be reviewed periodically to see if their carrying amounts exceed their fair values. This task falls well outside of the normal range of accounting activities, and so may be ignored. To improve the odds that impairment reviews will be conducted, formalize the following policy:

> All fixed assets having a carrying amount greater than $___ shall be tested for impairment at least once a year, or when it appears that the carrying amount may not be recoverable.

Asset impairment reviews can be quite expensive, both in terms of staff time and the cost of appraisers, so only review the most expensive fixed assets. There is only a small potential valuation decline in lower-cost assets, so there is no point in reviewing them. The cutoff point for conducting an asset impairment review may be much higher than the capitalization limit used to record fixed assets. For example, the capitalization limit might be $5,000, while the impairment review cutoff might be $100,000.

From time to time, fixed assets may be shifted from one department or location to another. If so, there is a strong risk that the accounting records will not reflect this change, so that the organization loses track of the assets. The following policy can remedy the situation:

The written approval of both the issuing and receiving managers is required for the transfer of fixed assets. The accounting department shall be notified of all fixed asset transfers.

A significant area of potential fraud is in the disposition of fixed assets. Employees could sell off fixed assets and pocket the funds. Alternatively, a disposition could simply be a bad business decision, where an asset should still be retained, or the price at which it sells is too low. These issues can be mitigated by requiring a review and approval for the disposition of all fixed assets exceeding a certain dollar value. For example:

> When a fixed asset with a carrying amount of greater than $___ is to be dispositioned, the approval of the executive director must be obtained in advance. When the carrying amount is greater than $[larger value], a formal disposition review must be conducted, with documentation of why the asset is no longer needed and whether the disposition price is reasonable.

Payables

There are a variety of ways in which to ensure that the majority of all purchases made by a nonprofit have been property authorized. This can be done by requiring purchase orders for larger amounts, and by requiring supervisory approval prior to payment of all invoices over a certain amount. Several applicable policies are:

> No invoices exceeding $___ shall be paid without prior supervisory approval.

> No invoices exceeding $___ shall be paid without an authorizing purchase order.

> Supervisors will receive a copy of all supplier invoices submitted for payment that exceed $___. Supervisors have five business days in which to protest these invoices; otherwise, the invoices will be paid.

A statement of unpaid invoices does not provide sufficient information for a payment, so the underlying supplier invoice must be obtained before there is sufficient evidence to justify a payment. This is pointed out by the following policy:

> No payments shall be made from supplier statements.

Expense reports are especially difficult to examine, since they may not contain sufficient supporting detail. This concern can be remedied by requiring that all requests for reimbursement be accompanied by a receipt. For example:

> Every expense submitted for reimbursement must be accompanied by a receipt.

> All cash payments listed on an expense report must be supported by a receipt.

It is much more time-consuming to create checks manually. In addition, the accounting staff may forget to record these checks in the accounting system or make a positive pay notification to the bank. Consequently, all check printing should be channeled through the check printing function of the accounting software. The following policy enforces the point:

> Manual checks are only to be used in emergencies, and must be authorized by the executive director.

As soon as an employee who is authorized to sign checks leaves the organization, contact the bank to remove them from the authorized check signer list. This also applies to the wire transfer approval list, as well as check signing privileges for payroll checks. A sample policy is:

> Check signers shall be removed from the authorized check signer list as soon as they leave the organization.

A potential source of cash leakage is petty cash, where small expenditures are supposed to be reimbursed from a small cash reserve, rather than forcing someone to go through the more complex accounts payable system. The following policies are intended to tighten the use of petty cash:

> Petty cash cannot be used to pay for invoices of more than $__.

> Employee advances and traffic citations cannot be reimbursed from petty cash.

Payroll

It can be quite difficult to convince some employees to submit time reports, which can result in delayed payroll processing or wage payments that are based on unconfirmed information. The following policy can be used to support a more rigorous enforcement of timesheet submissions:

> No employee shall be paid without the submission of a complete time sheet covering the entire pay period.

Since overtime involves a much higher rate of pay, employees will be more tempted to record overtime on their timesheets, and management will be less enthusiastic about paying it. A reasonable policy for controlling overtime is:

> No overtime shall be paid without prior supervisory approval.

A special problem faced by nonprofits is the possibility that management will encourage the paid staff to volunteer additional working hours to the organization. This approach is unlikely to stand up if legally challenged, so it would be better to compensate the paid staff for all hours worked, as encouraged by the following policy:

> The paid staff is not allowed to volunteer their time to the organization. They must be compensated for all hours worked.

Nonprofit-Specific Policies

In this section, we note why policies are needed to govern the handling of donor receipts, donated assets, investments, operations, joint ventures, lobbying, and tax filings, and provide sample policies.

Donor Receipts

Donors may request that a nonprofit provide a receipt for donate funds or assets. The receipt may include a statement of the value of the assets received. If this value is incorrect, a donor could use it to illegally reduce his or her income tax liability. The situation could be even worse – an employee of the nonprofit could issue a receipt when no assets were even received. To avoid this situation, have a policy that restricts who can complete a donor receipt. The following policy could be used:

> Only the executive director, development director, and controller are authorized to issue receipts to donors. All donor receipts shall be prenumbered, with copies kept of each issued receipt. These receipts shall be reviewed periodically by a designated member of the management team.

A nonprofit may solicit donations for programs that are not tax-exempt. If so, the solicitation should include a statement noting that any donations made in relation to the solicitation will not be tax deductible. Otherwise, the donations will reduce the tax receipts of the IRS. The issue is dealt with by the following policy:

> All solicitations issued shall include a statement that identifies whether solicited donations will be tax deductible.

Donated Assets

A third party may attempt to donate physical assets to a nonprofit. There should be a policy in place for whether these assets will be accepted, since some types of assets are difficult to dispose of, have little inherent value, and may impose a significant financial burden. For example, a building may require asbestos removal, or a plot of land may have a groundwater contamination problem. These issues can be avoided by instituting a policy that strictly defines the types of assets that a nonprofit will accept, such as:

> We will only accept as donations food and clothing that can be readily gifted to homeless shelters.

In cases where a nonprofit is willing to accept larger fixed assets, it can place the burden of inspections on the donor, as noted in the following policy:

> If a donor wishes to contribute land or a building, the donor will provide us with an inspector's report, stating the nature of any structural, wiring, plumbing, soil damage, or other issues that must be remediated.

Investments

A nonprofit may receive stock from donors. This may result in a nonprofit owning a broad array of equities, which can be a problem. Some of the shares may result in ownership of entities that are anathema to the mission of the nonprofit. For example, a lung cancer prevention nonprofit may find itself owning shares in a cigarette company. Or, the shares may be in a highly speculative company whose long-term prospects are poor. Nonprofits tend to invest their funds conservatively, so there is little risk of a catastrophic loss of funds, so the ownership of high-risk stock may conflict with a nonprofit's investment philosophy. In these situations, it can make sense for a nonprofit to conduct an immediate analysis of all donated stock and decide whether it wants to retain the stock or sell it and use the resulting cash to invest in more appropriate investments. The following policy is designed to address this issue:

> All donated stock shall be immediately forwarded to the investment committee for review. The committee shall review the stock in light of the entity's investment philosophy and mission statement, and decide whether the stock shall be retained or liquidated. If the decision is made to liquidate, the stock shall be forwarded to the entity's stock brokerage for sale within five business days.

The investment strategy for restricted funds may result in an investment loss. If so, the nonprofit may be compelled by the donor agreement to reconstitute the balance in the endowment fund. This issue can be addressed in advance by setting a standard policy that requires investment losses to be charged against endowment funds. The following policy demonstrates the concept:

> The entity shall include in its standard endowment agreement a clause requiring that investment losses be offset against the endowment balance. The executive director will not object if significant donors exclude this clause from the agreement.

This policy may not be allowable if there are state laws requiring nonprofits to reconstitute endowment balances.

Operations

If a nonprofit has branches or affiliates, the IRS' Form 990 tax return asks whether the nonprofit has a system of written policies and procedures that govern the activities of these branches and affiliates. Otherwise, they would be more likely to engage in activities inconsistent with the exempt purposes of the organization. A policy intended to alleviate the situation is:

> A set of policies and procedures governing the primary activities of the organization shall be constructed, reviewed periodically, disseminated to all branches and affiliates, and enforced through the use of periodic audits and reporting of the results to the audit committee.

The Form 990 asks whether a nonprofit has a written conflict of interest policy. This issue can arise regularly in a nonprofit, where employees, volunteers, and directors may engage in activities that are contrary to the interests of the entity's mission. The following policy can be used as the basis for a more customized conflict of interest policy that will mitigate the number and severity of these conflicts:

> A conflicts of interest questionnaire shall be issued to the board of directors annually. Directors shall disclose to the board any situations in which they have a conflict of interest with the entity. If necessary, a committee shall be appointed to investigate the reported conflict, and report back to the board with recommendations. Board members are prohibited from voting on any issues in which they stand to personally benefit. If a board member does not report a conflict of interest, the board may take appropriate disciplinary and corrective actions.

The Form 990 asks whether a nonprofit has a written whistleblower policy. This policy is needed to protect anyone from reporting fraud or other issues to the board of directors; otherwise, such issues are more likely to remain hidden. A sample policy is:

> The organization will not retaliate against any employee who has made a good faith protest against a business practice, on the grounds that it may be illegal or against public policy.

The Form 990 asks whether a nonprofit has a written document retention and destruction policy. This policy is needed to ensure that documents are retained long enough to provide evidence that the organization is operating as intended, but are not retained so long that they impose an excessive storage burden. A sample policy is:

> The organization shall retain documents for as long as needed for its own operations and as required by law. The following table contains mandated document storage periods.

Document Retention Requirements

Record Type	Retention Period
Accounting records	3 years
Age certification	While employed
Audit reports	Indefinite
Benefit payments	3 years
Board minutes	Indefinite
Compensation records	3 years
Contracts	3 years beyond the life of the agreement
Deductions from pay	2 years
Deeds, mortgages, and bills of sale	Indefinite
Disability status	1-2 years
Employee benefit plans	1 year after plan termination
Employment contracts	3 years
Employment test results	1 year
Financial statements	7 years
I-9 Form	Later of 3 years or 1 year after employment
Income tax withholding documentation	4 years
Insurance policies	Indefinite
Legal documents	10 years
Pension plan beneficiary designations	Indefinite
Pension plan descriptions and annual reports	6 years
Pension plan eligibility documentation	Indefinite
Personal information (name, address, social security number, gender, date of birth, occupation, and job classification)	3 years
Promotions and demotions	1 year
Reasonable accommodation requests	1 year
Records of hours worked	3 years
Records related to discrimination charges	Until resolved
Resumes	1 year
Salary calculations	3 years
Tax deductions	3 years
Tax records	7 years
Terminations	1 year
Veteran status	1-2 years
Wage records used to calculate retirement benefits	6 years

The Form 990 asks whether a nonprofit has a written policy for determining the compensation of the executive director, other officers, and key employees. This policy is needed to keep a nonprofit from adopting excessively large compensation packages for its employees. A sample policy is:

> The compensation committee shall determine the recommended compensation for the executive director and other key staff based on comparability data for the applicable labor market. This committee shall also document its deliberations and decision. The resulting recommendation and substantiating report shall be forwarded to the board of directors for approval.

Joint Ventures

The Form 990 asks whether a nonprofit has a policy or procedure for evaluating its participation in any joint venture arrangements. This oversight is needed to keep a nonprofit from engaging in activities that could cause it to lose its tax exempt status. The following policy applies to this situation:

> All proposed joint venture arrangements shall be examined by the board of directors to see if they substantially match the tax exempt activities of the organization. Also, existing joint ventures shall be examined in a similar manner at least once a year, or whenever there is a significant change in the direction of a joint venture's activities.

Lobbying and Political Campaigns

A nonprofit that has a 501(c)(3) designation is not allowed to participate in the political campaigns of candidates for public office, and can only engage in an insubstantial amount of lobbying activities in comparison to its total activities. If this is not the case, the IRS can retract the 501(c)(3) designation. Given the severity of the IRS response, it is of some importance to keep these two activities under control. The following two policies are examples of how to deal with the issue:

> A budget for lobbying expenditures shall be formulated in advance of each fiscal year, and must be formally approved by the board of directors before any funds are spent. Expenditures above the approved amount are prohibited.

> All activities by the organization that might be construed as participation in political campaigns are strictly prohibited. If there is a question about whether a proposed action can be construed as political campaign activity, the opinion of tax counsel must be obtained in advance.

Tax Filings

The Form 990 tax return asks whether a copy of the Form 990 was provided to all members of its governing body before filing the form. This question is presumably targeted at using the review by this additional group to improve the odds of filing an accurate tax return. The following policy enforces this distribution:

A complete copy of the annual Form 990, including all supporting schedules, shall be provided to all members of the board of directors at least ____ weeks prior to the expected filing date.

Summary

Though there are a number of policies that can be used to guide the operations of a nonprofit, there is a danger in formalizing too many of them. When there are dozens of policies in place, their sheer volume may reduce their individual impact; instead, it is possible that employees will be more likely to ignore them. To avoid this reaction, consider issuing only a set of policies that are most critical to how the organization functions, and weave them into the procedures used by employees. By doing so, it is more likely that the policies will be followed on a recurring basis.

Chapter 23
Analysis of a Nonprofit's Financial Health

Introduction

The financial health of a nonprofit is of great interest to its donors, lenders, and volunteers, since they all have a vested interest in the ability of the organization to continue in existence. Financial health can be discerned with a variety of tools, which are outlined in this chapter. We begin with the auditor's report, which provides general clues about financial health, and then drill down into more detailed analyses that provide specific information about revenue and expense trends, the proportion of expenses incurred, the quality of revenues, and the liquidity of an organization.

The Auditor's Report

An audit report is a written opinion of an auditor regarding whether an entity's financial statements fairly present its financial position, in accordance with GAAP. This report is written in a standard format, as mandated by generally accepted auditing standards (GAAS). GAAS requires or allows certain variations in the report, depending on the circumstances of the audit work that the auditor engages in. For example, the report may include a qualified opinion, depending upon the existence of any scope limitations based on the audit work or any issues found. The report may include an adverse opinion, in which the auditor points out that the financial statements were not prepared in accordance with GAAP.

Any qualifications or adverse opinions found in the auditor's report should be considered a large warning that something is wrong with the financial condition of the entity. At most, the report will only deliver a high-level indication of what that problem may be. To discern more information, it will be necessary to conduct the additional analyses noted through the remainder of this chapter.

A nonprofit does not always have its financial statements audited. It may instead use a compilation or review service. These alternatives provide far less assurance that the financial statements fairly present the financial position of a nonprofit, as the following two bullet points will make clear:

- *Compilation.* A compilation is a service to assist the management of an organization in presenting its financial statements. This presentation involves no activities to obtain any assurance that there are no material modifications needed for the financial statements to be in conformity with GAAP. Thus, a person engaged in a compilation does not use inquiries, analytical procedures, or review procedures, nor does he need to obtain an understanding of internal controls, or engage in other audit procedures. In short, compilation activities are not designed to provide any assurance regarding the information contained within the financial statements.

- *Review.* A financial statement review is a service under which an auditor obtains limited assurance that there are no material modifications that need to be made to an entity's financial statements for them to be in conformity with GAAP. A review does not require the auditor to obtain an understanding of internal control, or to assess fraud risk, or to use other types of audit procedures. The result is only a modest level of assurance regarding the fairness of presentation of the financial statements.

In short, audit opinions can provide a general indication of potential problems with the financial statements of a nonprofit, but only if a full audit has been conducted. A compilation is essentially useless for analyzing financial heath, while a review has not involved a sufficient level of audit activity to provide a decent level of assurance that all meaningful issues were found.

Horizontal Analysis

Horizontal analysis is the comparison of historical financial information over a series of reporting periods, or of the ratios derived from this information. The analysis is most commonly a simple grouping of information that is sorted by period, but the numbers in each succeeding period can also be expressed as a percentage of the amount in the baseline year, with the baseline amount being listed as 100%.

When conducting a horizontal analysis, it is useful to conduct the analysis for all of the financial statements at the same time, to see the complete impact of operational results on the nonprofit's financial condition over the review period. For example, as noted in the next two examples, the statement of activities analysis shows a nonprofit having an excellent second year, but the related statement of financial position analysis shows that it is having trouble funding growth, given the decline in cash, increase in accounts payable, and increase in debt.

Horizontal analysis of the statement of activities is usually in a two-year format such as the one shown below, with a variance also reported that states the difference between the two years for each line item. An alternative format is to simply add as many years as will fit on the page, without showing a variance, in order to see general changes by account over multiple years.

	20X1	20X2	Variance
Revenues	$1,000,000	$1,500,000	$500,000
Cost of programs	400,000	600,000	-200,000
Salaries and wages	250,000	375,000	-125,000
Office rent	50,000	80,000	-30,000
Supplies	10,000	20,000	-10,000
Utilities	20,000	30,000	-10,000

	20X1	20X2	Variance
Other expenses	90,000	110,000	-20,000
Total expenses	420,000	615,000	-195,000
Change in net assets	$180,000	$285,000	$105,000

Horizontal analysis of the statement of financial position is also usually in a two-year format, such as the one shown below, with a variance stating the difference between the two years for each line item. An alternative format is to add as many years as will fit on the page, without showing a variance, in order to see general changes by account over multiple years.

	20X1	20X2	Variance
Cash	$100,000	$80,000	-$20,000
Pledges receivable	350,000	525,000	175,000
Investments	150,000	275,000	125,000
Total current assets	600,000	880,000	280,000
Fixed assets	400,000	800,000	400,000
Total assets	$1,000,000	$1,680,000	$680,000
Accounts payable	$180,000	$300,000	$120,000
Accrued liabilities	70,000	120,000	50,000
Total current liabilities	250,000	420,000	170,000
Notes payable	300,000	525,000	225,000
Total liabilities	550,000	945,000	395,000
Net assets without donor restrictions	200,000	200,000	0
Net assets with donor restrictions	250,000	535,000	285,000
Total net assets	450,000	735,000	285,000
Total liabilities and net assets	$1,000,000	$1,680,000	$680,000

Vertical Analysis

Vertical analysis is the proportional analysis of a financial statement, where each line item on a statement is listed as a percentage of another item. Typically, this means that every line item on a statement of activities is stated as a percentage of revenues, while every line item on a statement of financial position is stated as a percentage of total assets.

The most common use of vertical analysis is within a financial statement for a single time period, to see the relative proportions of account balances. Vertical analysis is also useful for timeline analysis, to see relative changes in accounts over time, such as on a comparative basis over a five-year period. For example, if compensation has a history of being 40% of revenues in each of the past four years, then a new percentage of 48% would be a cause for alarm. An example of vertical analysis for a statement of activities is shown in the far right column of the following condensed statement of activities:

	$ Totals	Percent
Revenues	$1,000,000	100%
Program costs	400,000	40%
Salaries and wages	250,000	25%
Office rent	50,000	5%
Supplies	10,000	1%
Utilities	20,000	2%
Other expenses	90,000	9%
Total expenses	420,000	42%
Change in net assets	$180,000	18%

The information provided by this statement of activities format is primarily useful for spotting spikes in expenses.

The central issue when creating a vertical analysis of a statement of financial position is what to use as the denominator in the percentage calculation. The usual denominator is the asset total, but the total of all liabilities can also be used when calculating all liability line item percentages, and the total of all net asset accounts when calculating all net asset line item percentages. An example of vertical analysis is shown in the far right column of the following condensed statement of financial position:

	20X1	Percent
Cash	$100,000	10%
Accounts receivable	350,000	35%
Pledges receivable	150,000	15%
Total current assets	600,000	60%
Fixed assets	400,000	40%
Total assets	$1,000,000	100%

	20X1	Percent
Accounts payable	$180,000	18%
Accrued liabilities	70,000	7%
Total current liabilities	250,000	25%
Notes payable	300,000	30%
Total liabilities	550,000	55%
Net assets without donor restrictions	200,000	20%
Net assets with donor restrictions	250,000	25%
Total net assets	450,000	45%
Total liabilities and net assets	$1,000,000	100%

The information provided by this statement of financial position format is useful for noting changes in a nonprofit's investment in working capital and fixed assets over time, which may indicate an altered business model that requires a different amount of ongoing funding.

Expense Proportions Analysis

A nonprofit is constantly judged by its donors based on the proportion of its total expenses that are used in programs, fundraising, and management and administration. Ideally, spending 80% of total expenses on programs indicates a lean organization that makes effective use of donations. Conversely, a much lower percentage may drive away potential donors. The following notes pertain to the use of these ratios:

- The total program expense to total expense ratio is commonly demanded by donors, which means that management is under pressure to force expenses into the programs classification. This can lead to fraudulent behavior to over-allocate expenses into program expenses.
- Some expenses are required to maintain the general operations of a nonprofit, so it may be necessary to educate donors regarding the need for a certain level of management and administration expenses.
- Donors are less excited about seeing their contributions being used to raise more money, which places management under pressure to report the minimum amount of fundraising expenditures, usually by shifting them into the management and administration area. It is better to educate donors about the need for fundraising, and then segregate and report the actual level of fundraising expenses being incurred.
- Management and administration expenses are subject to step costs (such as hiring more accounting staff) as a nonprofit expands in size. Thus, opera-

tions may initially appear quite lean for a smaller organization, and then comparatively more bloated as an executive director and various support staff are hired.

Three ratios commonly used to monitor nonprofit expense levels are:

$$\frac{\text{Total program expenses}}{\text{Total expenses}}$$

$$\frac{\text{Total fundraising expenses}}{\text{Total expenses}}$$

$$\frac{\text{Total management and administration expenses}}{\text{Total expenses}}$$

Though these ratios appear simple enough, the accounting staff must be careful to maintain the same listing of accounts that feed into each ratio. If the chart of accounts is altered, this can result in a sudden shift of expenses into a different classification. Conversely, if the accounts used to feed into a particular ratio are deliberately altered, be sure to run the new formulation back through the ratio calculation for all periods presented, to show to users a consistent formulation for all time periods.

EXAMPLE

Teton Helicopter Rescue calculates the following expense proportions for the past three years:

	Year 1	Year 2	Year 3
Total program expenses	$1,800,000	$1,950,000	$2,050,000
Total fundraising expenses	100,000	125,000	140,000
Total management and administration expenses	350,000	425,000	470,000
Total expenses	$2,250,000	$2,500,000	$2,660,000
Program expenses ratio	80%	78%	77%
Fundraising expenses ratio	4%	5%	5%
Management and administration ratio	16%	17%	18%

The expense proportions analysis reveals a common problem with nonprofits, where increased size tends to result in a gradual increase in non-program expenses. In this case, Teton must hire additional administrative support staff as its program revenues increase.

Fundraising Effectiveness Ratio

A continual concern in any nonprofit is the effectiveness of fundraising activities. Is the organization earning back a sufficient amount of contributions in exchange for the cost of its fundraising activities? This concern can be quantified by comparing contributions received to the cost of fundraising. The formula is:

$$\frac{\text{Contributions received}}{\text{Total fundraising expense}}$$

A major concern with this analysis is that it may take a long time to bring a donor to the point of making a large contribution, in which case the cost incurred in the current period does not really reflect the total effort required to obtain the contribution. There are two ways to deal with this issue:

- Calculate the ratio on a trailing 12-month basis, so that the comparison covers a longer period of time.
- Present the ratio for a number of reporting periods, so that the general trend in fundraising effectiveness can be ascertained.

Another concern with this measurement is that it aggregates the results of all types of fundraising activities into a single measurement that may mask unusually fine or poor results for certain types of fundraising activities. The following example illustrates the point.

EXAMPLE

Teton Helicopter Rescue engages in cold calling, mailers, and art shows to raise money. In aggregate, the nonprofit received $2,000,000 in contributions in the last year, as opposed to $200,000 of fundraising expense, which represents a 10x fundraising effectiveness ratio. However, when the results are broken down by type of fundraising activity, the following picture emerges:

	Contributions Received	Fundraising Expense	Effectiveness Ratio
Cold calling	$50,000	$40,000	1.25x
Mailers	250,000	100,000	2.5x
Art show	1,700,000	60,000	28.3x
Totals	$2,000,000	$200,000	10x

The table reveals that Teton is gaining a positive return from all of its fundraising activities, but that the art show generates by far the largest amount of contributions. Given the minimal effectiveness of the cold calling alternative, Teton's management might want to consider terminating the cold calling campaign and trying other methods.

Revenue Concentration Analysis

A financially healthy nonprofit is one that obtains revenue from a large number of sources, so that a decline in contributions from a few donors will not have a large negative effect on total revenues. Conversely, if the bulk of all contributions come from a small number of donors, a nonprofit is at a substantially greater risk of a significant revenue decline.

There are several ways to conduct a revenue concentration analysis. One is to create a sorted itemization of donors, based on the total amount contributed, and determine how many donors are generating 80% of all contributions. If the number is a small one, the board of directors should discuss a new fundraising approach that will broaden the base of large donors.

On a more forward-looking basis, it can also be useful to examine the possibility of new nonprofits in the same market space absorbing some of the contributions from existing and potential donors. This analysis can be particularly relevant when key donors have expressed dissatisfaction with how the organization is using their funds, or have agreed to serve on the board of directors of one of the competing nonprofits.

Revenue concentration analysis is mostly targeted at contributions, since these funds represent pure income to a nonprofit. However, if funding is mostly derived from program revenues, it may be necessary to conduct the same analysis for the largest customers. Again, if there are a small number of customers from whom most revenues are derived, a precautionary reaction could be to search for new customers. The same logic applies to government grants.

EXAMPLE

Archimedes Education's executive director is conducting an analysis of revenue concentration. Most Archimedes funding comes from individual donors, with contributions ranging from $25 to $100,000. Total contributions in the past year were $10,000,000. Of that amount, 30 donors contributed $8,000,000, and 2,000 donors contributed the remaining $2,000,000. A more detailed analysis of the 30 donors reveals that all of them are graduates of Archimedes programs that later became rich and decided to send money back to the entity that provided them with an education.

The executive director realizes that this finding represents an ideal opportunity. She investigates all Archimedes graduates from the past 20 years, and realizes that 400 are now high net worth individuals. She immediately initiates a long-term program to maintain contact with these other individuals, to see if they would be willing to make substantial contributions.

Traffic Light Revenue Analysis

A key element of any revenue analysis is the risk associated with gaining revenues. Some contributions and program revenues will appear, year after year, without a great deal of effort. This revenue comes from long-time supporters and long-term program participants. Other revenues will require considerable effort to obtain, and may be at continual risk of loss, perhaps due to competition from other nonprofits, or variable funding availability or shifting priorities by donors. This range of risk can be translated into the colors in a traffic light – "green" revenues are considered completely reliable, "red" revenues are at risk, and "yellow" revenues lie somewhere in between. Analyzing revenues in this manner can reveal important insights regarding the overall risk to which a nonprofit is subjected. A likely outcome is that the annual budget is redesigned to associate the most essential programs with "green" revenues, so that these programs can provide crucial services, year after year. Less-critical services are formally associated with "yellow" or "red" revenues, so that they can be more readily scaled back if those revenues do not materialize.

EXAMPLE

The core service provided by Newton Education is mathematics training, which comprises 50% of all the classes that Newton teaches, at a cost of $3,500,000 per year. This cost nicely coincides with the "green" revenue that Newton receives each year. In addition, Newton's fundraising staff estimates that $1,500,000 of revenues are in the "yellow" classification, while the remaining $2,500,000 of revenues are in the "red" classification. Accordingly, Newton associates all math class funding with "green" revenues, so that these classes will be conducted, irrespective of changes in the receipt of "yellow" and "red" revenues.

Traditional Ratio Analysis

The preceding analyses were targeted specifically at nonprofits. In addition, there are several more broad-based ratio analyses that can be applied to a nonprofit's financial statements in order to derive additional information. The following five ratios are all intended to provide some insight into the liquidity of a nonprofit. Liquidity is the ability of an entity to pay its bills in a timely manner.

Current Ratio

One of the first ratios that a lender or supplier reviews when examining a nonprofit is its current ratio. The current ratio measures the short-term liquidity of a nonprofit. A ratio of 2:1 is preferred, with a lower proportion indicating a reduced ability to pay in a timely manner. Since the ratio is current assets divided by current liabilities, the ratio essentially implies that current assets can be liquidated to pay for current liabilities.

To calculate the current ratio, divide the total of all current assets by the total of all current liabilities. The formula is:

$$\frac{\text{Current assets}}{\text{Current liabilities}}$$

The current ratio can yield misleading results under the following circumstances:

- *Inventory component.* When the current assets figure includes a large proportion of inventory assets, since these assets can be difficult to liquidate. This can be a particular problem if management is using aggressive accounting techniques to apply an unusually large amount of overhead costs to inventory, which further inflates the recorded amount of inventory.
- *Paying from debt.* When an organization is drawing upon its line of credit to pay bills as they come due, which means that the cash balance is near zero. In this case, the current ratio could be fairly low, and yet the presence of a line of credit still allows the nonprofit to pay in a timely manner.

EXAMPLE

A supplier wants to learn about the financial condition of Teton Helicopter Rescue. The supplier calculates the current ratio of Teton for the past three years:

	Year 1	Year 2	Year 3
Current assets	$8,000,000	$16,400,000	$23,400,000
Current liabilities	$4,000,000	$9,650,000	$18,000,000
Current ratio	2:1	1.7:1	1.3:1

The sudden rise in current assets over the past two years indicates that Teton has undergone a rapid expansion of its operations. Of particular concern is the increase in accounts payable in Year 3, which indicates a rapidly deteriorating ability to pay suppliers. Based on this information, the supplier elects to restrict the extension of credit to Teton.

Quick Ratio

The quick ratio formula matches the most easily liquidated portions of current assets with current liabilities. The intent of this ratio is to see if a nonprofit has sufficient assets that are immediately convertible to cash to pay its bills. The key elements of current assets that are included in the quick ratio are cash, marketable securities, and accounts receivable. Inventory is not included in the quick ratio, since it can be quite difficult to sell off in the short term. Because of the exclusion of inventory from the formula, the quick ratio is a better indicator than the current ratio of the ability of a nonprofit to pay its obligations.

To calculate the quick ratio, summarize cash, marketable securities and trade receivables, and divide by current liabilities. Do not include in the numerator any excessively old receivables that are unlikely to be paid. The formula is:

$$\frac{\text{Cash} + \text{Marketable securities} + \text{Accounts and pledges receivable}}{\text{Current liabilities}}$$

Despite the absence of inventory from the calculation, the quick ratio may still not yield a good view of immediate liquidity, if current liabilities are payable right now, while receipts from receivables are not expected for several more weeks.

EXAMPLE

Suture Indigent Medical Care appears to have a respectable current ratio of 4:1. The breakdown of the ratio components is:

Item	Amount
Cash	$100,000
Marketable securities	50,000
Accounts receivable	420,000
Inventory	3,430,000
Current liabilities	1,000,000
Current ratio	4:1
Quick ratio	0.57:1

The component breakdown reveals that nearly all of Suture's current assets are in the inventory area, where short-term liquidity is questionable. This issue is only visible when the quick ratio is substituted for the current ratio.

Days Sales in Accounts Receivable

Days sales in accounts receivable is the number of days that a customer invoice is outstanding before it is collected. The measurement is usually applied to the entire set of invoices that a nonprofit has outstanding at any point in time, rather than to a single invoice. The point of the measurement is to determine the effectiveness of an organization's credit and collection efforts in allowing credit to reputable customers, as well as its ability to collect from them. When measured at the individual customer level, it can indicate when a customer is having cash flow troubles, since the customer will attempt to stretch out the amount of time before it pays invoices.

There is not an absolute number of accounts receivable days that represents excellent or poor accounts receivable management, since the figure varies considerably by industry and the underlying payment terms. Generally, a figure of 25% more than the standard terms allowed may represent an opportunity for improvement. Conversely, an accounts receivable days figure that is very close to the payment terms granted to a customer probably indicates that a nonprofit's credit policy is too tight.

The formula for accounts receivable days is:

(Accounts receivable ÷ Annual revenue) × Number of days in the year

For example, if a nonprofit has an average accounts receivable balance of $200,000 and annual sales of $1,200,000, its accounts receivable days figure is:

$$(\$200{,}000 \text{ Accounts receivable} \div \$1{,}200{,}000 \text{ Annual revenue}) \times 365 \text{ Days}$$

$$= 60.8 \text{ Accounts receivable days}$$

The calculation indicates that the entity requires 60.8 days to collect a typical invoice.

An effective way to use the accounts receivable days measurement is to track it on a trend line, month by month. Doing so shows any changes in the ability of the organization to collect from its customers. If a business is highly seasonal, a variation is to compare the measurement to the same metric for the same month in the preceding year; this provides a more reasonable basis for comparison.

No matter how this measurement is used, remember that it is usually compiled from a large number of outstanding invoices, and so provides no insights into the collectability of a specific invoice. Thus, it should be supplemented with an ongoing examination of the aged accounts receivable report and the collection notes of the collection staff.

Days Sales in Inventory

Days sales in inventory (DSI) is a way to measure the average amount of time that it takes for an organization to convert its inventory into sales. A relatively small number of days sales in inventory indicates that an entity is more efficient in selling off its inventory, while a large number indicates that a nonprofit may have invested too much in inventory, and may even have obsolete inventory on hand.

To calculate days sales in inventory, divide the average inventory for the year by the cost of goods sold for the same period, and then multiply by 365. For example, if an organization has average inventory of $1.5 million and an annual cost of goods sold of $6 million, then its days sales in inventory is calculated as:

$$= (\$1.5 \text{ million inventory} \div \$6 \text{ million cost of goods sold}) \times 365 \text{ days}$$

$$= 91.3 \text{ days sales in inventory}$$

The days sales in inventory figure can be misleading, for the following reasons:

- An entity could post financial results that indicate a low DSI, but only because it has sold off a large amount of inventory at a discount, or has written off some inventory as obsolete. An indicator of these actions is when net assets decline at the same time that the number of days sales in inventory declines.

- A nonprofit could change its method for calculating the cost of goods sold, such as by capitalizing more or fewer expenses into overhead. If this calculation method varies significantly from the method the organization used in the past, it can lead to a sudden alteration in the results of the measurement.

- The person creating the metrics might use the amount of ending inventory in the numerator, rather than the average inventory figure for the entire measurement period. If the ending inventory figure varies significantly from the average inventory figure, this can result in a sharp change in the measurement.
- A nonprofit may switch to contract manufacturing, where a supplier produces and holds goods on behalf of the entity. Depending upon the arrangement, the organization may have no inventory to report at all, which renders the DSI measurement useless.

Days Payables Outstanding

The accounts payable days formula measures the number of days that an organization takes to pay its suppliers. If the number of days increases from one period to the next, this indicates that the entity is paying its suppliers more slowly. A change in the number of payable days can also indicate altered payment terms with suppliers, though this rarely has more than a slight impact on the total number of days. If a nonprofit is paying its suppliers very quickly, it may mean that the suppliers are demanding short payment terms because they are suspicious of the organization's ability to pay.

To calculate days payables outstanding, summarize all purchases from suppliers during the measurement period, and divide by the average amount of accounts payable during that period. The formula is:

$$\frac{\text{Total supplier purchases}}{(\text{Beginning accounts payable} + \text{Ending accounts payable}) \div 2}$$

This formula reveals the total accounts payable turnover. Then divide the resulting turnover figure into 365 days to arrive at the number of accounts payable days.

The formula can be modified to exclude cash payments to suppliers, since the numerator should include only purchases on credit from suppliers. However, the amount of up-front cash payments to suppliers is normally so small that this modification is not necessary.

As an example, an executive director wants to determine his organization's accounts payable days for the past year. In the beginning of this period, the beginning accounts payable balance was $800,000, and the ending balance was $884,000. Purchases for the last 12 months were $7,500,000. Based on this information, the executive director calculates the accounts payable turnover as:

$$\frac{\$7,500,000 \text{ Purchases}}{(\$800,000 \text{ Beginning payables} + \$884,000 \text{ Ending payables}) \div 2}$$

$$=$$

$$\frac{\$7,500,000 \text{ Purchases}}{\$842,000 \text{ Average accounts payable}}$$

$$= 8.9 \text{ Accounts payable turnover}$$

Thus, the nonprofit's accounts payable is turning over at a rate of 8.9 times per year. To calculate the turnover in days, the executive director divides the 8.9 turns into 365 days, which yields:

$$365 \text{ Days} \div 8.9 \text{ Turns} = 41 \text{ Days}$$

Organizations sometimes measure accounts payable days by only using the cost of programs in the numerator. This is incorrect, since there may be a large amount of administrative expenses that should also be included. If an entity only uses the cost of programs in the numerator, this creates an excessively small number of payable days.

A significant failing of the days payables outstanding measurement is that it does not factor in all of the short-term liabilities of a nonprofit. There may be substantial liabilities related to payroll and interest that exceed the size of payables outstanding. This issue can be eliminated by incorporating all short-term liabilities into the days payable outstanding measurement.

Free Cash Flow

Free cash flow is the net change in cash generated by the operations of an organization during a reporting period, minus cash outlays for working capital and capital expenditures during the same period. Thus, the calculation of free cash flow is:

$$\text{Operating cash flow} \pm \text{Working capital changes} - \text{Capital Expenditures}$$

The "operating cash flow" component of that equation is calculated as:

$$\text{Net income} + \text{Depreciation} + \text{Amortization}$$

Free cash flow is important because it is an indicator of the financial health of an entity, and particularly of its ability to invest in new programs. However, there can be a variety of situations in which a nonprofit can report positive free cash flow, and which are due to circumstances not necessarily related to a healthy long-term situation. For example, positive free cash flow can be caused by:

- Selling off major assets
- Cutting back on or delaying capital expenditures
- Delaying the payment of accounts payable
- Accelerating receivable receipts with high-cost early payment discounts
- Cutting back on key maintenance expenditures
- Reducing fundraising expenditures
- Curtailing scheduled pay increases

In these examples, management has taken steps to reduce the long-term viability of a nonprofit in order to improve its short-term free cash flows. Thus, one should be aware of the general condition and strategic direction of an organization when evaluating whether the state of its free cash flows is beneficial or not.

The Profitability Conundrum

In a for-profit environment, a corporation is constantly trying to increase the amount of profit that it generates, so that it can enhance its cash reserves and prove to investors that the strategy of the organization is robust. This is not the case in a nonprofit, where constant increases in net assets may very well be frowned upon by donors. A donor wants a nonprofit to employ contributions to achieve the maximum effect in a targeted area, not increase its cash reserves. Consequently, a well-managed nonprofit is considered to be one that generally reports a slight net asset increase or decrease, year after year. By doing so, a nonprofit's management is essentially saying that it is avoiding any cash hoarding, instead focusing on meeting the main nonprofit objectives of the organization.

The focus on an essentially minimal change in net assets does not always work in the short term. If a nonprofit receives an unusually large contribution from a donor, it may require several years to find an effective use for the funds. If so, the result may be a sudden increase in net assets that reflects the initial receipt of cash, followed by a decline in net assets over several years, as the nonprofit uses the funds.

Summary

The essential tools to ascertain financial health have been divulged in this chapter, with a particular emphasis on revenues and liquidity. However, financial health is really an outcome of a number of other processes and systems that are not so easily quantified. These other factors include the number and quality of volunteer hours contributed, the quality and support level of the donor base, the unity of the board of directors in supporting the organization, and the ability of the management team to stay on target in fulfilling the mission of the organization. These issues can only be understood by discussing a nonprofit with all concerned parties over an extended period of time. Thus, the analysis of financial health really only provides a quantification of current conditions; it does not provide insights into the long-term health of a nonprofit, which is largely based on nonfinancial considerations.

Glossary

A

Accounting equation. The concept that total assets must equal the total of all liabilities and net assets.

Accrual basis of accounting. The concept of recording revenues when earned and expenses as incurred.

Accumulated depreciation. The sum total of all depreciation expense recognized to date on a depreciable fixed asset.

Acquisition method. The process used to account for the acquisition of an entity by the acquirer.

Active market. A market in which there is a sufficiently high volume of transactions to provide ongoing pricing information.

Adjusting entry. A journal entry used to adjust the balances in various accounts to more accurately report results.

Affiliate. Where an entity controls, is controlled by, or is under common control with another entity.

Allowance for uncollectible pledges. An estimate of the amount of pledges receivable that will not be collected.

B

Bargain purchase option. An option in a lease agreement that allows the lessee to buy a leased asset for a below-market price.

Board-designated funds. Funds set aside by the board of directors for a specific purpose.

C

Calendar year. The reporting period that begins on January 1 and ends on December 31.

Capitalization limit. The amount paid for an asset, above which the item is recorded as a fixed asset.

Carryover method. The process of combining the assets and liabilities of merging nonprofit entities for reporting purposes.

Cash basis of accounting. The concept that revenue is recorded when cash is received, and expenses are recorded when cash is paid.

Cash equivalent. A short-term, very liquid investment that is easily convertible into a known amount of cash.

Chart of accounts. The listing of all accounts used by an entity to record business transactions.

Cliff vesting. When an employee becomes fully vested in pension benefits on a specific date.

Closing entry. A journal entry used to flush out the balances in temporary accounts at the end of a reporting period.

Collection. Art works that are for public use, are safeguarded and cared for, and are protected by a policy to replace items that are sold from the collection.

Consolidation. When the financial statements of two or more entities are merged, net of any transactions between the organizations.

Contribution. An unconditional transfer of assets to an entity, or the settlement of liabilities in a nonreciprocal transfer, where the granting entity is not the owner.

Curtailment. When a benefit plan is reduced or terminated earlier than expected.

D

Deferral. A journal entry intended to defer the recognition of revenue or expenses.

Defined benefit plan. A pension plan in which the employer pays a pre-determined periodic payment to employees after they retire.

Defined contribution plan. A pension plan in which the employer has no obligation other than an initial payment into the plan.

Depreciation. The gradual charging to expense of an asset's cost over its expected useful life.

Determination letter. A letter issued by the Internal Revenue Service, establishing the status of an entity as a 501(c)(3) tax-exempt organization.

Direct expenses. Expenses that are directly traceable to programs.

Double entry accounting. A recordkeeping system under which every transaction is recorded in at least two accounts.

E

Economic interest. A situation in which a nonprofit has significant assets that must be used for the purposes of another entity, or it is responsible for the liabilities of the other entity.

Employer identification number. A unique identifying number issued by the Internal Revenue Service to a business entity.

Equity method. A method of accounting for a significant ownership interest in a for-profit entity that involves recognizing a portion of the financial results of the investee.

Exchange value. The value of an item or service given to a donor in exchange for a contribution.

F

Fair value. The price at which an asset could be sold or a liability settled in an orderly transaction between independent market participants.

Finance lease. A leasing arrangement in which ownership of the underlying asset effectively passes to the lessee by the end of the lease. This designation is used by the lessee.

Fiscal year. The twelve-month period over which an entity reports on the activities that appear in its annual financial statements.

G

General and administrative. Those revenues and expenses not related to the fundraising or program elements of a nonprofit.

Generally accepted accounting principles (GAAP). A group of accounting standards and common industry usage that is used to organize and report financial information.

Goodwill. An intangible asset that represents the future benefits arising from assets acquired in a business combination.

Gross receipts. The total amounts an organization receives from all sources during its tax year, without subtracting any expenses.

Gross income. Gross receipts minus the cost of goods sold.

I

Indirect expenses. Expenses that are allocated to programs.

Indirect rate. An overhead charge applied to a program funded by a government grant.

Inherent contribution. When an acquirer gains control of an acquiree whose fair value is greater than the consideration paid for it.

Irrevocable. An agreement that cannot be terminated by a party to the agreement.

J

Joint activity. An activity that is part of the fundraising function and which has elements of other functions used by a nonprofit.

Joint costs. Costs that are not specifically identifiable with a single activity.

Journal entry. A method used to enter an accounting transaction into the accounting records of an entity.

K

Kick-out rights. The rights of the limited partners of a limited partnership to dissolve a limited partnership or remove the general partners without cause.

L

Lead interest. The right to the use of or cash flows from assets during the term of a split-interest agreement.

Lease. An arrangement where the lessor agrees to allow the lessee to use an asset for a stated period of time in exchange for one or more payments.

Lease liability. The obligation by a lessee to make payments arising from a lease, as calculated on a discounted basis.

Lessee. The user of a leased asset.

Lessor. The owner of a leased asset.

Liquidity. The ability of an entity to pay its bills in a timely manner.

Lower of cost or market. An accounting rule mandating that the recorded cost of inventory be no higher than its market value.

M

Management and administration. Those revenues and expenses not related to the fundraising or program elements of a nonprofit.

N

Net assets with donor restrictions. That portion of net assets subject to donor-imposed restrictions.

Net assets without donor restrictions. That portion of net assets not subject to donor-imposed restrictions.

Net realizable value. The selling price of inventory, minus disposal costs.

Noncontrolling interest. That portion of the net assets of a subsidiary that cannot be attributed to the parent entity.

Nonprofit. An entity that has no ownership interests, has an operating purpose other than to earn a profit, and receives significant contributions from third parties that do not expect a return.

O

Operating lease. The rental of an asset from a lessor, but not under terms that would classify it as a capital lease.

P

Participating rights. The rights of the limited partners of a limited partnership to block or participate in certain financial and operating decisions of the entity.

Petty cash. A small amount of cash that is kept on the premises to pay for minor cash needs.

Pledge. A promise by a donor to make a contribution on a future date.

Posting. The process of shifting the totals in a ledger account to the general ledger.

Program. The type of service provided by a nonprofit.

Projected benefit obligation. The actuarial present value of future benefits attributed to services already rendered by employees.

Q

Quid pro quo. When a nonprofit gives goods or services to a donor in exchange for a contribution.

R

Realized. When a gain or loss is derived from the sale of an asset.

Receipts and disbursements method. A detailed method for deriving a short-term cash forecast.

Recipient entity. A nonprofit that accepts assets from donors and which agrees to employ the assets as directed by the donor.

Remainder interest. The right to the use of or cash flows from assets following the term of a split-interest arrangement.

Reporting unit. An operating segment or one level below an operating segment.

Restricted stock. An ownership interest that has a restriction placed on the ability of the owner to sell the stock.

Reversing entry. A journal entry that will be reversed in the next accounting period.

Revocable. An agreement that can be terminated by a party to the agreement.

Right-of-use asset. A lessee's right to use an asset over the term of a lease.

S

Sale-leaseback. An arrangement in which the owner of a property sells it to a third party and then leases it back from the buyer.

Security. A financial instrument that represents an ownership position in a business or a creditor relationship with a borrower.

Settlement. When lump-sum payments are made to employees in exchange for their rights to receive pension benefits.

Short-term lease. A lease that has a term of 12 months or less as of the commencement date.

Special purpose entity. A legal entity created to fulfill a specific objective.

Split-interest agreement. An arrangement under which a nonprofit splits the benefits of assets with other entities.

Step costing. A cost that does not change steadily in response to changes in activity, but rather at discrete points.

Sublease. A transaction in which the primary lease remains in effect, while the lessee re-leases the underlying asset to a third party.

T

Target balance. A minimum level of cash that is kept on hand to guard against emergency needs.

Temporary account. An account used to hold balances for revenue, expense, gain, or loss transactions.

Trustee. An entity that is required to hold and manage assets for the benefit of a beneficiary.

U

Unconditional promise to give. A promise to give assets or settle liabilities that will be granted on demand or through the passage of time.

Underwater endowment fund. A donor-restricted endowment fund for which the fund's fair value is less than the original gift amount or the amount that the donor or the law requires be maintained.

Unrealized. When a gain or loss is derived from the change in value of an asset that is still held.

Useful life. The time period over which an asset is expected to be productive.

V

Variance power. The unilateral power to redirect funds.

W

Wage base limit. The maximum amount of wages to which the social security tax is applied.

Z

Zero-base analysis. A budgeting methodology under which managers are required to justify all of their proposed expenditures, rather than only justifying incremental changes from the preceding year.

Index

Made in the USA
Monee, IL
07 January 2020